BEAT THE PRESS WITH A BOX MIDFIELD

Build Up Play and Sessions from Guardiola, Alonso and Arteta's Tactics

Written by
Athanasios Terzis

Published by

BEAT THE PRESS WITH A BOX MIDFIELD

Build Up Play and Sessions from Guardiola, Alonso and Arteta's Tactics

First Published April 2025 by SoccerTutor.com
info@soccertutor.com | www.SoccerTutor.com

UK: 0208 1234 007 | **US:** (305) 767 4443 | **ROTW:** +44 208 1234 007
ISBN: 978-1-910491-78-2

Copyright: SoccerTutor.com Limited © 2025. All Rights Reserved.

All rights reserved. No part of this publication may be reproduced, stored in a retrieval system, or transmitted in any form or by any means, electronic, mechanical, photocopy, recording or otherwise, without prior written permission of the copyright owner. Nor can it be circulated in any form of binding or cover other than that in which it is published and without similar condition including this condition being imposed on a subsequent purchaser.

Author: Athanasios Terzis

Editor: Alex Fitzgerald - SoccerTutor.com

Diagrams designed by SoccerTutor.com
All diagrams in this book have been created using Tactics Manager Software
- Available from www.SoccerTutor.com

Note: While every effort has been made to ensure the technical accuracy of the content of this book, neither the author nor publishers can accept any responsibility for any injury or loss sustained as a result of the use of this material.

Contents

CONTENTS

Meet the Author: Athanasios Terzis 7
Introduction: Build Up from the Goalkeeper with a Box Midfield 8
Coaches Studied to Produce the Tactical Analysis for this Book 9
Diagram Key & Coaching Format 11

Build Up Play Factors: Essential Skills and Opposition Pressing Tactics with Different Formations 12

Build Up Play Factors 13
1. Essential Goalkeeper Skills During Build Up Play 13
2. Essential Defender and Defensive Midfielder Skills During Build Up Play 14
Why does this Pressing Section Analyse Opposition Tactics Against the 4-3-3? ... 15
3. Different Types of High Pressing (High or Ultra-Aggressive) 16
4. How the Numerical Situation in the Low Area Affects the Team Building Up ... 18
5. Different Types of Defending Used During High Pressing 22

Tactical Analysis: Box Midfield Build Up - Positional Rotations to Play Out from Goalkeeper 27

Positional Rotations to Build Up from Goalkeeper with Box Midfield 28
1. Full Back Shifts into Centre to Create a Box Midfield from 4-3-3 Formation .. 28
2. Centre Back Pushes Forward to Create a Box Midfield from 4-3-3 Formation ... 29
3. Winger Drops Back and Inside into Attacking Midfield to Create a Box Midfield from 4-2-3-1 Formation 30
4. Defenders Shift to the Right to Create a Box Midfield from 3-4-2-1 Formation ... 31

Tactical Analysis: Box Midfield Build Up - Break Lines vs High Press Zonal Defending 32

Box Midfield Build Up Play Principles and Objectives 33
Build Up with Box Midfield vs High Pressing with Zonal Defending (2 at Back) .. 34
Options for Breaking the First and Second Pressing Lines (2 at Back) 36
Drawing Press with a Pass and Exploit Gaps Created (2 at Back) 43
Options for Breaking the First and Second Pressing Lines (3 at Back) 45
Drawing Press with a Pass and Exploit Gaps Created (3 at Back) 50
Drawing Pressure with Centre Back Dribbling Forward (3 at Back) 52

Contents

Box Midfield Training Session 1: Break Lines vs High Press Zonal Defending 54
1. Passing Decisions to Break Lines Depending on Opposition Pressing 55
2. Moving the Ball Beyond the Lines Based on Defender Reactions 7 (+GK) v 2 Functional Practice 57
3. Breaking Lines Against a High Press in a 9 (+GK) v 6 Positional Game 59
4. Break Lines Through Turning, Recycling the Ball, or Dribbling Forward 3 Zone Conditioned Game 61

Tactical Analysis: Box Midfield Build Up - Goalkeeper's Passing Over Pressing Lines 62
Goalkeeper's Passing Over Second Pressing Line 63
Goalkeeper's Passing Over Second Pressing Line (2 at Back) 64
Goalkeeper's Passing Over Second Pressing Line (3 at Back) 67

Box Midfield Training Session 2: Goalkeeper's Passing Over Pressing Lines 69
1. Goalkeeper's Passing Over Pressing Lines and Decisions to Play in Behind 70
2. Goalkeeper's Passing Over Second Pressing Line Functional Practice with Target Zones 73
3. Goalkeeper's Passing Over Second Pressing Line 10 (+GK) v 8 Functional Practice with Target Zones 75
4. Goalkeeper's Passing Over Second Pressing Line Conditioned Tactical Game 77

Tactical Analysis: Box Midfield Build Up - Strong Side Advantage vs High Press Zonal Defending 78
Numerical Situations vs High Pressing with Zonal Defending (2 at Back) 79
Finding the Free Player Around the Ball Area (3 at Back) 82
Numerical Situations vs High Pressing with Zonal Defending (3 at Back) 85

Box Midfield Training Session 3: Strong Side Advantage vs High Press Zonal Defending 86
1. Exploiting Numerical Advantage to Find the Free Player Continuous Possession Game 87
2. Exploiting 4v3 Numerical Advantage 3-Team Small Sided Game 89
3. Build Up with Numerical Advantage on Strong Side with Box Midfield Dynamic Game (2 at Back) 90
4. Build Up with Numerical Advantage on Strong Side with Box Midfield Split-Pitch Game (3 at Back) 91

Contents

5. Build Up with Numerical Advantage on Strong Side with Box Midfield 11v11 Conditioned Game 93

Tactical Analysis: Box Midfield Build Up - Strong Side Equality vs High Press Zonal Defending 94
Switching Play from Strong to Weak Side (2 at Back) 95
Strong Side Build Up with Numerical Equality (2 at Back) 98
Strong Side Build Up with Numerical Equality (3 at Back) 102
Weak Side Build Up with Numerical Equality (3 at Back) 103

Box Midfield Training Session 4: Strong Side Equality vs High Press Zonal Defending 104
1. Box Midfield Build Up Combinations and Switching Play with Target Areas 105
2. Box Midfield Build Up with Equal Numbers and Switch Play in a Dynamic 3-Team Game 107
3. Split-Pitch Box Midfield Build Up Tactical Game with Equal Numbers 109
4. Box Midfield Build Up with Equal Numbers 11v11 Conditioned 3 Zone Game 111

Tactical Analysis: Box Midfield Build Up - Against High Press with Zonal Defending and Man Marking 113
Build Up Against High Press with Zonal Defending and Man Marking 114
Build Up Against High Press with Zonal Defending and Man Marking (2 at Back) ... 115
Build Up Against High Press with Zonal Defending and Man Marking (3 at Back) ... 120

Box Midfield Training Session 5: Against High Press with Zonal Defending and Man Marking 124
1. Box Midfield Passing Combinations and Movements Against a Double Pivot 125
2. Goalkeeper's Long Pass and Box Midfield Support Play Combinations Against a Single Pivot 126
3. Find the Free Midfielder with 3-at-the-Back Box Midfield 6 (+GK) v 4 (+1) Positional Game 127
4. Find the Free Midfielder with 2-at-the-Back Box Midfield 5 (+GK) v 4 Positional Game 128
5. Find the Free Midfielder Against a High Press with Zonal Defending and Man Marking Conditioned Game 129

Tactical Analysis: Box Midfield Build Up - Against Ultra-Aggressive Pressing with Zonal Defending and Man Marking 130
Build Up Against Ultra-Aggressive Pressing with Zonal Defending and Man Marking (Principles) 131

Contents

Build Up Against Ultra-Aggressive Pressing with Zonal Defending and Man Marking (3 at Back) 132

Build Up Against Ultra-Aggressive Pressing with Zonal Defending and Man Marking (2 at Back) 139

Box Midfield Training Session 6: Against Ultra-Aggressive Pressing with Zonal Defending and Man Marking 141

1. Passing Combinations to Move the Ball to the Free Player via a Link Player 142
2. Using the Link Player to Move the Ball to the Free Player Continuous 3v2 Wave Game 143
3. Moving the Ball to the Free Player Directly or via Link Player and Finish 3v2 (+GK) Game 145
4. Finding Free Player Against Ultra-Aggressive Pressing 8+1 (+GK) v 7 Game (3-at-the-Back Box Midfield) 146
5. Finding Free Player Against Ultra-Aggressive Pressing 7+1 (+GK) v 6 Game (2-at-the-Back Box Midfield) 147
6. Finding the Free Player Against Ultra-Aggressive Pressing 11v11 Game (3-at-the-Back Box Midfield) 148

Tactical Analysis: Box Midfield Build Up - Against Full Pitch Man Marking 149

Box Midfield Build Up Solutions Against Full Pitch Man Marking (2 at Back) 150
Box Midfield Build Up Solutions Against Full Pitch Man Marking (3 at Back) 153

Box Midfield Training Session 7: Against Full Pitch Man Marking ... 157

1. Beating a Full Pitch Man Marking Press by Finding the Free Player Support Play Zones 158
2. Beating a Full Pitch Man Marking Press with a Long Pass and Support Runs Functional Combinations 159
3. Beating an Ultra-Aggressive Man Marking Press with a Box Midfield in a Half Pitch Game 160
4. Beating a Full Pitch Man Marking Press with the Goalkeeper's Long Pass 7v7 (+GKs) Game 162
5. Reading Tactical Triggers to Beat the Press Against Full Pitch Man Marking Game .. 164

Final Message for Coaches 165

MEET THE AUTHOR: ATHANASIOS TERZIS

- Football Tactics Expert and Award Winning Author
- UEFA 'A' Coaching Licence
- Greek Football Federation Instructor (HFF)
- PAOK U23 Assistant Coach
- Analyst (Pundit) for Cosmote TV
- Former Coach of Professional Teams in Greece
- M.S.C. - Coaching and Conditioning
- Former Technical Director of DOXA Dramas Academy (Greek 2nd division)
- Former Professional Football Player

Athanasios Terzis is a football tactics expert and instructor for many coaching seminars and workshops around the world. Athanasios has written many best selling football coaching books published by **SoccerTutor.com** in multiple languages (English, Spanish, German, Italian, Greek, Japanese, Korean and Chinese) including:

- Pep Guardiola - Coaching High Pressing Tactics & Sessions Against Different Formations
- Marcelo Bielsa Attacking Tactics and Sessions
- Diego Simeone Attacking and Defending Tactics from Atlético Madrid's 4-4-2
- Pep Guardiola's Attacking Tactics - Tactical Analysis and Sessions from Manchester City's 4-3-3
- Creative Attacking Play - From the Tactics of Conte, Allegri, Simeone, Mourinho, Wenger & Klopp
- Marcelo Bielsa - Coaching Build Up Play Against High Pressing Teams
- Coaching the Juventus 3-5-2 - Tactical Analysis and Sessions: Attacking and Defending
- Jürgen Klopp's Attacking and Defending Tactics from Borussia Dortmund's 4-2-3-1
- FC Barcelona Training Sessions: 160 Practices from 34 Tactical Situations
- Jose Mourinho's Real Madrid - A Tactical Analysis: Attacking and Defending in the 4-2-3-1
- FC Barcelona - A Tactical Analysis: Attacking and Defending

Introduction

INTRODUCTION: BUILD UP FROM THE GOALKEEPER WITH A BOX MIDFIELD

In modern football, technical proficiency has reached new levels, allowing players to perform under intense time and space pressure. As a result, **more coaches are adopting build up play from the goalkeeper as a fundamental strategy**.

A **key development in this area is the box midfield**, which provides structural advantages in build up by creating **numerical superiorities in central areas**.

This book provides an in-depth analysis of build up tactics using the box midfield and its variations, with tactical insights drawn from these top coaches and teams:

- **Pep Guardiola** (Manchester City)
- **Xabi Alonso** (Bayer Leverkusen)
- **Mikel Arteta** (Arsenal)

The tactical analysis included focuses on how these teams:

- **Manipulate space and create passing options**
- **Progress the ball effectively through pressing structures**
- **Use the box midfield to generate numerical advantages in key areas**

The first two sections examine the key factors that affect build up play:

- **Essential player skills during build up play**
- **Opposition pressing tactics with different formations**

Examining the pressing strategies used by opponents helps to understand the challenges teams face in the build up phase, and teaches your players how to defend/press when they are in that role during training, allowing the team to best prepare for the competitive matches. We explore the defensive principles used in pressing, focusing on:

- **Zonal defending**
- **Pressing with man marking**
- **Zonal defending and man marking (hybrid)**

Based on the type of pressing and defensive structure, specific tactical solutions can be applied to create a successful build up phase.

This book details how to:

- **Create numerical advantages in key areas of the pitch**
- **Exploit pressing triggers to progress the ball forward**
- **Break the first and second pressing lines**
- **Build up play against high pressing**
- **Build up play against zonal defending**
- **Build up play against man marking**

For a broader understanding of build up play tactics, a second volume will follow this book focusing on the 4-3-3 and 4-2-3-1 formations, featuring analysis taken from **Hansi Flick** (FC Barcelona), **Jürgen Klopp** (Liverpool), and **Unai Emery** (Aston Villa). Together, these two book volumes provide a complete tactical analysis of modern build up play across different structures.

COACHES STUDIED TO PRODUCE THE TACTICAL ANALYSIS FOR THIS BOOK

Pep Guardiola

Manchester City's 2022–23 Season:

- Pep's City team adopted a box midfield shape as part of their build up and attacking structure.
- The formation evolved into a 3-2-2-3, providing central overloads and fluid progression from the back.
- The box was created by a full back (e.g. Rico Lewis) shifting inside to join the defensive midfielder, or a centre back (e.g. John Stones) stepping into midfield.
- This approach became a defining feature of Pep Guardiola's positional play throughout the season.
- Manchester City won a historic treble of the Premier League, FA Cup, and UEFA Champions League.

Manchester City's 2023–24 Season:

- Manchester City continued to use the box midfield, maintaining a similar 3-2-2-3 structure.
- There was greater tactical variation depending on opposition and player availability.
- John Stones, Manuel Akanji, and Rico Lewis were used in hybrid roles to form or support the box shape.
- While other shapes were occasionally used, the box midfield remained a key part of their build up strategy.
- Manchester City won the Premier League again (fourth time in a row), the UEFA Super Cup, and the FIFA Club World Cup.

Impact of the Box Midfield:

- The use of the box midfield was central to Manchester City's success, providing control, flexibility, and dominance in key areas of the pitch.

Coaches Studied to Produce the Tactical Analysis for this Book

Xabi Alonso

- **Bayer Leverkusen's 2022-23 Season:**
  Xabi Alonso took over as manager in October 2022 and quickly transformed the team, guiding them from 17th to a 6th-place finish using the 3-4-3 formation.

- **Bayer Leverkusen's 2023-24 Season:**
  Alonso introduced a 3-4-2-1 formation with a box midfield. The build up became a lopsided 2-4-2-2, creating strong and weak sides based on ball position. This allowed Bayer to dominate central areas and build up play from the goalkeeper effectively.

- **Impact of the Box Midfield:**
  The box midfield has been key for Leverkusen's control, progression, and compact transitions. They went unbeaten in the Bundesliga to win their first-ever league title, won the DFB-Pokal (German Cup) and reached the UEFA Europa League final.

Mikel Arteta

- **Arsenal's 2022-23 Season:**
  Influenced by his time as an assistant at Manchester City, Arteta used a box midfield with a 3-2-2-3 shape. Zinchenko moved inside alongside the defensive midfielder, allowing Xhaka to push higher. This structure improved Arsenal's control and build up play.

- **Arsenal's 2023-24 Season:**
  The box midfield remained, now formed by a left winger (Martinelli or Trossard) shifting inside to support Ødegaard. It continued to provide central overloads and attacking fluidity.

- **Impact of the Box Midfield:**
  The box midfield was fundamental to Arsenal's build up play and positional dominance. They finished 2nd in the Premier League in both seasons, which was a big improvement in performance.

Diagram Key & Coaching Format

DIAGRAM KEY & COACHING FORMAT

- BALL MOVEMENT
- PLAYER MOVEMENT
- MOVEMENT WITH BALL

Created using SoccerTutor.com Tactics Manager

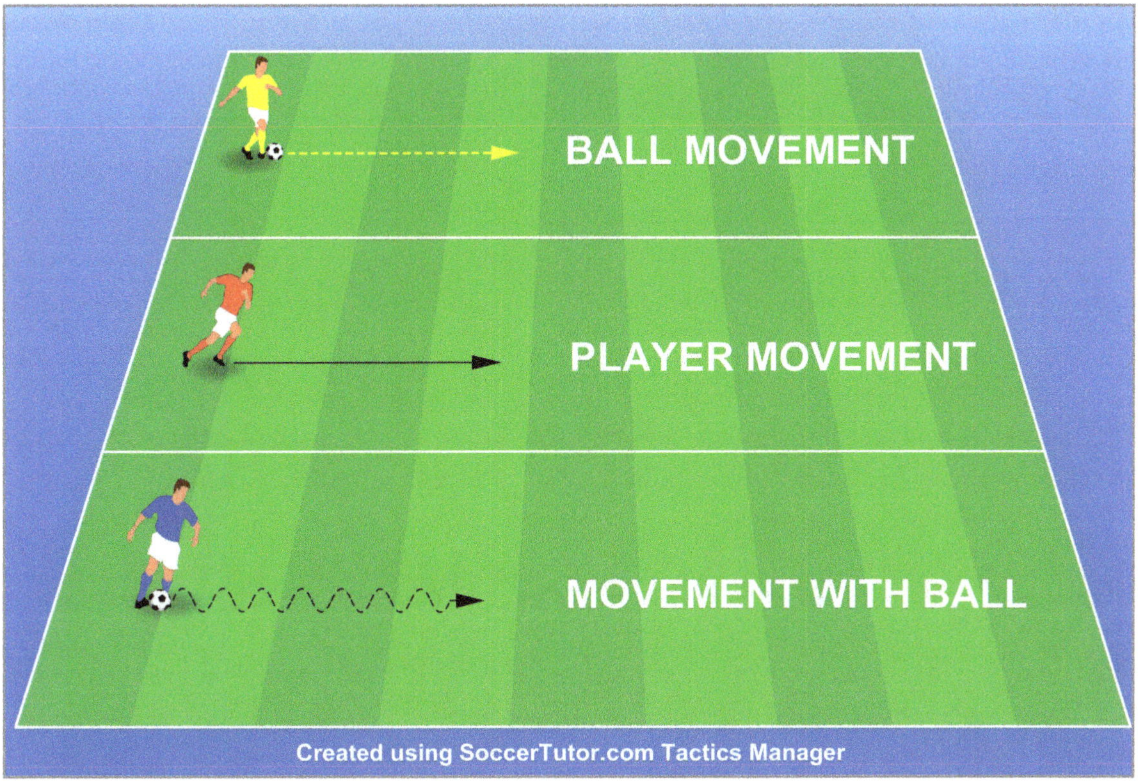

TACTICAL ANALYSIS

- All of the analysis in this book is based on recurring patterns of play observed within **Pep Guardiola's Manchester City**, **Xabi Alonso's Bayer Leverkusen**, and **Mikel Arteta's Arsenal** teams. Once the same phase of play is observed multiple times across many matches, the tactics are seen as a pattern.
- Each action, pass, movement (on or off the ball), and positioning of each player on the pitch, including body shape, is presented with a full description.

TRAINING SESSIONS BASED ON THE TACTICS

- Technical, Functional and Tactical Practices
- Functional Games / Conditioned Games
- Name/Objective, Full Description, Rules/Conditions, Restrictions, Variations, Progressions, and Coaching Points (if applicable)

BUILD UP PLAY FACTORS

Technical Requirements and Opposition Analysis

Essential Skills and Opposition Pressing Tactics with Different Formations

Build Up Play Factors

There are several factors that affect a team's success when building up play from the goalkeeper and defence:

1. **Skills of the goalkeeper**.
2. **Skills of defenders and midfielders (especially the defensive midfielder/s)**.
3. **Type of pressing**.
4. **The numerical situation in the low area of the team building up play**.
5. **Type of defending used during pressing**.

1. Essential Goalkeeper Skills During Build Up Play

The **goalkeeper plays a crucial role** in building up play from the back. If they lack the necessary technical abilities, the team's ability to progress play effectively is compromised, making build up a high risk strategy for the coach. This is why **coaches who implement these tactics place a strong emphasis on selecting or developing a goalkeeper with the right skill set**. If a goalkeeper does not meet these technical demands, teams often invest in signing one who does, as seen when Pep Guardiola brought in Ederson from Benfica (replacing Joe Hart) to fit Manchester City's playing style.

A goalkeeper who is proficient in build up play **must be comfortable on the ball and capable of executing various types of passes under pressure**. This includes high level skills in receiving, ball control, and changing direction with the ball when necessary.

The ability to remain composed when pressed allows the team to retain possession and find progressive passing options.

Passing range is another essential trait. A goalkeeper must be able to play:

- **Short passes** with accuracy to defenders, ensuring smooth ball circulation in the first phase of the build up.
- **Through passes** that break at least one and sometimes two lines of pressure, enabling the team to bypass or break through the opposition's press.
- **Medium-range passes** that travel over two lines of pressure, allowing the team to quickly switch play or progress the ball to midfielders in space.
- **Long passes** that are accurately played behind the opposition's defensive line, providing a direct route to goal when necessary.

An effective goalkeeper must now be a **key distributor**, acting as the foundation for the possession phases. Their **technical ability and composure when pressed directly influence the success of a team's build up play**, making them an integral part of modern tactical systems.

Build Up Play Factors: Essential Skills and Opposition Pressing Tactics

2. Essential Defender and Defensive Midfielder Skills During Build Up Play

The defenders play a crucial role in building up play from the back, forming the second line of the team's attacking structure, with the goalkeeper acting as the first line. As the primary receivers of the goalkeeper's initial pass, defenders must be highly competent in:

- **Receiving**
- **Dribbling**
- **Passing the ball with precision**

Their ability to **remain composed under pressure and distribute effectively** is essential for maintaining possession and progressing the play forward. To execute build up play efficiently, defenders must be able to:

- **Comfortably receive the ball in tight spaces while under pressure from pressing opponents**
- **Carry the ball forward when space is available**
- **Draw out opponents to create passing lanes**

Accurate short and medium-range passing is crucial, enabling the defenders to connect with teammates and bypass the first line of pressure. Their **decision making must be quick and precise**, ensuring they do not invite unnecessary risk while playing out from the back.

Defensive midfielders must possess similar technical qualities, as they frequently receive the ball in congested areas. In addition to their ability to pass and receive under pressure, they **must excel in scanning their surroundings** before receiving passes. Studies have shown that **elite players scan the pitch 6-8 times in the 10 seconds before receiving the ball**, allowing them to:

- **Anticipate opposition movements**
- **Locate teammates**
- **Identify available space**

This level of awareness enables them to make quick, informed decisions, ensuring smooth ball progression.

Defenders and defensive midfielders must be proactive in possession, **constantly making themselves available to receive the ball**. They should adopt positions that provide passing options for teammates, creating angles that allow for fluid ball circulation. After playing a pass, they must immediately reposition themselves to offer further support, ensuring continuity in possession. This constant movement and awareness helps to **maintain the team's structure and allow the team to advance the ball efficiently while minimising the risk of losing possession**.

The **ability to combine technical skills with intelligent movement is fundamental to build up play effectively**. Defenders and defensive midfielders who can execute these principles consistently provide their team with greater control in possession, making them less vulnerable to opposition pressing and better equipped to transition into attacking phases.

Why does this Pressing Section Analyse Opposition Tactics Against the 4-3-3?

Before the following sections of this book focus on build up play using a box midfield, **this section first examines how pressing is applied by opponents against a more traditional formation, the 4-3-3. This choice is deliberate and serves an important purpose in the overall structure of the book**.

The 4-3-3 is one of the most widely used formations in modern football and is easily recognisable to players, coaches, and analysts at all levels. Its balanced and familiar structure makes it ideal for explaining the fundamental defensive behaviours of the opposition, including zonal marking, man marking, and hybrid systems that combine elements of both. By using a familiar shape, the key characteristics of each pressing approach can be seen more clearly and understood more easily.

This section also lays essential groundwork for analysing how numerical situations develop during build up play. Understanding how teams create or concede numerical superiority, particularly in the defensive third of the pitch, is crucial to grasping the challenges of building out from the back. By starting with a straightforward formation, the **reader can observe these dynamics without the additional complexity introduced by the box midfield**.

Once these foundational ideas are established, the book transitions into its main focus of how to build up effectively using a box midfield shape. At that point, the pressing concepts introduced earlier are revisited and re-analysed, but this time in the context of how the opposition adapts their pressing strategy to deal with the positional advantages and unique characteristics of the box midfield.

The aim is to provide the necessary clarity and context to understand the tactical concepts explored throughout the rest of the book.

Build Up Play Factors: Essential Skills and Opposition Pressing Tactics

3. Different Types of High Pressing (High or Ultra-Aggressive)

A. High Pressing (On First Receiver) with 4-4-2

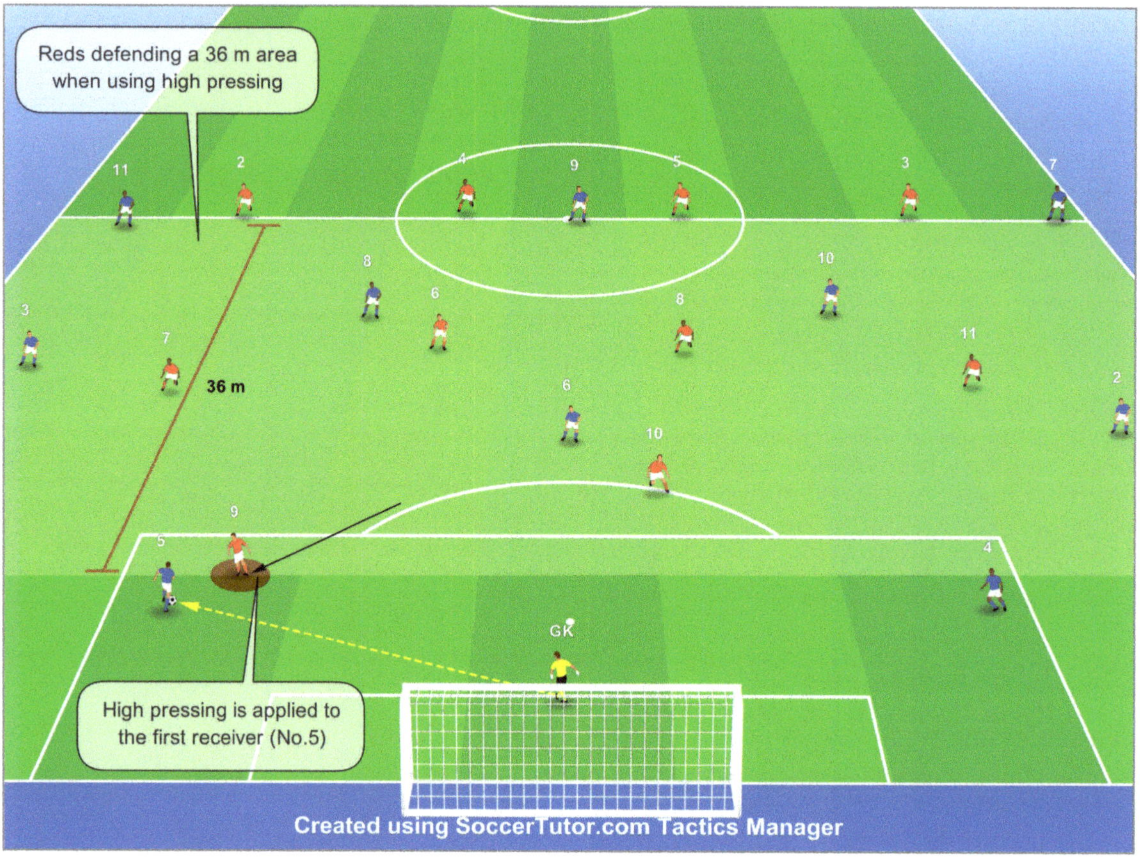

Reds defending a 36 m area when using high pressing

36 m

High pressing is applied to the first receiver (No.5)

The **type of pressing used by the opposition heavily influences how build up play is executed** and the tactics needed to overcome it. Coaches must analyse their next opponent's pressing approach during scouting to prepare effective solutions.

There are **2 types of high pressing** (**high pressing and ultra-aggressive high pressing**). High pressing is applied after the first pass from the goalkeeper to the receiver, which is usually a defender.

Generally, during high pressing, the **defending team has to control less space compared to applying ultra-aggressive high pressing** (up to the goalkeeper).

In the diagram, we show that a team has to defend in an area of approximately 36 metres. This is because the first receiver (blue Nº5 in this example) is usually positioned higher than the goalkeeper.

BEAT THE PRESS WITH A BOX MIDFIELD

Build Up Play Factors: Essential Skills and Opposition Pressing Tactics

B. Ultra-Aggressive High Pressing (On Goalkeeper) with 4-4-2

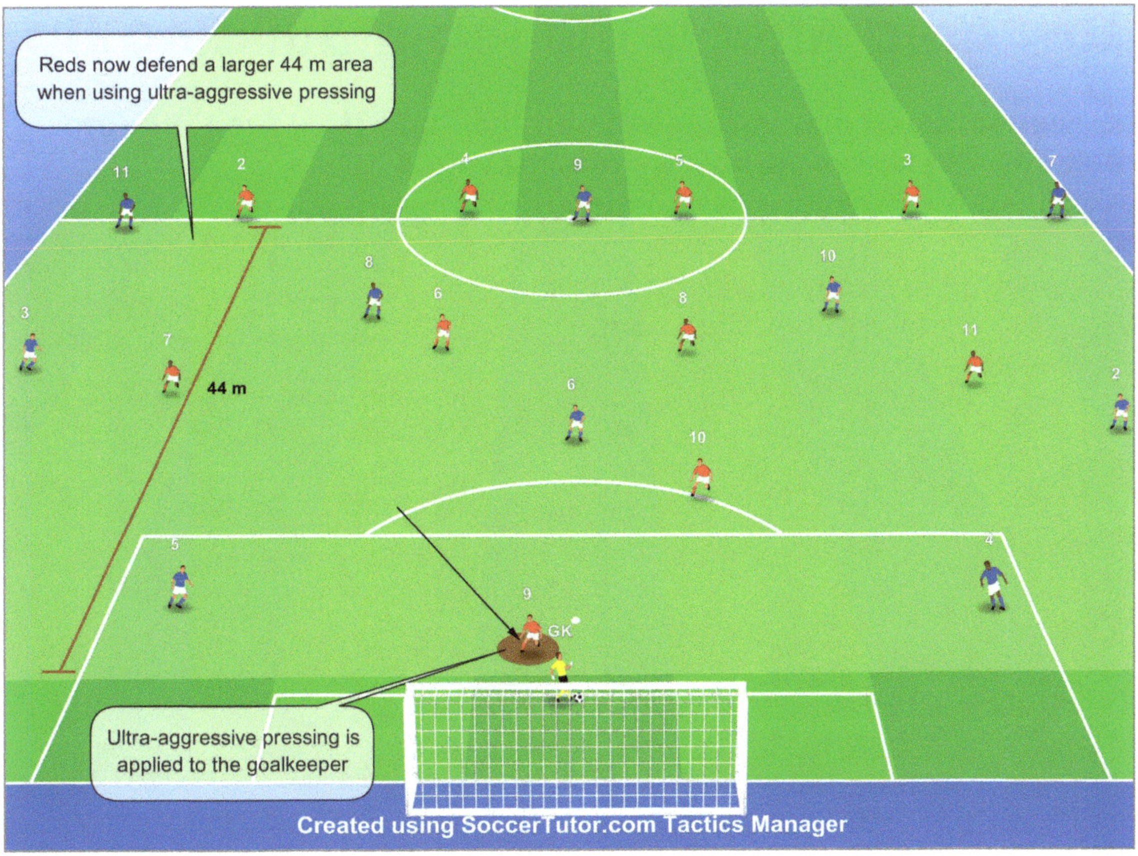

Ultra-aggressive high pressing is applied up to the goalkeeper.

As the goalkeeper is most often the deepest positioned player, the **defending team has to control a bigger space compared to when applying high pressing**.

In the diagram, the red defending team has to control and defend an area of approximately 44 metres, compared with 36 metres against high pressing on the first receiver (see previous page).

As each team has 10 outfield players, when the goalkeeper is pressed, there is always **at least 1 outfield player on the attacking team (blues) who will be free of marking**.

The defending team has to deal with this free player.

Additionally, with ultra-aggressive high pressing stretching the defensive shape, **more attacking players position themselves between the lines** compared to high pressing.

The extended defensive structure creates gaps and allows attackers more time and space to receive and progress play. As a result, the **defending team must not only manage the free player created by pressing the goalkeeper but also stay compact** to prevent the attacking team from exploiting these spaces.

BEAT THE PRESS WITH A BOX MIDFIELD

Build Up Play Factors: Essential Skills and Opposition Pressing Tactics

4. How the Numerical Situation in the Low Area Affects the Team Building Up

A. Numerical Disadvantage High Up the Pitch (Low Area of Team Building Up) Before Applying Pressing with 4-2-3-1

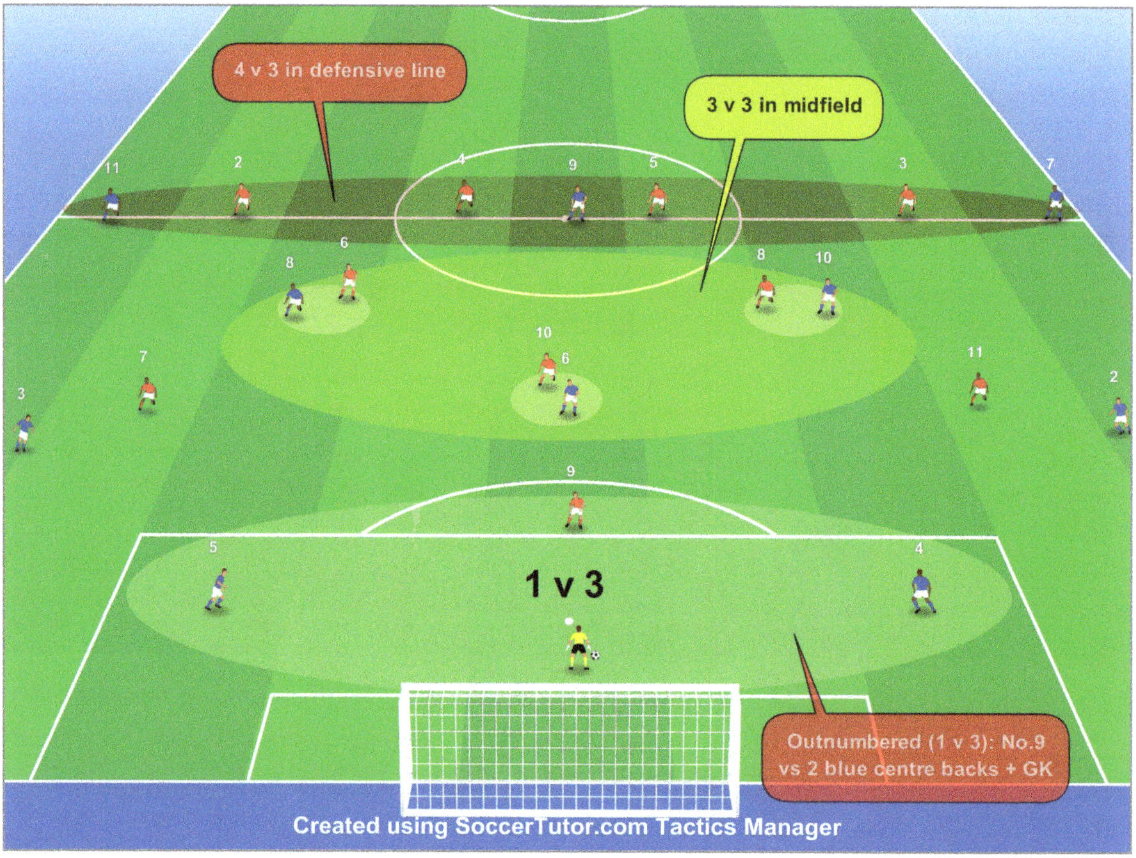

The **numerical situation in the low area is crucial** for the team building up (blues). If the defending team (reds) want to press effectively, the numerical balance should not tilt too much in favour of the blues. Ideally, numbers should be equal (e.g. 2v2 or 3v3), or the **reds should only be 1 player down (e.g. 1v2 or 2v3)**.

In the diagram, the reds have a 4v3 advantage in the defensive line and 3v3 in midfield.

However, the **blues have a 3v1 advantage against the pressing forward (red N°9)**.

With only 1 red forward pressing 2 blue centre backs and the goalkeeper, the reds struggle to apply consistent pressure.

This gives the blues more time and space to build up, allowing their centre backs to circulate the ball comfortably, disrupting the press and forcing reactive defending.

©SOCCERTUTOR.COM

BEAT THE PRESS WITH A BOX MIDFIELD

Build Up Play Factors: Essential Skills and Opposition Pressing Tactics

B. Forward is Unable to Control Both Centre Backs Allowing them to Find Space (4-2-3-1)

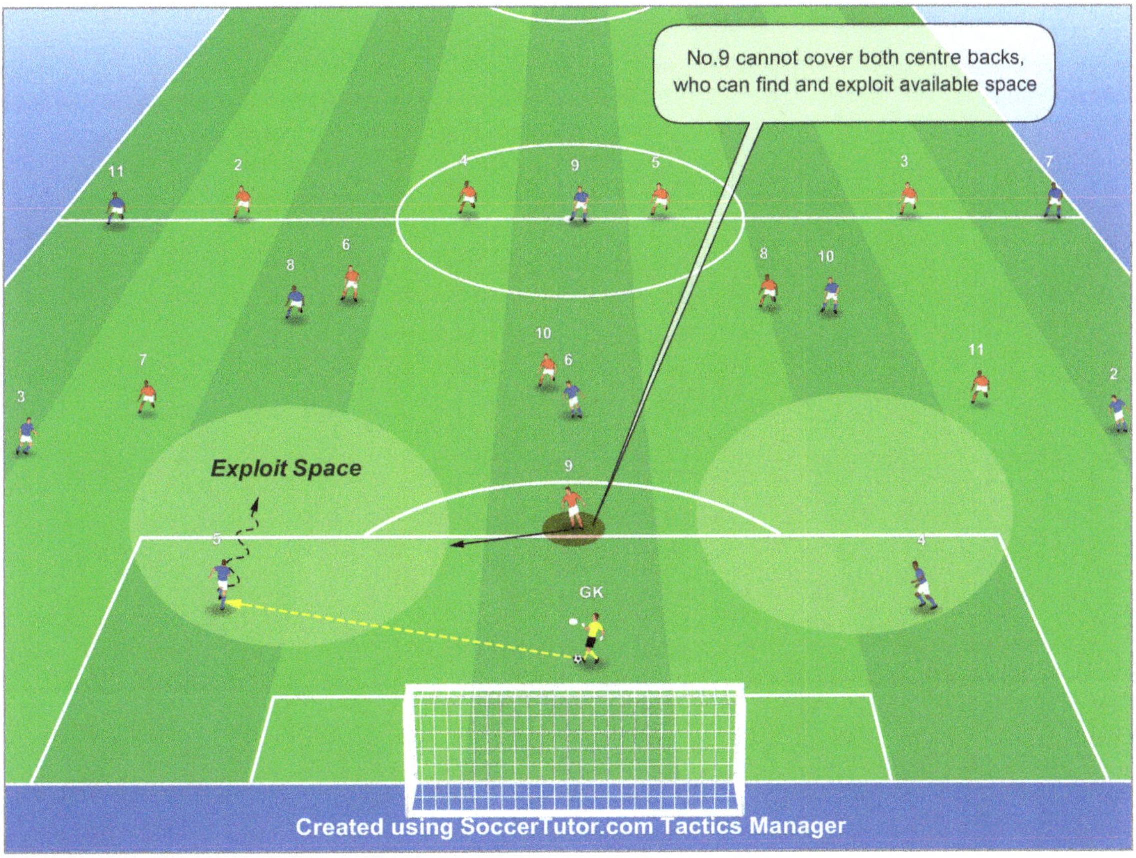

No.9 cannot cover both centre backs, who can find and exploit available space

The key issue when pressing with 1 forward (Nº9) is that they cannot effectively cover both centre backs.

With no additional support, the **centre backs are often able to find and exploit available space**, particularly if the forward fails to close down quickly when the goalkeeper plays the first pass.

This **lack of immediate pressure allows the blues to dictate the tempo of their build up**, making it easier to play through the press.

Without defensive adjustments, the blue centre backs have time to receive, turn, and pick out passing options, enabling their team to **bypass the press and progress into midfield** with relative ease.

Note: If the **red forward (Nº9)** does not press aggressively or cut off passing lanes, the blue defenders can comfortably shift the ball between themselves, drawing the press before switching play to the weak side, where additional space may be available.

BEAT THE PRESS WITH A BOX MIDFIELD

Build Up Play Factors: Essential Skills and Opposition Pressing Tactics

C. Forward Presses the Centre Back as Ball is Switched to Free Weak Side Centre Back (4-2-3-1)

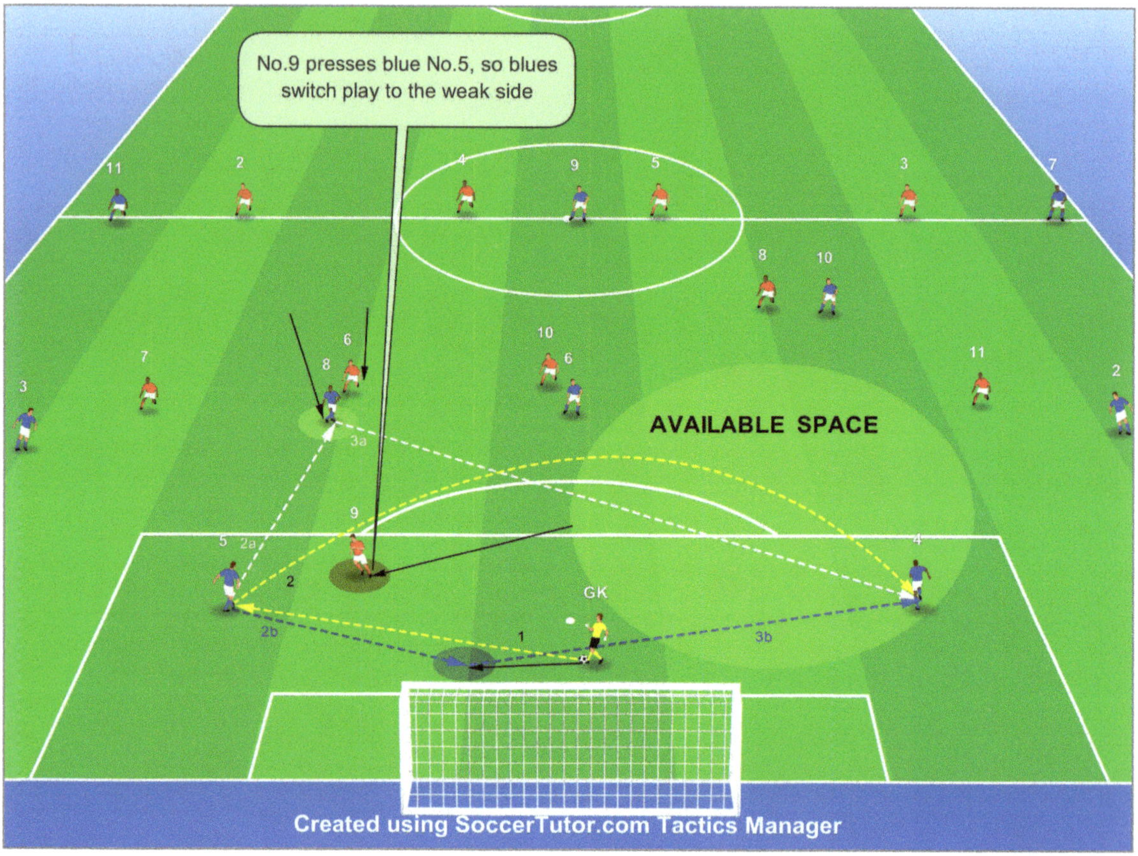

No.9 presses blue No.5, so blues switch play to the weak side

AVAILABLE SPACE

If the pressing **forward (red Nº9)** is proactive and moves quickly to press the centre back receiving the first pass from the goalkeeper (Nº5 in diagram), the **blue team can still exploit the weak side**.

By shifting the ball across the defensive line, either directly (yellow arrows) or through a link player (blue and white arrows), the weak side centre back (Nº4) will be available in a large space and can advance to continue the build up.

If the red defending team does not react quickly, the **blues can take advantage of this open space to progress forward with minimal resistance**.

The **pressing team (reds) must recognise this positional weakness and adjust accordingly to prevent easy switches of play**. This may involve:

- The nearest midfielder shifting across to close down passing lanes.
- The weak side winger adjusting their positioning to anticipate the switch and press the receiving defender.

Note: Without these adjustments, the blue team can comfortably move the ball into dangerous areas with little disruption.

©SOCCERTUTOR.COM   BEAT THE PRESS WITH A BOX MIDFIELD

Build Up Play Factors: Essential Skills and Opposition Pressing Tactics

D. Adjusting the 4-2-3-1 to a 4-4-2 Defensive Shape to Apply More Effective Pressing

To overcome the numerical disadvantage in the high press, an adjustment is needed. The **red attacking midfielder (N°10) pushes higher and creates a 2 v 3 situation** against the blue team's 2 centre backs and goalkeeper (highlighted in diagram).

The **red team increase their ability to disrupt the build up phase while limiting the space and time available for the blue defenders** to play forward.

This tactical shift transforms the defensive shape into a **4-4-2, allowing the 2 most advanced players to press both blue centre backs (N°4 and N°5) simultaneously**, reducing their time and space on the ball.

With this structure, more effective pressing can be applied, forcing rushed decisions, inaccurate passes, or long balls when put under pressure.

Note 1: By cutting off passing options and closing down space more efficiently, the **likelihood of forcing the blues into errors in their own defensive third increases**, as does winning possession higher up the pitch, and countering to score.

Note 2: 4-4-2 pressing restricts space for centre backs or full backs (key receivers) effectively. Without this, they could play forward without pressure.

BEAT THE PRESS WITH A BOX MIDFIELD

Build Up Play Factors: Essential Skills and Opposition Pressing Tactics

5. Different Types of Defending Used During High Pressing

A. Zonal Defending: Controlling Space in a Pressing System

Defensive zones of responsibility

Pressing can be applied with different types of defending:

A. **Zonal Defending**

B. **Man Marking with Numerical Advantage at the Back**

C. **Full Pitch Man Marking**

D. **Zonal Defending and Man Marking (Hybrid)**

Each type of defending has advantages and disadvantages. Teams that apply pressing with **zonal defending prioritise controlling space rather than directly marking individual opponents**, aiming to disrupt the opposition's build up while maintaining defensive organisation.

The diagram shows zones of responsibility for players in a 4-4-2 formation with zonal defending. **Each player is responsible for defending a specific area (zone) of the pitch.** The zones of responsibility are dynamic and change according to the position of the ball.

©SOCCERTUTOR.COM

BEAT THE PRESS WITH A BOX MIDFIELD

Build Up Play Factors: Essential Skills and Opposition Pressing Tactics

B1. Man Marking with Numerical Advantage at the Back (Option 1)

[Diagram showing tactical setup with annotations:
- 7 blue outfield players marked (1 v 1)
- 2 v 1 in centre of defence
- 2 v 3
- Controls 2 players which creates a weakness in the pressing structure
- 2 v 3: GK remains unmarked]

In this setup, the red team maintain a numerical advantage at the back, where there is a **2v1 situation in the centre of defence**.

As shown, the blue forward (N°9) is covered by **2 red centre backs (N°4 and N°5)**, ensuring control in this zone and minimising the threat of direct play through the centre.

The **red right winger (N°7)** pushes forward to apply pressure on the blue left centre back (N°5), creating a **2v3 situation in the highlighted area for the blue team's initial build up play from the back**.

Across the rest of the pitch, the reds are committed to man marking, resulting in multiple **1v1 duels against the remaining 7 blue outfield players**.

Note: 1 red player (**winger N°7** in diagram) is forced to cover 2 blue players, which creates a weakness in the defensive setup. Also, the blue goalkeeper (GK) is left unmarked, providing a free outlet for the blue team when needed.

BEAT THE PRESS WITH A BOX MIDFIELD

Build Up Play Factors: Essential Skills and Opposition Pressing Tactics

B2. Man Marking with Numerical Advantage at the Back (Option 2)

[Diagram: Tactical board showing red team pressing blue team's build-up. Labels: "3 v 3: Chances of forcing errors or recovering possession in advanced areas is increased"; "2 v 1 in centre of defence"; "Higher position"; "Controls 2 players" (left and right); "3 v 3" in central build-up area.]

The second option retains a numerical advantage at the back while **shifting into a more balanced structure across the rest of the pitch**.

As shown in the diagram, the reds continue to control the blue forward (N°9) with their **2 centre backs (N°4 and N°5)**, preserving the same **2 v 1 situation in the centre of defence**.

In contrast to the first option, there is now a **3 v 3 situation in the highlighted area for the blue team's initial build up play from the back**. This is achieved with the central positioning of the **red forward (N°9)** and the advanced positioning of both **wingers (N°7 and N°11)**.

N°7 and **N°11** mark the 2 blue centre backs (N°5 and N°4), while **N°9** has the role of pressing the goalkeeper (GK). This structure allows the reds to apply **ultra-aggressive pressing (up to the goalkeeper)** with more balance across the pitch.

With all key outfield players marked and pressure being applied to the goalkeeper, the **chances of forcing errors or recovering possession in advanced areas is increased** without creating significant numerical disadvantages elsewhere on the pitch.

Note: 2 red players (**wingers N°7 and N°11**) are forced to cover 2 blue players, which creates 2 points of weakness.

Build Up Play Factors: Essential Skills and Opposition Pressing Tactics

C. Full Pitch Man Marking (Equal Numbers at the Back)

The second form of man marking creates 1v1 situations for every outfield player including in the defensive line. Every defending team player is matched directly with 1 opponent, as shown.

Unlike structures that retain a spare player at the back, this approach ensures that **every defending player is directly responsible for marking an opponent** (1v1), leaving no extra cover.

As shown in the diagram, **one of the centre backs (red Nº4) pushes forward to mark an opposing midfielder (blue Nº8)**, maintaining balance while ensuring tight marking throughout the pitch.

This results in a **3v3 situation in the defensive line**, where each red defender must track their direct opponent closely.

This setup forces the possession team (blues) into constant individual battles, restricting their space and time on the ball. However, as every defender is occupied, there is an **increased risk if an opponent manages to evade their marker**, as there is no extra cover to provide support.

Note: Defensive discipline, anticipation, and physical duels are essential for successfully applying full pitch man marking.

BEAT THE PRESS WITH A BOX MIDFIELD

Build Up Play Factors: Essential Skills and Opposition Pressing Tactics

D. Zonal Defending and Man Marking (Hybrid)

Balanced position: Reds are outnumbered 2 v 3 in midfield, so No.8 must cover 2 opponents

2 v 3

This defensive approach combines zonal defending and man marking, requiring players to **mark opponents within their designated zones while adjusting to opposition movement**.

When the **defending team is outnumbered in a specific area (e.g. 2 v 3 in midfield), 1 player must adopt a balanced position to cover 2 opponents** instead of marking a single player.

In the diagram example, a **red central midfielder (N°6)** marks a blue attacking midfielder (N°8), while the **other central midfielder (N°8)** is positioned between the other blue attacking midfielder (N°10) and the defensive midfielder (N°6).

This positioning **allows red N°8 to react based on the blue team's movement**, ensuring that the team remains compact while still applying effective pressing.

Note: The success of this approach relies on defensive awareness, communication, and the ability to adjust positioning quickly based on opposition movement.

©SOCCERTUTOR.COM　　　BEAT THE PRESS WITH A BOX MIDFIELD

BOX MIDFIELD BUILD UP

Tactical Analysis

Positional Rotations to Play Out from Goalkeeper

Build up play patterns from Guardiola, Alonso, and Arteta's teams

BEAT THE PRESS WITH A BOX MIDFIELD

Box Midfield Build Up: Positional Rotations to Play Out from Goalkeeper

Positional Rotations to Build Up from Goalkeeper with Box Midfield

1. Full Back Shifts into Centre to Create a Box Midfield from 4-3-3 Formation

Change from 4-3-3 to Box Midfield shape with 2 at the back (No.5 + GK)

BOX MIDFIELD

Created using SoccerTutor.com Tactics Manager

The **box midfield has become key** in recent years for **Pep Guardiola (Manchester City)**, **Xabi Alonso (Bayer Leverkusen)**, and **Mikel Arteta (Arsenal)**. It is created through positional adjustments in the 4-3-3 and 4-2-3-1 formations and exists naturally in the 3-4-2-1 (Bayer Leverkusen).

The box midfield is **4 players in a box shape**. In a 4-3-3 setup, one way to create this structure is by **shifting a full back into central midfield (inverted)**.

As shown in the diagram, the **right back (N°2 - RB)** moves centrally and the **defensive midfielder (N°6 - DM)** shifts to the left. At the same time, the **goalkeeper (GK)** moves wider into the **right centre back's (N°4 - RCB)** position and **N°4** shifts into a right back role.

This adjustment **forms a 2-at-the-back shape with the left centre back (N°5)** and the goalkeeper positioned deepest.

©SOCCERTUTOR.COM · BEAT THE PRESS WITH A BOX MIDFIELD

Box Midfield Build Up: Positional Rotations to Play Out from Goalkeeper

2. Centre Back Pushes Forward to Create a Box Midfield from 4-3-3 Formation

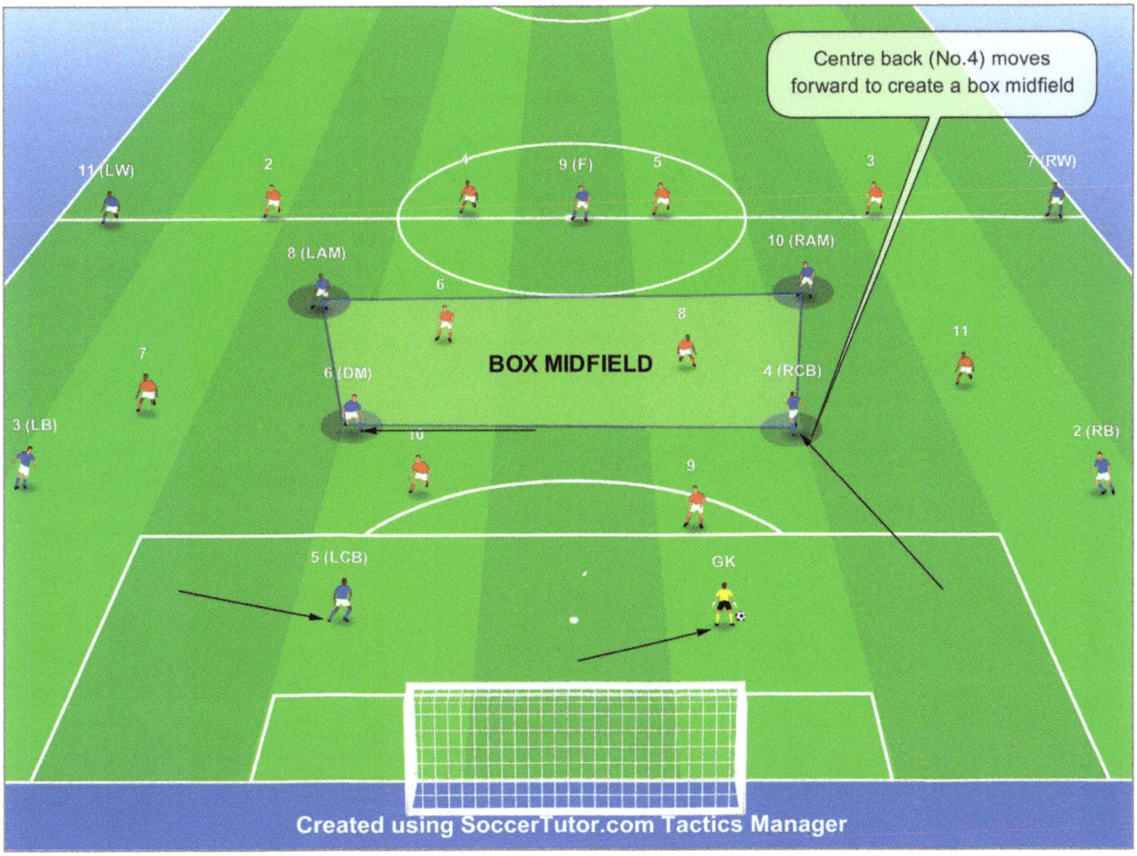

Another way to form a box midfield is by pushing a centre back into midfield. This has been done **most notably by Pep Guardiola and Manchester City with John Stones**.

As shown in the diagram, the **right centre back (N°4)** moves forward and the **defensive midfielder (N°6)** shifts across to the left.

Once again, the **goalkeeper (GK)** moves wider to take up the right centre back position, ensuring balance at the back. This **creates the same 2-at-the-back shape, with the left centre back (N°5) and GK** positioned deepest.

Note: In both situations (1 & 2), the **goalkeeper takes a centre back's position, so the team gain an extra player in an advanced area**. In addition, these adjustments help create a numerical advantage on the strong side, allowing the team to find the free player, a concept that will be analysed later in the book.

BEAT THE PRESS WITH A BOX MIDFIELD

Box Midfield Build Up: Positional Rotations to Play Out from Goalkeeper

3. Winger Drops Back and Inside into Attacking Midfield to Create a Box Midfield from 4-2-3-1 Formation

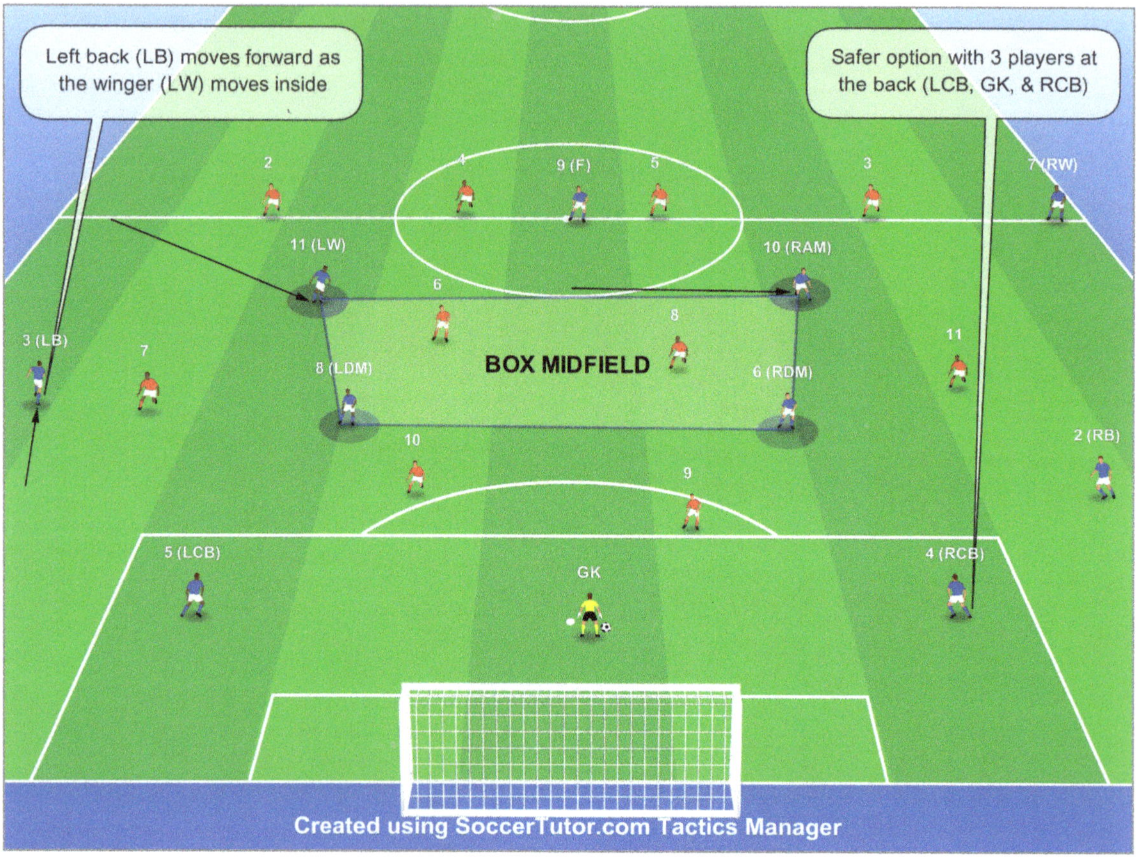

The box shape in midfield can also be formed from the 4-2-3-1 formation with a **winger dropping back and shifting inside into an attacking midfielder's position**.

This increases the numbers in midfield and leaves **3 players at the back (goalkeeper + 2 centre backs), making it a safer option** than the 2-at-the-back setup. However, it does weaken one of the flanks (left in diagram).

In this example, the **left winger's (Nº11)** movement inside is coordinated with the **attacking midfielder (Nº10)** shifting to the right side. To counter this and restore balance, the **left back (Nº3)** moves forward to provide width on the left flank.

Note 1: **This adjustment creates a weak side with 1 wide player on the left (Nº3) and a strong side with 2 wide players on the right (Nº2 and Nº7).**

It is essential that **Nº11** can operate effectively in tight spaces, while **Nº3** must possess strong attacking qualities to ensure the most effective combination of player attributes.

Note 2: **The box midfield can also be created (from 4-2-3-1) with a full back shifting into a central position, while the respective defensive midfielder moves into an attacking midfielder position.**

BEAT THE PRESS WITH A BOX MIDFIELD

Box Midfield Build Up: Positional Rotations to Play Out from Goalkeeper

4. Defenders Shift to the Right to Create a Box Midfield from 3-4-2-1 Formation

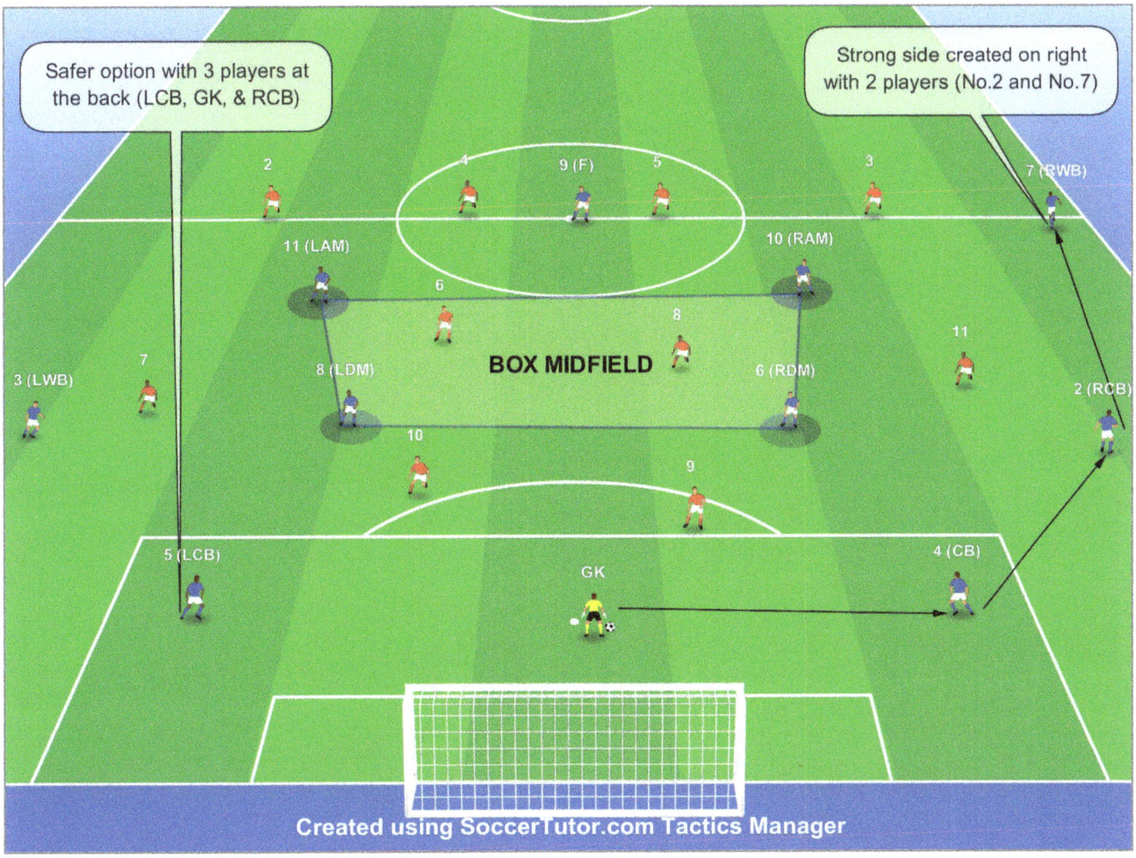

The 3-4-2-1 formation follows the same structure as previous 4-2-3-1 example. The key difference is that **there are already 2 attacking midfielders (N°11 and N°10) and 2 defensive midfielders (N°8 and N°6)**, eliminating the need for a wide player to shift inside. When the goalkeeper has the ball, the defensive line shifts towards one side to create a structured build up phase.

In the diagram, the **right centre back (N°4) moves right and triggers a chain reaction**:

- The **right wing back (N°7 - RWB)** advances into a right winger position.
- The **right centre back (N°2 - RCB)** shifts into a right back position.

- The **middle centre back (N°4 - CB)** moves into a right centre back position.

This movement forms a 3-at-the-back shape with the **left centre back (N°5 - LCB)**, the **goalkeeper (GK)**, and **N°4**.

Note: The blues establish a strong right side and a weaker left side where there are fewer attacking players.

BEAT THE PRESS WITH A BOX MIDFIELD

BOX MIDFIELD BUILD UP

Tactical Analysis

Break Lines vs High Press Zonal Defending

Build up play patterns from Guardiola, Alonso, and Arteta's teams

Box Midfield Build Up Play Principles and Objectives

Build Up Play from the Back

Build up play refers to progressing the ball from the defensive third against organised pressing. This book focuses on build up starting from the goalkeeper, typically against a high defensive block.

Different types of defending tactics influence how teams build up play, as do defensive formations which shift based on pressing intensity, requiring teams to adapt accordingly.

Please see the earlier section in the book for full details (*Build Up Play Factors: Essential Skills and Opposition Pressing Tactics*).

Principles of Build Up Play

Effective build up play relies on key principles to ensure controlled progression and attacking fluidity:

- **Numerical Superiority:** Creating overloads in key areas to maintain possession and break through pressing.
- **Effective Positioning:** Players must position themselves between opposition lines to create passing lanes.
- **Decision Making and Awareness:** Recognising space, anticipating defensive movements, and executing quick passing decisions.
- **Ball Circulation and Patience:** Moving the ball efficiently to wait for the right moment to penetrate defensive lines.
- **Support and Movement:** Off-the-ball adjustments to maintain passing options and avoid being isolated.

Objectives of Build Up Play

Main Objective: **Break defensive lines, advance play, and create goal scoring opportunities**.

To achieve this, teams must:

- **Beat the Press:** Find free players or use link players to progress play through or around pressing lines.
- **Exploit Space:** Use intelligent positioning and quick ball movement to take advantage of defensive gaps.
- **Ensure Defensive Stability:** Maintain balance at the back to best prepare for potential counter attacks.
- **Transition Efficiently:** Once past the first or second defensive lines, capitalise on attacking opportunities.

Note: By applying these principles, teams using a box midfield can successfully play through high pressing opponents, ensuring control and structured progression.

Box Midfield Build Up: Break Lines vs High Press Zonal Defending

Build Up with Box Midfield vs High Pressing with Zonal Defending (2 at Back)

1. Available Spaces Between the Lines vs High Pressing with Zonal Defending

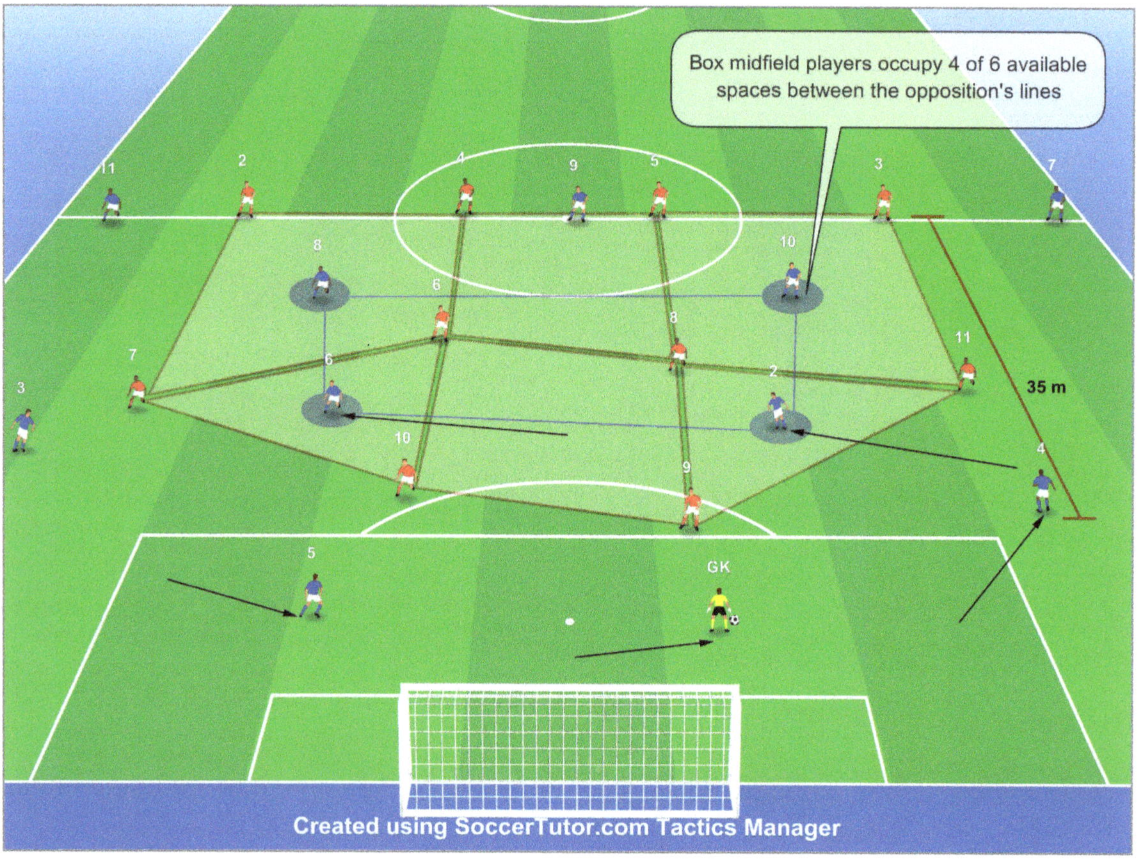

In this example, the box midfield build up shape is formed by an **inverted full back (Nº2)** adjusting from the 4-3-3 formation *(see page 28)*.

This setup occupies 4 of 6 available spaces between the opposition's lines, increasing passing options for the goalkeeper.

A 4-4-2 zonal defensive setup defends in 3 lines of pressure (forwards, midfielders, and defenders).

The first defensive line (forwards) is positioned just outside the box and the third line (defenders) is on the halfway line.

Note: A compact zonal defending team in a middle or low block typically has 17-18m of space between their lines. During the pressing application, the distance increases significantly, allowing the players positioned in midfield (blue Nº8, Nº10, Nº6 and Nº2) to exploit gaps effectively.

BEAT THE PRESS WITH A BOX MIDFIELD

Box Midfield Build Up: Break Lines vs High Press Zonal Defending

2. Optimal Box Midfield Positioning to Exploit the Spaces Between the Lines

Box midfield players stay equally distanced from closest opponents to find the most space

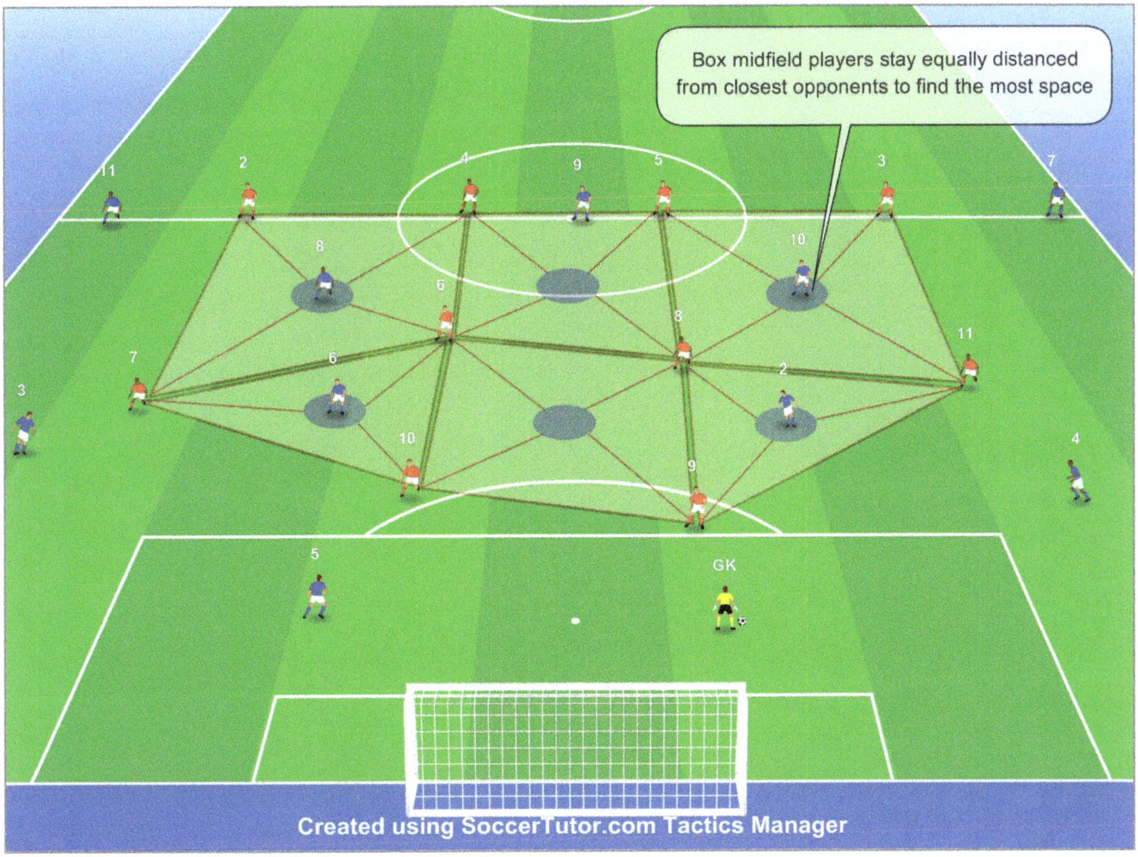

The **central area of the pitch is more important than wide areas** as it offers more passing options.

To exploit available spaces between the opposition's lines:

1. Midfielders position themselves effectively between the lines to maximise space.
2. Midfielders must stay equally distanced from their closest opponents to find the most space.
3. The goalkeeper or defenders try to move the ball to one of the midfielders.

A box midfield provides an advantage over a normal 4-3-3 or 4-2-3-1 shape because it allows 4 players to occupy spaces between the lines.

In this example, the **defensive midfielder (N°6), inverted full back (N°2) and attacking midfielders (N°8 and N°10) position themselves centrally between multiple opponents**. The blue circles show the effective positions that the midfielders can take between lines and players.

Note: When gaps open up, the **midfielders must adjust their positioning to maximise space** and receive in effective areas.

BEAT THE PRESS WITH A BOX MIDFIELD

Box Midfield Build Up: Break Lines vs High Press Zonal Defending

Options for Breaking the First and Second Pressing Lines (2 at Back)

1. Goalkeeper's Options to Pass Through or Over Pressing Lines

GK's options to play through or over pressing lines to box midfield players

Once players take up effective positions, the next step is to **break the first line of pressure by playing through or over the pressing lines**, depending on the defending team's approach.

The box midfield shape does not favour the **goalkeeper (GK)** moving forward, as the red forward (N°9) is positioned directly in front. Instead, **GK must quickly assess the situation and identify the best passing option**.

Good passing angles are available to the 2 players in defensive midfield positions:

1. **Defensive midfielder (N°6)**
2. **Inverted right back (N°2)**

They must be well positioned to receive and progress the play forward. If the opposition block these options, supporting players must adjust to provide alternative options e.g., aerial passes to the **attacking midfielders (N°8 or N°10)**, as shown.

BEAT THE PRESS WITH A BOX MIDFIELD

Box Midfield Build Up: Break Lines vs High Press Zonal Defending

2. Creating Free Players Behind the Second Pressing Line and Forcing Defensive Decisions (Marking vs Balanced Positioning)

Opposing defenders stay to mark the forward and wingers, so attacking midfielders are left in space

Following on from the previous page, the **defensive midfielder (N°6)** has received from the **goalkeeper (GK)** behind the first pressing line. By turning, the 2 red forwards have been neutralised.

The **next step is to break the second line**, ideally by passing to free players positioned in between the oppositions' midfield and defensive lines, who can receive and turn.

So, first of all, the **blues have to create free players behind the second pressing line**. To do this, players must position themselves strategically and **force opposing defenders into difficult marking decisions**.

The **attacking midfielders (N°8 and N°10) maintain positions between lines and between opponents** (see red lines). The **wingers (N°11 and N°7)** and **forward (N°9)** create dilemmas for the red full backs (N°2 and N°3) and centre backs (N°4 and N°5), as they have 2 players to control within their zone of responsibility.

The **red defenders must decide whether to mark a player or hold a balanced position**. Typically, they stay closer to the more dangerous player, leaving space for others. As the wingers and the forward pose the biggest threat, **attacking midfielders often find more room to operate**.

BEAT THE PRESS WITH A BOX MIDFIELD

Box Midfield Build Up: Break Lines vs High Press Zonal Defending

3a. Advancing the Ball Beyond the Second Pressing Line to an Attacking Midfielder Between the Lines

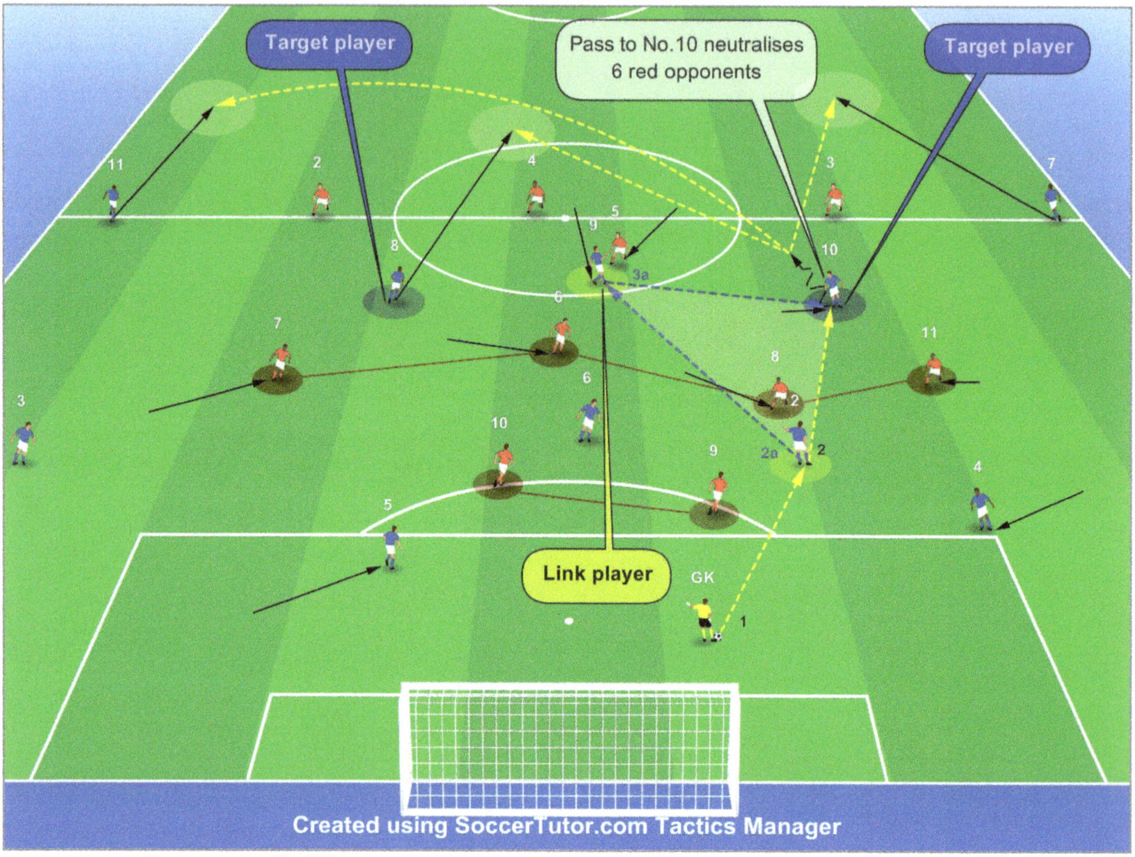

If passes to the base of the box midfield (to **N°6** or **N°2**) are successful, the first pressing line is bypassed, allowing the receiver to turn and play forward.

From there, **N°6 or N°2 can pass directly to an attacking midfielder (target players N°8 or N°10)** or use the forward (**N°9**) **as a link player**. The positioning of the players behind the second pressing line **challenges the opposing red defenders' decision making** and increases the number of available passing options. The players behind the second line move in different available passing lanes so there are **at least 2 passing options (triangle shape)**.

When **blue N°2** receives and turns, **N°10's** position between the lines, along with the movements of the **winger** (**N°7**) and **N°9** create uncertainty for the red centre backs.

The ball can be played to **N°10** directly (yellow arrow) or via the link player **N°9** (blue arrows). If successful, the **first 2 pressing lines will be broken and 6 red players neutralised**. **N°10's** 3 options for passing in behind the defensive line are shown (yellow arrows).

Note: The blue centre backs (**N°5** and **N°4**) shift inside and provide greater defensive balance in case possession is lost.

Box Midfield Build Up: Break Lines vs High Press Zonal Defending

3b. Exploiting Passing Lanes to Beat the Second Pressing Line and Play to Attacking Midfielders Between the Lines

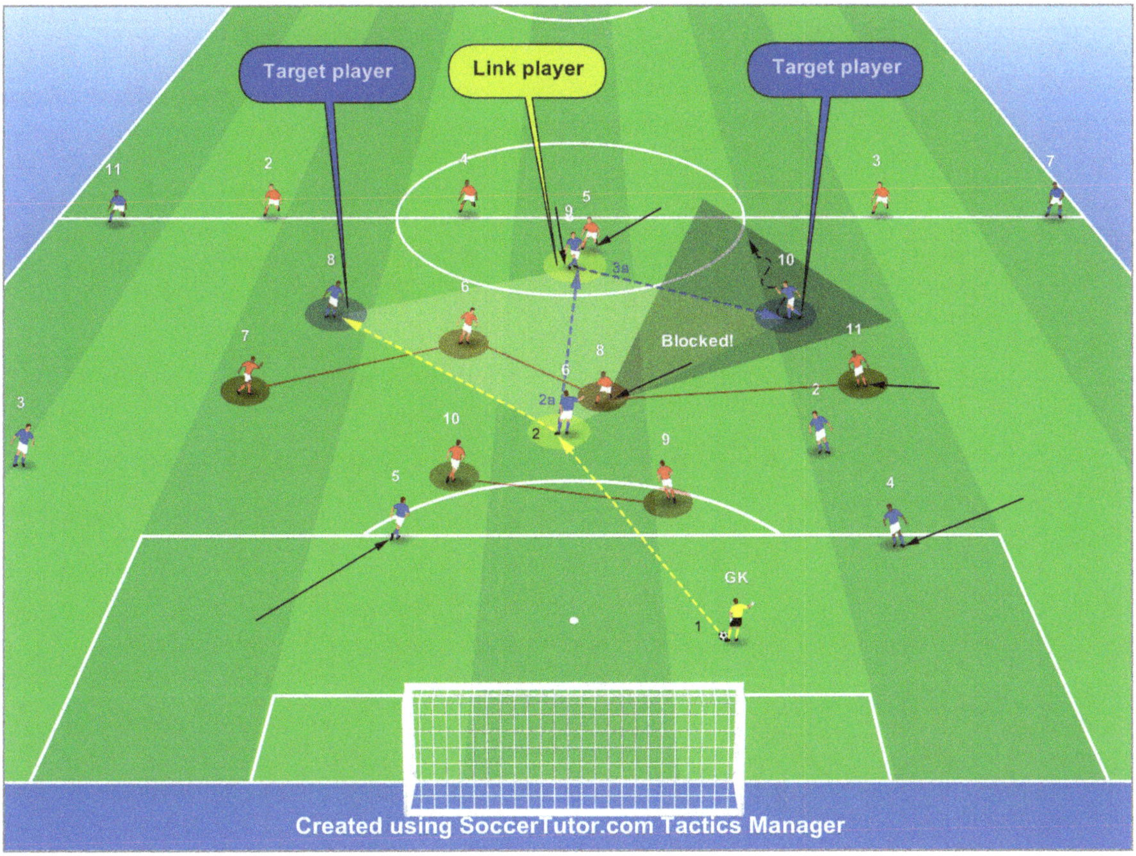

In this variation of the previous example, the **defensive midfielder (N°6)** receives from the **goalkeeper (GK)** in the centre and **both attacking midfielders (N°8 and N°10) are target players between the lines**. Their advanced positioning provides immediate passing options, helping the team progress beyond the second pressing line.

Note: **The movement and positioning of N°8, N°10, and the forward (N°9) in different passing lanes further increase the chances of finding a way to play forward. These players behind the second line create 2 passing triangles, which form a diamond shape (highlighted).**

Even though a red central midfielder (N°8) blocks the direct pass to **blue N°10**, there are still effective solutions available.

N°6 can play directly to the other **attacking midfielder N°8** (yellow arrow) or use the **forward (N°9)** as a link player to move the ball to **N°10** (blue arrows).

Note: If executed quickly, this **ball movement disrupts the defending team's defensive shape**, drawing them out of position and creating opportunities to break beyond the second pressing line.

BEAT THE PRESS WITH A BOX MIDFIELD

Box Midfield Build Up: Break Lines vs High Press Zonal Defending

4. Alternative Passing Options for the Goalkeeper when Passing to the Defensive Midfielders is Too Risky

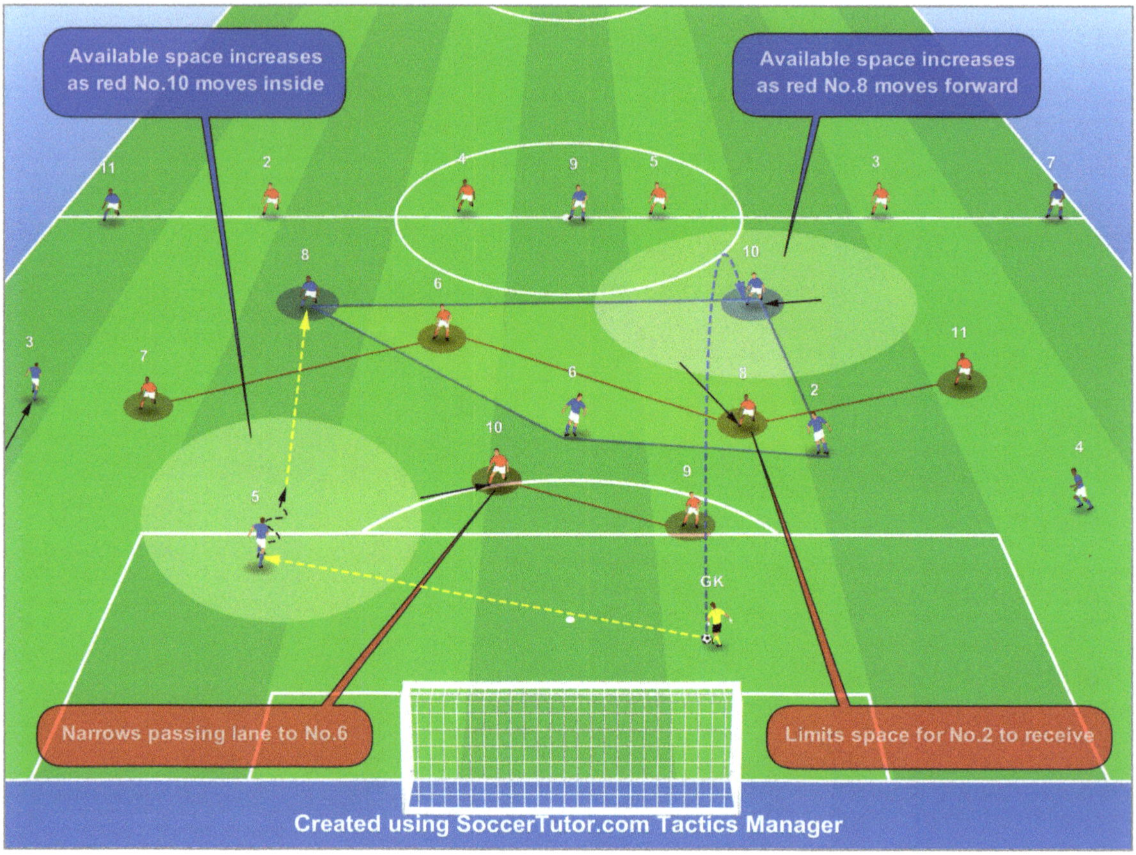

Game Situation: The red N°10 shifts centrally to narrow the passing lane to the **blue defensive midfielder (N°6)**.

Option 1 (Yellow Arrows): As more space opens up for the **left centre back (N°5)**, the **goalkeeper (GK)** passes to him.

The **aim is then to move the ball to a free player behind the second line**, with the **left attacking midfielder (N°8)** in a good position to receive directly from **N°5**.

If the red winger (N°7) shifts inside to block the pass to **blue N°8**, an alternative option is to pass wide to the **left back (N°3)**, who will have space to receive and advance.

Option 2 (Blue Arrows): Initially, on the right, no red players are positioned to block a pass to the **inverted right back (N°2)**, so he could receive and turn freely. To prevent this, the **red central midfielder (N°8) steps forward to restrict N°2's space**.

This movement creates a **large area of available space for the attacking midfielder and target player (N°10) to receive a direct aerial pass from GK** (blue arrow).

Note: In both situations, if the goalkeeper or N°5 execute their passes effectively, the first 2 pressing lines are broken, which neutralises 6 red opponents.

©SOCCERTUTOR.COM   BEAT THE PRESS WITH A BOX MIDFIELD

Box Midfield Build Up: Break Lines vs High Press Zonal Defending

5a. Utilising the Centre Back in a Wide Position to Break the Second Pressing Line when Passing to Defensive Midfielders is Too Risky

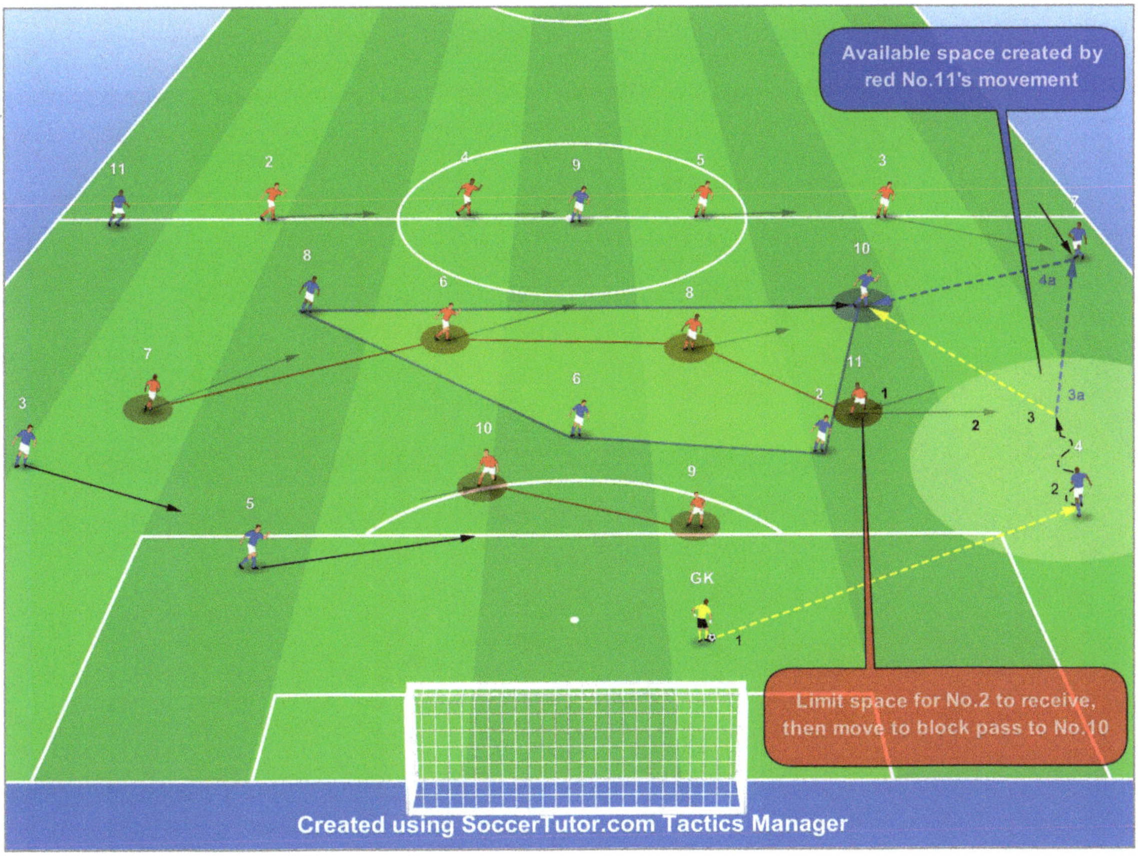

In this example, the red left winger (N°11) moves forward to mark the **blue defensive midfielder (N°2)**. The **centre back (N°4)** finds available space and becomes a viable passing option.

Once **N°4** receives from the **goalkeeper (GK)**, the **primary focus is on breaking the second pressing line** and progressing the play. The **best option is to find the attacking midfielder (N°10)**, who is positioned between the lines and in space to receive.

If the direct passing lane to **N°10** is open, then **N°4** should play a quick, accurate pass directly to him (yellow arrow).

However, if red N°11 cuts off this direct passing option, **N°4** must use the **right winger (N°7)** as a link player to move the ball to **N°10** (blue arrows).

Note: **This quick combination disrupts the opposition's defensive setup, forcing them to shift out of their positions and create opportunities for the blues to advance play into the final third.**

BEAT THE PRESS WITH A BOX MIDFIELD

Box Midfield Build Up: Break Lines vs High Press Zonal Defending

5b. Winger Drops Deep to Create Space for the Run of the Attacking Midfielder in Behind the Defensive Line

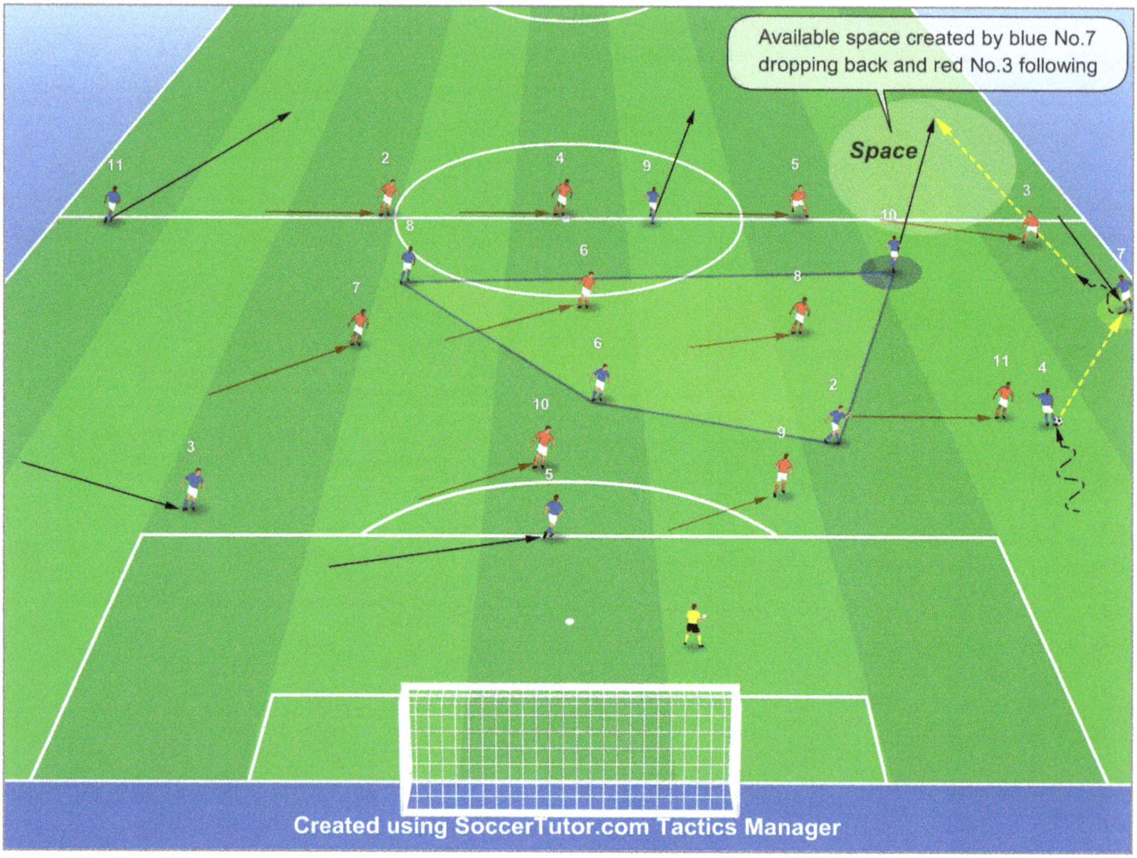

In this variation of the previous example, we again have the **right centre back (N°4)** with the ball in a wide position. Another way to create a free player behind the second pressing line is with the **winger (N°7)** dropping back into space where the opposing full back will struggle to follow.

As the red left back (N°3) does not track **blue N°7's** movement, he is able to receive and turn. The blues are able to **bypass the first 2 pressing lines very easily in this situation and neutralise 5 or 6 red players**. The next step is to advance the ball in behind the defensive line, with **N°10's** movement playing a key role in progressing towards the final third.

As **N°7** receives, the red left back (N°3) is forced to close him down. The **attacking midfielder (N°10) makes a run in behind red N°3** to receive with plenty of space ahead in the opposition's half.

Note 1: A player is considered free behind a defensive line if they can receive and turn without pressure.

Note 2: If red N°3 follows blue N°7 and marks him closely, the pass from N°4 can be played directly into the available space behind for the run of N°10.

Box Midfield Build Up: Break Lines vs High Press Zonal Defending

Drawing Press with a Pass and Exploit Gaps Created (2 at Back)

1. Exploiting Space After Drawing Press: GK to Inverted Full Back for Pass Wide to Centre Back (to Bypass Press)

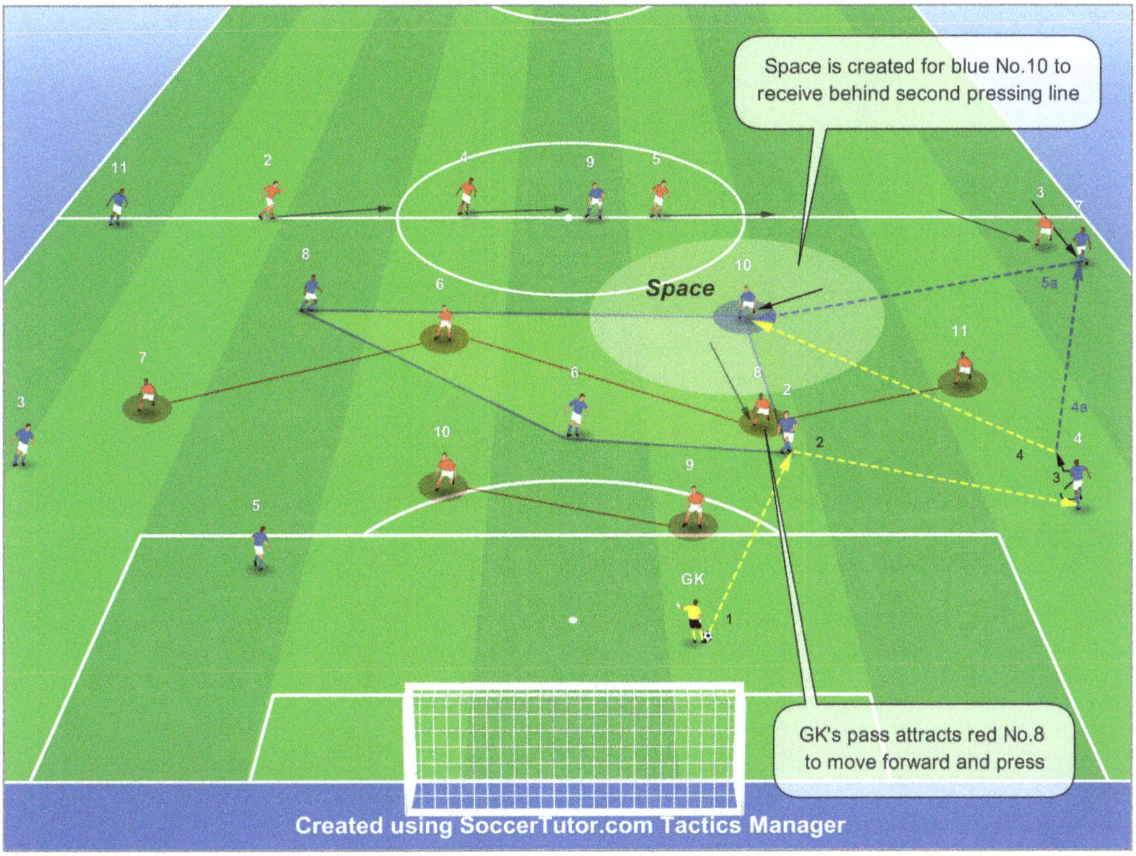

Another way to create space behind the second pressing line is to draw pressure with a pass. The **goalkeeper (GK)** passes to the **inverted full back (N°2)** behind the first pressing line. The **pass draws the red central midfielder (N°8) to move forward and press blue N°2** and prevent him from turning. Under pressure, **N°2** passes back to the **centre back (N°4)**. The reaction from red N°8 creates available space in behind the second pressing line.

The **aim is to move the ball to the attacking midfielder (N°10)**. If the direct through pass (yellow arrow) is blocked, **N°4** uses the **right winger (N°7)** as a link player to move the ball to **N°10** (blue arrows).

2 Key Principles:

1. **Quickly recognise which side the press is coming from**.
2. **Move the ball into the available space as quickly as possible**.

BEAT THE PRESS WITH A BOX MIDFIELD

Box Midfield Build Up: Break Lines vs High Press Zonal Defending

2. Variation: GK to Defensive Midfielder, Back to GK, and Quick Pass Wide to Centre Back for Line Breaking Pass

Space is created for blue No.8 to receive behind second pressing line

GK's pass attracts red No.6 to move forward and press

In this variation, the **goalkeeper (GK) passes to the defensive midfielder (N°6)** in the centre. Once this pass is played, the red central midfielder (N°6) moves forward to press him. The **blues quickly recognise the situation and look to exploit the space created behind red N°6 by moving the ball to the attacking midfielder (N°8)** in behind the second pressing line.

Option 1 (Yellow Arrows): Back pass to **GK**, who directs the ball into an area with available space, which is a pass to the **centre back (N°5)** in this example. N°5 dribbles the ball forward quickly and passes to N°8 before any opponents can move to block the passing lane.

If the red winger (N°7) manages to block the lane, the **blue left back (N°3)** will have more space and receives instead.

Option 2 (Blue Arrows): A **quicker but riskier option is a pass to the inverted right back (N°2 - defensive midfield position)**. If N°2 receives, a through pass to **N°8** best exploits the situation.

Note: A box midfield with 2-at-the-back boosts forward passing but leaves only 1 deep centre back. Passes must be safe and N°4 should shift centrally for balance. As play advances, the outfield players' shape shifts into a 3-2-2-3.

©SOCCERTUTOR.COM

BEAT THE PRESS WITH A BOX MIDFIELD

Box Midfield Build Up: Break Lines vs High Press Zonal Defending

Options for Breaking the First and Second Pressing Lines (3 at Back)

1. Effective Positioning with 3-at-the-Back Box Midfield

With 3-at-the-back shape, GK has option to move forward with the ball before passing

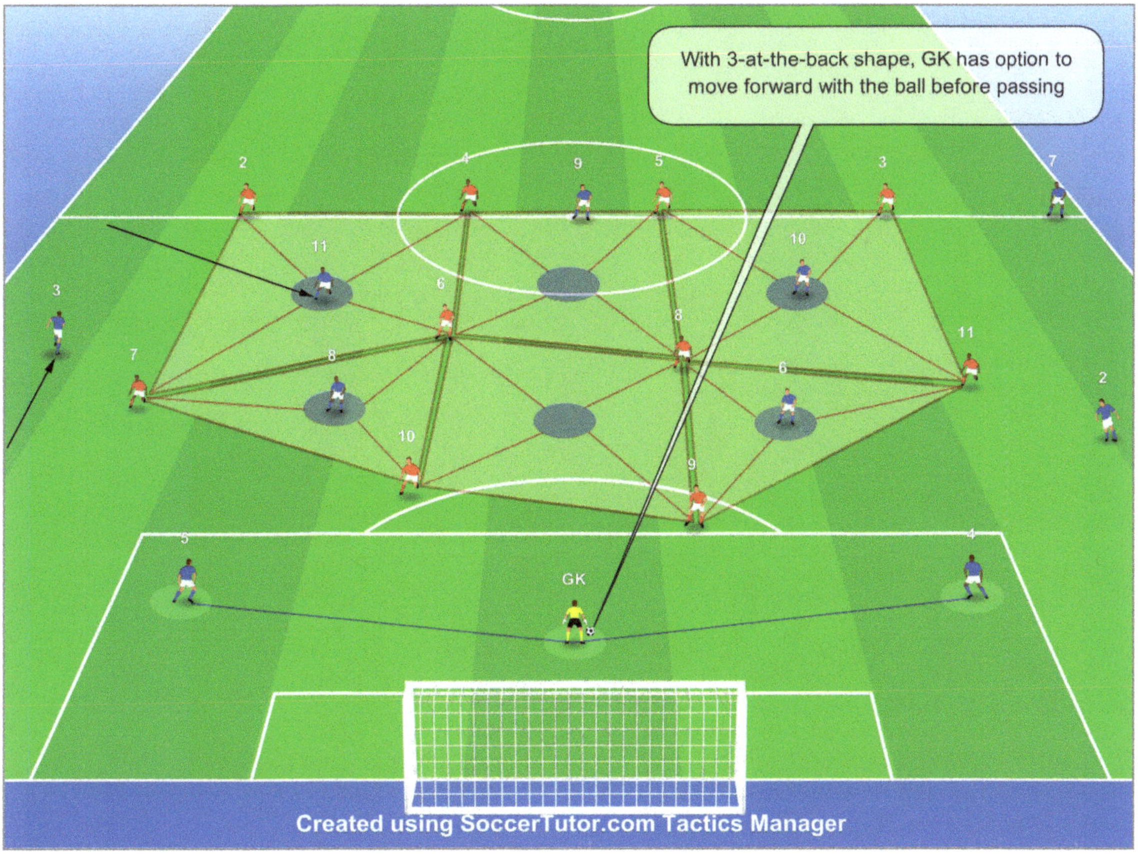

With the 3-at-the-back box midfield, 4 of the 6 spaces between the opposition's lines are occupied.

See page 30 for full details of how this build up shape is formed from the 4-2-3-1 formation (it can also be from 3-4-2-1).

To break as many lines as possible, the **goalkeeper (GK)** must play accurate passes, which **relies on effective positioning from the 4 midfielders**.

The longer and more precise the pass, the more defensive lines are bypassed, which neutralises more opponents. Unlike with 2-at-the-back, the 3-at-the-back shape has **GK between the 2 red forwards (N°9 and N°10), allowing him to move forward with the ball and reduce the passing distance to the target players**. This increases the likelihood of an accurate forward pass, making it easier to progress play while maintaining control.

©SOCCERTUTOR.COM BEAT THE PRESS WITH A BOX MIDFIELD

Box Midfield Build Up: Break Lines vs High Press Zonal Defending

2a. Playing Out from Goalkeeper Through the Centre and Create Free Players Behind the Second Pressing Line

Diagram labels:
- Moves forward and creates dilemma for red No.2
- Decision: Mark No.11 or stay?
- Target player
- Target player
- Shifts towards the left to provide balance after No.3 moves forward

Created using SoccerTutor.com Tactics Manager

If the ball is played behind the first pressing line to a **defensive midfielder** (**Nº6 or Nº8**) and they can turn, the next aim is to break the second line. To do this, the attacking team has to create free players behind the second pressing line. The **players should position themselves in a way that forces defenders to make difficult choices**.

With the **blue winger** (**Nº11**) positioned centrally as an attacking midfielder in the box midfield build up shape, the red right back (Nº2) may choose to move forward and mark him. This can be exploited by pushing the **left back** (**Nº3**) forward into the space left behind.

The blue **defensive midfielder** (**Nº8**) shifts across to provide defensive cover in case possession is lost.

This setup normally results in the opposing defenders choosing to stay back and cover the threat of the blue attacking players (**Nº9**, **Nº7** and **Nº3**). Most often, the result is that both players in the attacking midfield positions at the top of the box midfield (**Nº10** and **Nº11**) are left free of marking between the lines.

The diagrams to follow will show how to move the ball to these 2 target players.

BEAT THE PRESS WITH A BOX MIDFIELD

Box Midfield Build Up: Break Lines vs High Press Zonal Defending

2b. Moving the Ball to the Attacking Midfielders (Target Players) Behind the Second Pressing Line

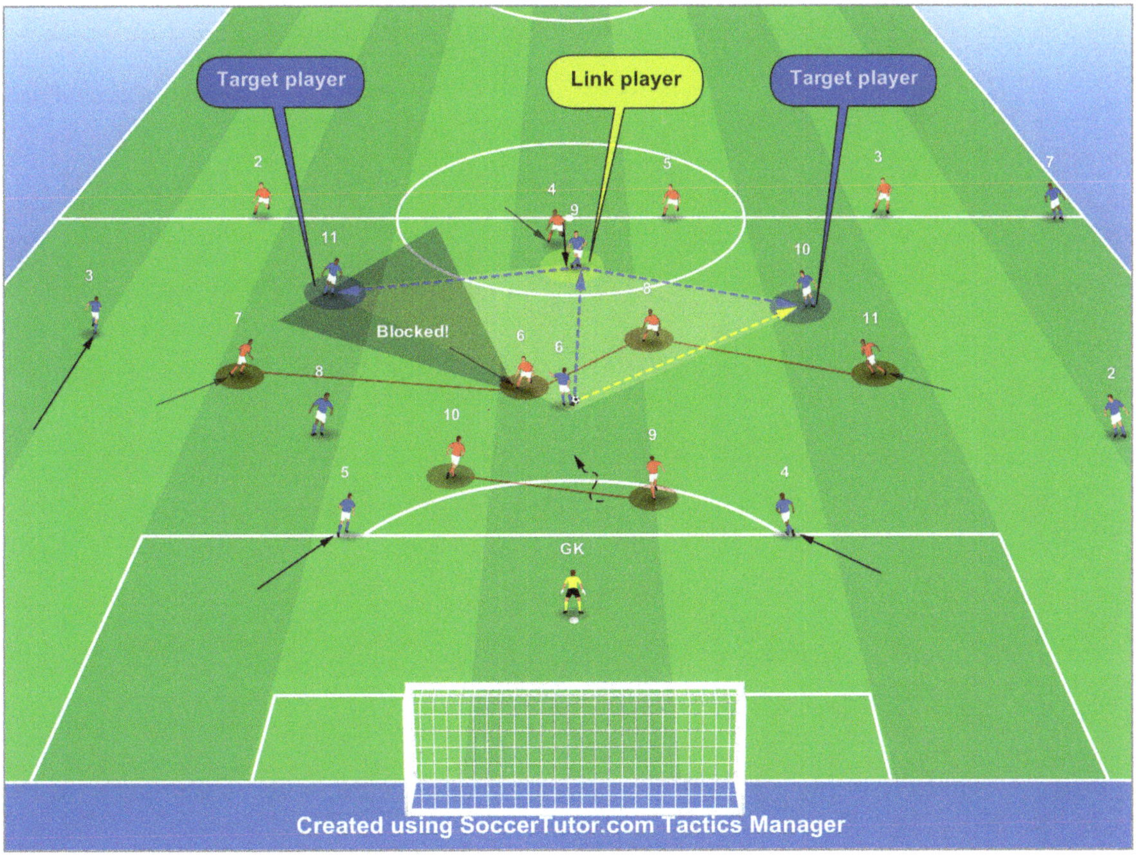

Once a player receives unmarked behind the first pressing line (**N°6** in diagram) and free players are positioned behind the second line (**N°11** and **N°10**), the next step is to create more passing options for the player in possession.

The **players behind the second line move into different passing lanes to create at least 2 passing options for the ball carrier**, ideally in a triangle shape.

As red N°6 presses the ball, the **forward** (**N°9**) and **attacking midfielders** (**N°11** and **N°10**) position themselves to form 2 triangles (1 diamond shape).

Although red N°6 blocks the direct pass to **blue N°11**, the ball can still reach the **other target player** (**N°10**) directly (yellow arrow) or either target player via the **link player** (**N°9** - blue arrows).

After **N°11** or **N°10** receive in space behind the second pressing line, the next action is to pass in behind the defensive line for a run of an attacker.

BEAT THE PRESS WITH A BOX MIDFIELD

Box Midfield Build Up: Break Lines vs High Press Zonal Defending

3a. Playing Out from Goalkeeper to the Side and Create Free Players Behind the Second Pressing Line

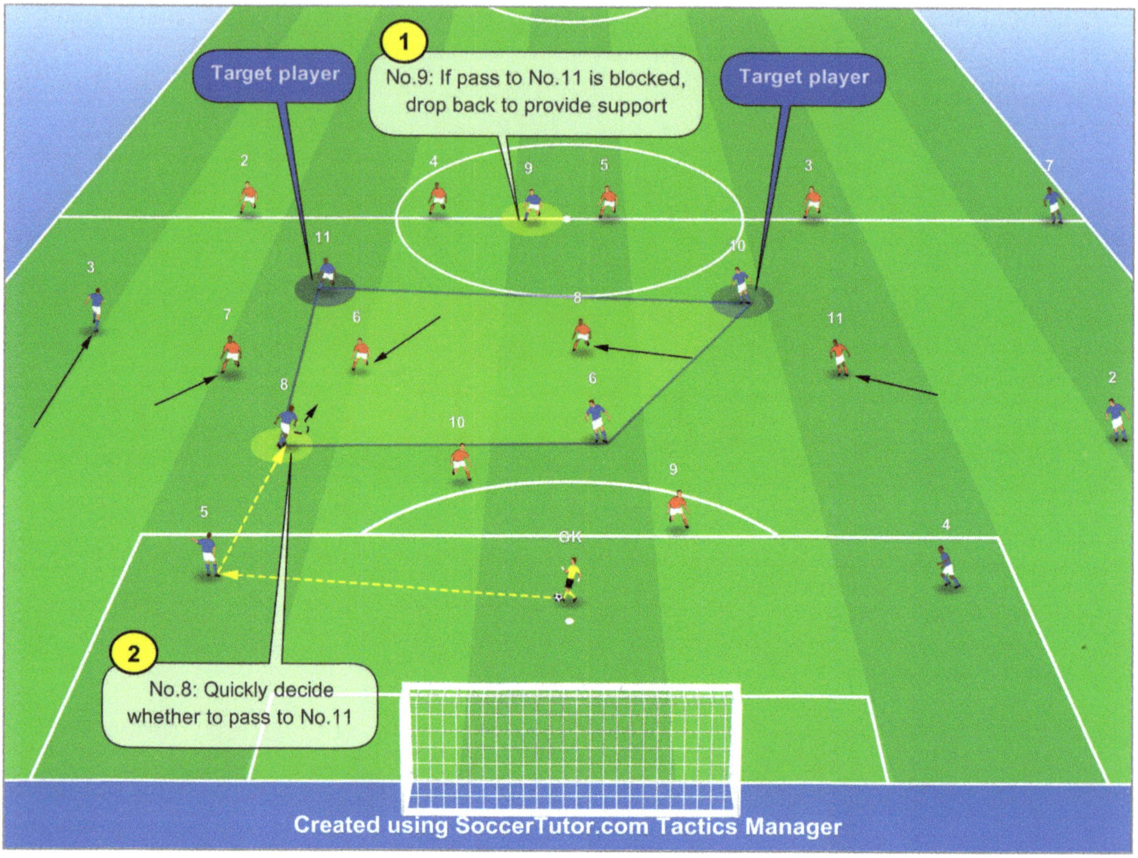

If the ball is played to the **defensive midfielder (N°8)** behind the first pressing line and the player can turn, the **next aim is to break the second pressing line**. This can be achieved by creating free players behind the second line and moving the ball to them. As both **N°11 and N°10 are free**, the **primary aim is to move the ball to the attacking midfielder on that side (N°11)**.

As the red midfielders shift and press, **N°8 must quickly decide whether to pass to N°11**. If the pass is clearly on and **N°11** can turn, the **forward (N°9)** should stay high and later make a diagonal run to receive in behind the defensive line.

If the pass is blocked or too risky, **N°9 should drop back, increase the passing options for the player in possession, and act as a link player** to move the ball to **N°11** or **N°10**.

Note: N°9 must read the situation well to provide support and help progress the attack effectively. The timing and body shape of the key players is essential to beating the press.

Box Midfield Build Up: Break Lines vs High Press Zonal Defending

3b. Moving the Ball to the Attacking Midfielders (Target Players) Behind the Second Pressing Line

Following on from the previous page, as **N°8** dribbles forward and red N°6 and N°7 shift to close the passing lane to **N°11**, **N°9 becomes the key link player** to beat the second pressing line.

N°9 drops back to act as the link player to move the ball to either attacking midfielder (N°11 or N°10), depending on who is free (yellow arrows).

Alternatively, the other **defensive midfielder (N°6) can be used as a link player to move the ball to N°10** on the weak side (blue arrows).

The **left back (N°3)**, positioned high after forward movement, may also become an option if the central route is totally blocked off. The **team must always read defensive shifts and circulate the ball quickly** to exploit openings.

Once either **N°11 or N°10** receive, the next step is to play a through pass in behind the opposition's defensive line.

Box Midfield Build Up: Break Lines vs High Press Zonal Defending

Drawing Press with a Pass and Exploit Gaps Created (3 at Back)

1. Draw Pressure from Midfielder to Create Space Behind Second Pressing Line for <u>Left Attacking Midfielder</u> to Receive

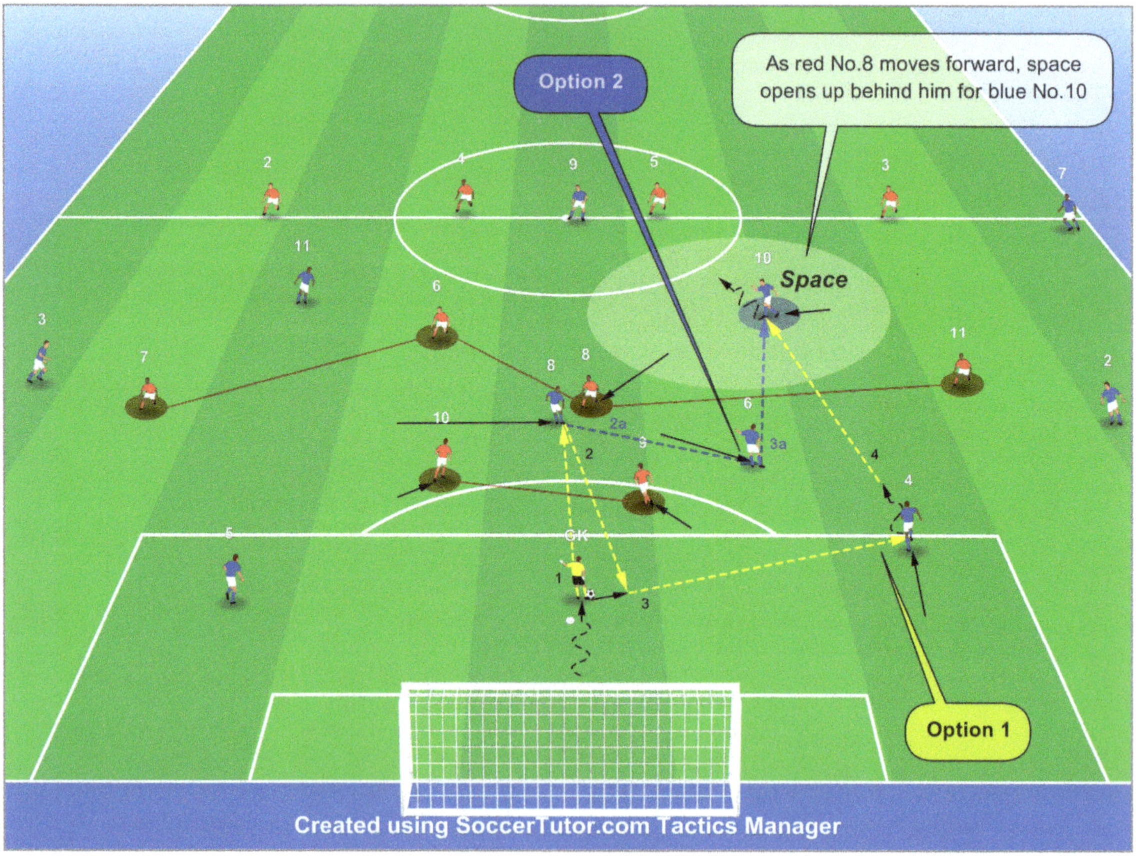

With 3-at-the-back, the **goalkeeper (GK)** is positioned between 2 pressing forwards and can play through the first line easier. As the potential receiver usually has their back to goal, the **through pass typically draws pressure**. This can be on purpose and is guided with these principles:

A. **Quick read of the situation and where the available space is.**

B. **Move the ball into this space as quickly as possible.**

GK plays a through pass to Nº8. As **red Nº8 moves to press, space opens up behind for blue Nº10** to receive behind.

Option 1 (Yellow Arrows): Nº8 passes back to **GK**, then to **centre back (Nº4)**, who finds **Nº10** before the opposition shifts.

Option 2 (Blue Arrows): A quicker but riskier option is for **Nº8** to pass to **Nº6**, who then finds **Nº10**.

BEAT THE PRESS WITH A BOX MIDFIELD

Box Midfield Build Up: Break Lines vs High Press Zonal Defending

2. Draw Pressure from Midfielder to Create Space Behind Second Pressing Line for <u>Left Attacking Midfielder</u> to Receive

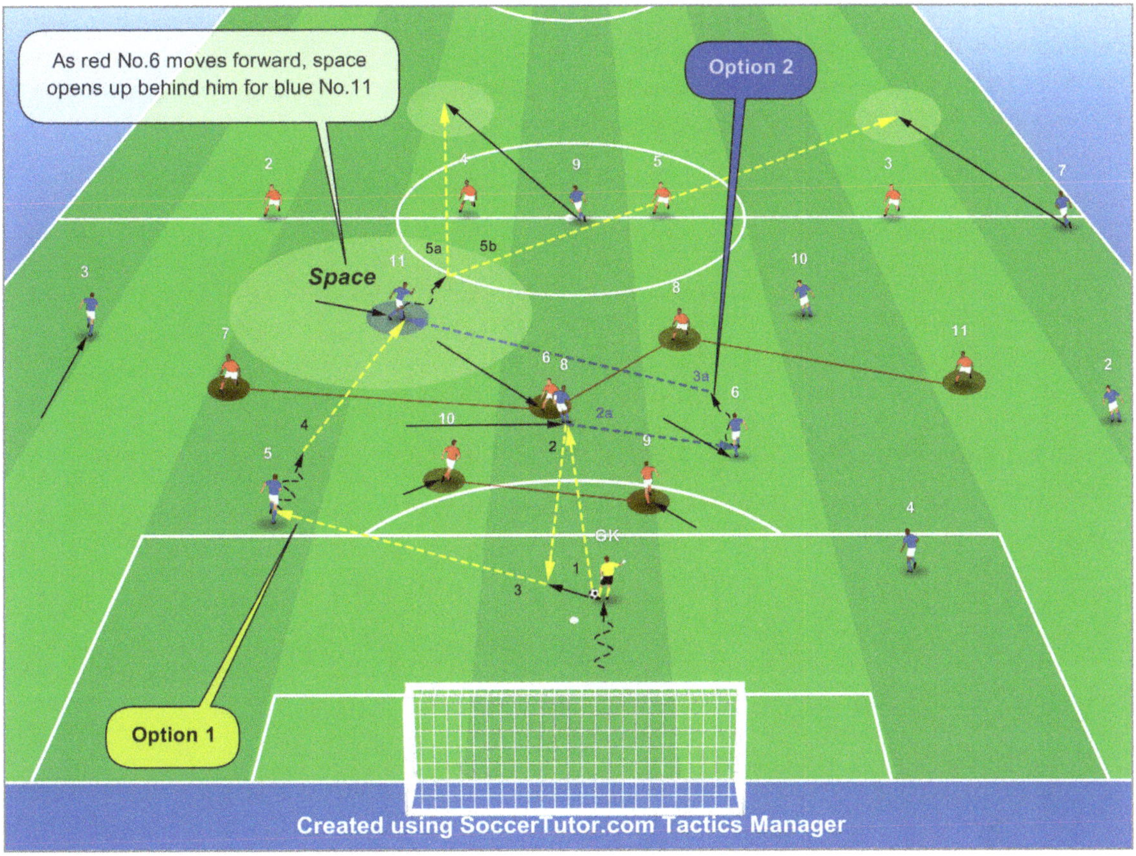

In this variation of the previous example, the **goalkeeper (GK)** passes to the **left defensive midfielder (N°8)** and the **opposing red central midfielder (N°6)** presses. Space opens up for the **left attacking midfielder (N°11 - target player)** to receive in between the lines.

This can be done in 2 ways.

Option 1 (Yellow Arrows): N°8 passes back to **GK**, then to **centre back (N°5)**, who dribbles forward and passes to **N°11**.

Option 2 (Blue Arrows): A quicker but riskier option is for **N°8** to pass to **N°6**, who moves forward and passes to **N°11**.

Note: Quick decision making and timing are vital to take advantage of the space before the red defending players recover for both options. In this example, the ball must move at speed to exploit the opening created by red N°6's pressing.

BEAT THE PRESS WITH A BOX MIDFIELD

Box Midfield Build Up: Break Lines vs High Press Zonal Defending

Drawing Pressure with Centre Back Dribbling Forward (3 at Back)

1. Opposing Forwards Narrow the Central Passing Lanes which Creates Space for the Centre Backs to Receive and Dribble Forward

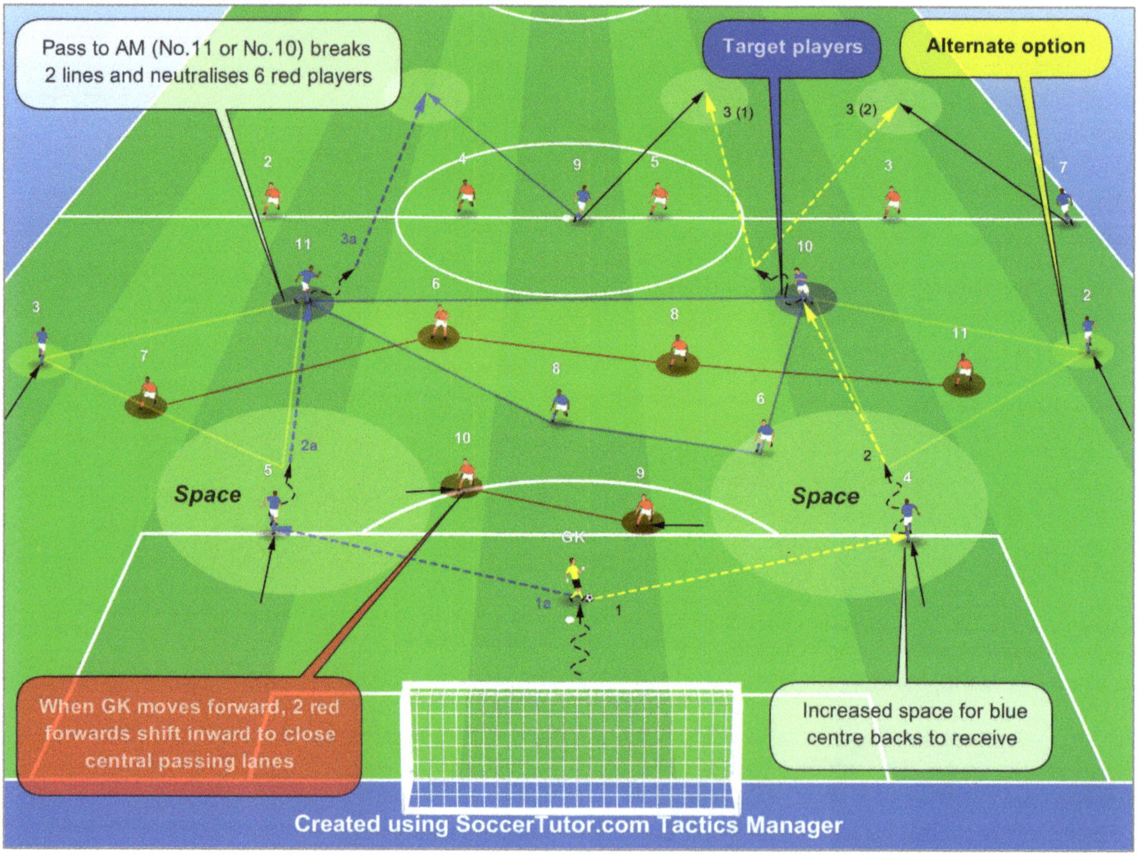

[Diagram: Pass to AM (No.11 or No.10) breaks 2 lines and neutralises 6 red players. Target players. Alternate option. Space. Space. When GK moves forward, 2 red forwards shift inward to close central passing lanes. Increased space for blue centre backs to receive.]

When the **goalkeeper (GK) carries the ball forward between 2 red forwards, they instinctively shift inward** to close the central passing lanes.

This movement **pulls them away from their original positions and increases the space available for the 2 blue centre backs (N°4 and N°5)** to receive. As the first pressing line collapses centrally, passing lanes to both centre backs open up.

The **full backs (N°3 and N°2)** push forward and create triangle shapes.

If a wide passing lane opens up to the attacking midfielders (N°11 or N°10), a direct pass can break 2 lines and neutralise 6 red players. If the red wingers (N°7 and N°11) shift inside to block the passing lanes, the ball can instead be played to the **full backs (N°3 or N°2)**, who will have time and space to progress play forward.

BEAT THE PRESS WITH A BOX MIDFIELD

Box Midfield Build Up: Break Lines vs High Press Zonal Defending

2. Full Backs Exploit Space Created by Central Pressing to Break the Second Pressing Line and Progress Play Wide

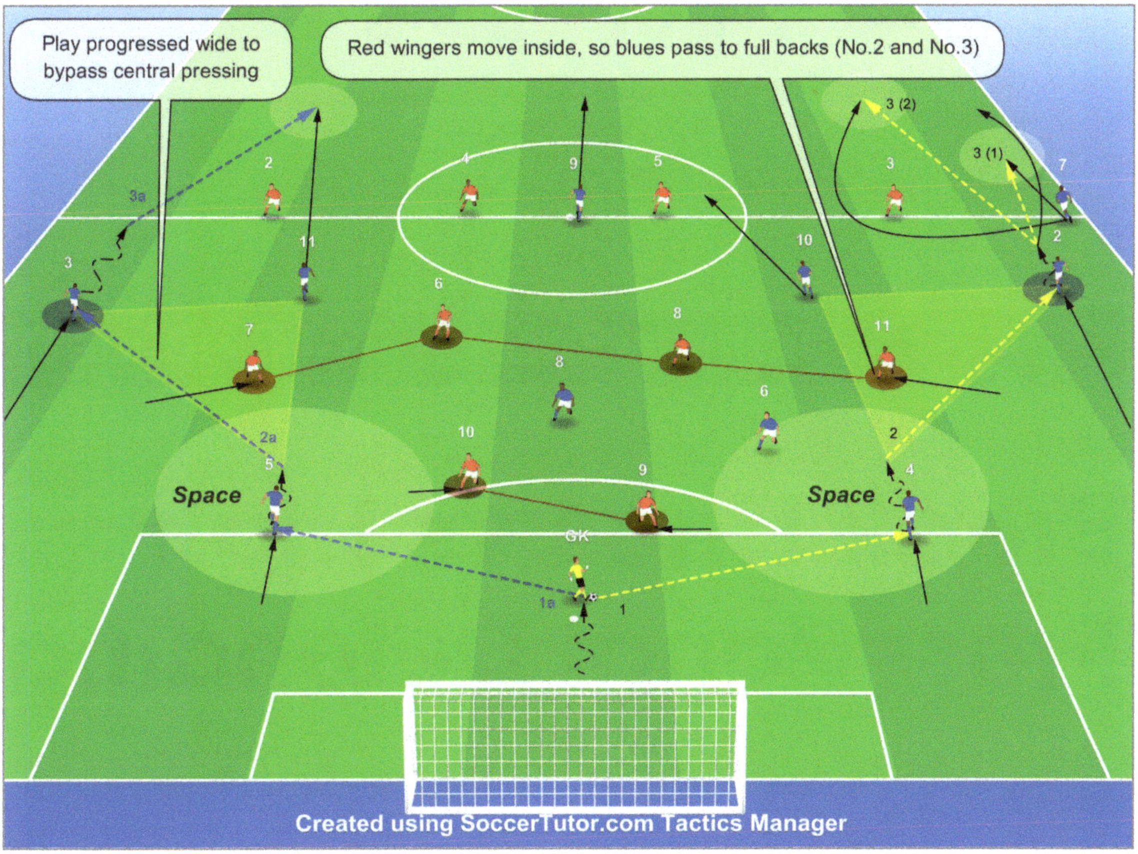

Play progressed wide to bypass central pressing

Red wingers move inside, so blues pass to full backs (No.2 and No.3)

In this variation, the **red wingers (N°7 & N°11) shift centrally to block inside passes, so space opens wide for the blue full backs (N°3 & N°2)** to break the second pressing line by exploiting the 2v1 situation.

Left Side: The **centre back (N°5)** can pass to the **left back (N°3)**, neutralising 2 pressing lines (6 red players).

The **left attacking midfielder (N°11)** makes a run in behind the red right back (N°2), the **forward (N°9)** runs forward, and the **right attacking midfielder (N°10)** runs centrally.

This central overload stops the red centre backs from supporting the full backs, allowing play to progress down the flank.

Right Side: The **centre back (N°4)** can find the **right back (N°2)** in space.

If **N°2** carries the ball forward, the **right winger (N°7)** moves inside and attacks the space behind red N°3 to receive in behind. Another option is for **N°2** to pass to **N°7** and make an overlapping run. Both options exploit the 2v1 situation wide, while **N°10** stays in a central position and becomes a potential receiver of a key pass or cross.

Note: In both of these situations (left and right), the build up play is progressed out wide by bypassing the opposition's central pressing.

BOX MIDFIELD SESSION

Training Session 1 (4 Practices)

Break Lines vs High Press Zonal Defending

Based on Guardiola, Alonso, and Arteta build up patterns

BEAT THE PRESS WITH A BOX MIDFIELD

Box Midfield Session 1: Break Lines vs High Press Zonal Defending

TRAINING SESSION (4 PRACTICES)
1. Passing Decisions to Break Lines Depending on Opposition Pressing

Variation 1: Midfield Decision Making Based on Opponent's Pressing

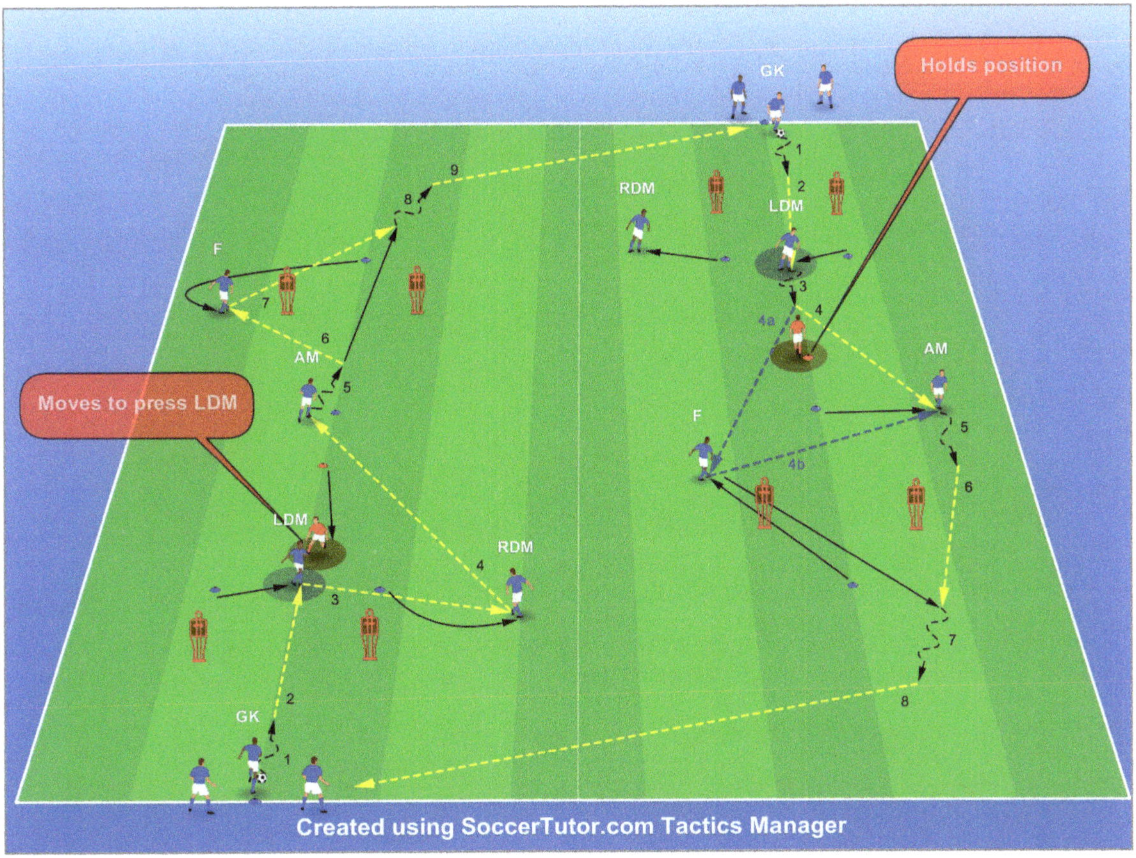

Practice Description (Variation 1)

- **Objective:** Decision making for whether to turn or pass back (to exploit space).
- The mannequins mark the first and third pressing lines and the red player is in the second line.
- **Left Side: GK** passes to **LDM**, who must assess the red player's reaction. If pressed, **LDM** passes to **RDM** and the ball is quickly played to **AM** behind the red player.

- **AM** turns and plays a one-two with **F** around the mannequin before passing to the other group.
- **Right Side:** If not pressed, **LDM** turns. The ball is either played to **AM** directly or via the link player **F** (blue arrows). **F** then runs in between the mannequins to receive **AM's** through pass and pass to the other group.
- **Player Rotations: GK → LDM → RDM → AM → F → GK (Other Group).**

BEAT THE PRESS WITH A BOX MIDFIELD

Box Midfield Session 1: Break Lines vs High Press Zonal Defending

Variation 2: Using Centre Back as Link Player

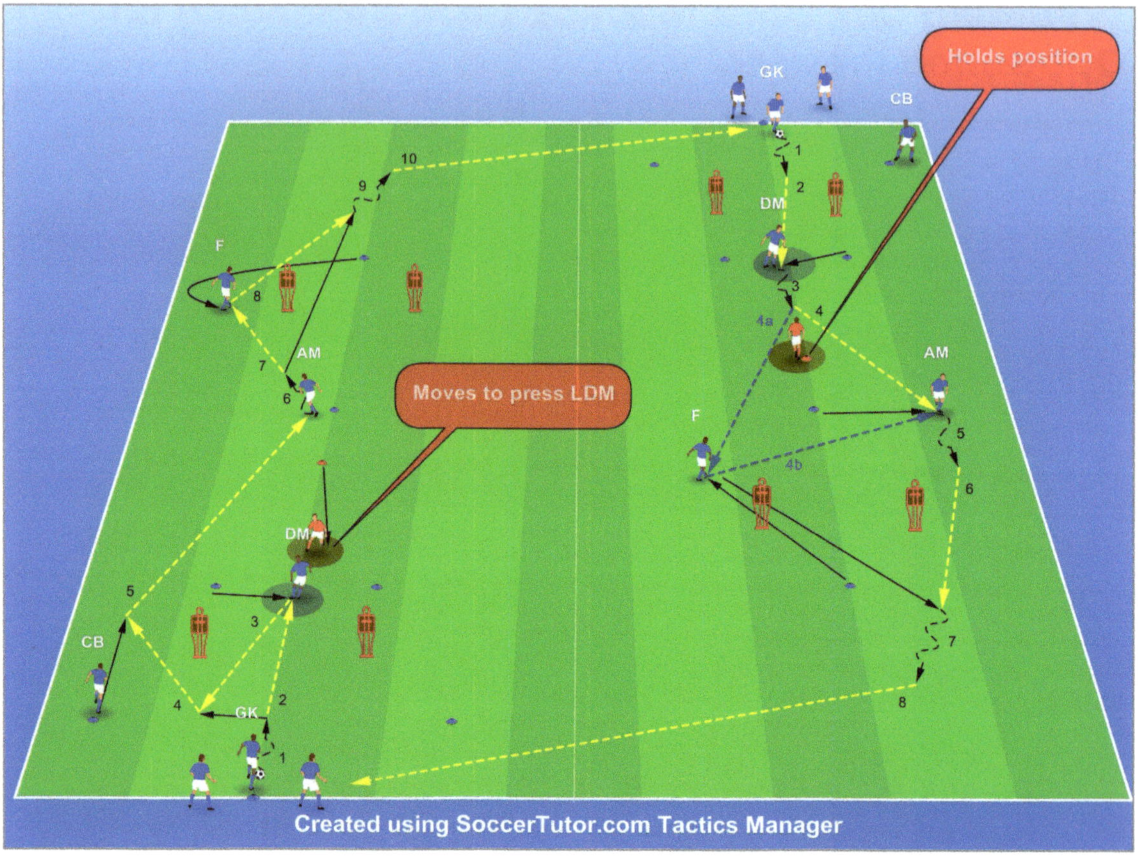

Practice Description (Variation 2)

- In this variation, we replace the right defensive midfielder (**RDM**) with a centre back (**CB**).

- **Left Side:** **GK** passes to **DM** and if pressed, the ball is returned back to **GK**. **GK** passes to **CB**, who passes to **AM**. **AM** turns and plays a one-two with **F** around the mannequin before passing to the other group.

- **Right Side:** If not pressed, **DM** turns. The ball is either played to **AM** directly or via **F**, who acts as a link player (blue arrows). **F** then runs in between the mannequins to receive **AM's** through pass before passing to the other group.

- **Player Rotations:** GK → CB → DM → AM → F → GK (Other Group).

Coaching Points

1. **Scan early** to decide whether to turn or pass back under pressure.
2. Support with **clear communication** e.g. "turn", "pass", "man-on".
3. **Move the ball quickly** to exploit space and break lines.
4. **Time support runs** to create clear passing options.

BEAT THE PRESS WITH A BOX MIDFIELD

Box Midfield Session 1: Break Lines vs High Press Zonal Defending

PROGRESSION

2. Moving the Ball Beyond the Lines Based on Defender Reactions 7 (+GK) v 2 Functional Practice

Variation 1: Receive + Turn When Not Pressed (3-at-Back-Box Midfield)

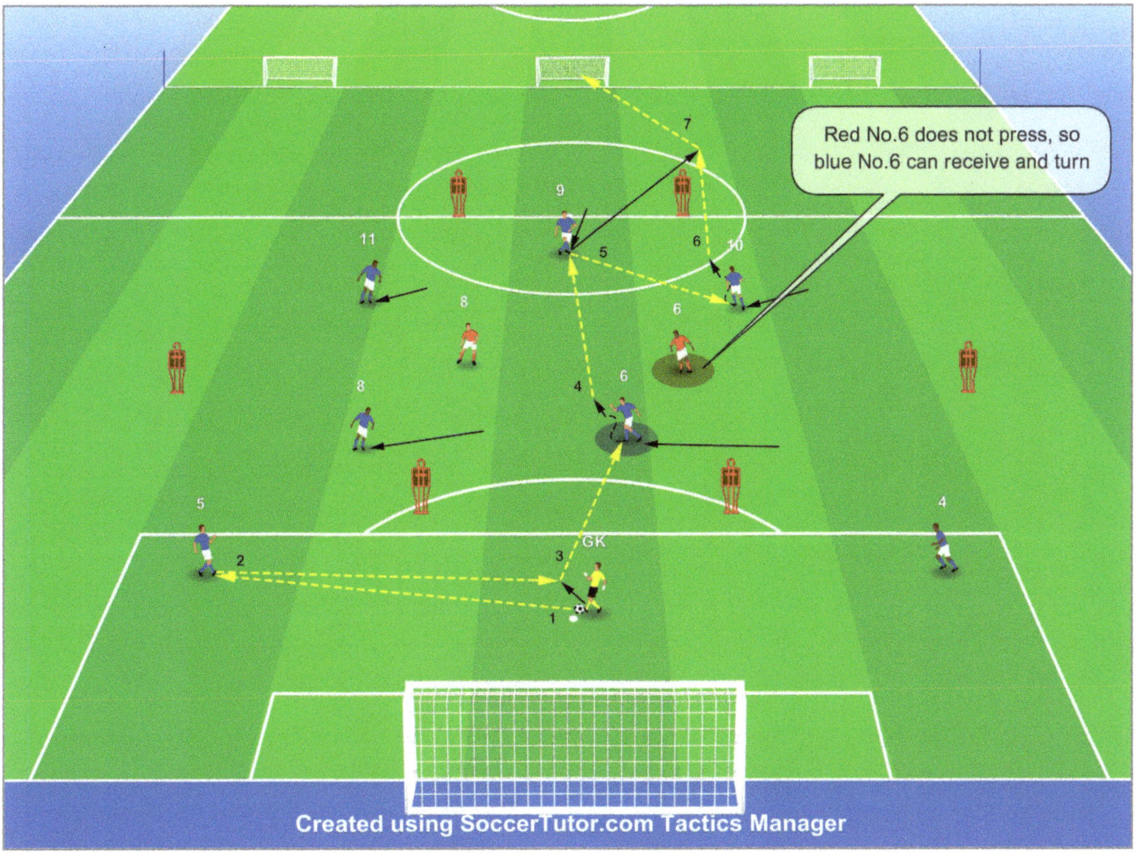

Red No.6 does not press, so blue No.6 can receive and turn

Practice Description (Variation 1)

- The blues have the goalkeeper, 2 centre backs, the box midfield, and the forward.
- The reds have 2 central midfielders and the mannequins form the rest of the defensive formation.
- **GK** starts and circulates the ball with the **centre backs (N°5 and N°4)** before passing to a **defensive midfielder (N°6 in diagram)** behind the first pressing line, who must scan before receiving.

- If the nearest **red midfielder (N°6) holds their position (Variation 1)**, **blue N°6 receives on the half-turn** and passes forward.
- Nearby teammates quickly offer passing options to progress the attack, ideally forming a triangle or diamond shape.
- In this example, the **forward (N°9)** plays a give-and-go with the **attacking midfielder (N°10)** to receive in behind the defensive line and score.

BEAT THE PRESS WITH A BOX MIDFIELD

Box Midfield Session 1: Break Lines vs High Press Zonal Defending

Variation 2: Exploit Space Behind Press (3-at-Back-Box Midfield)

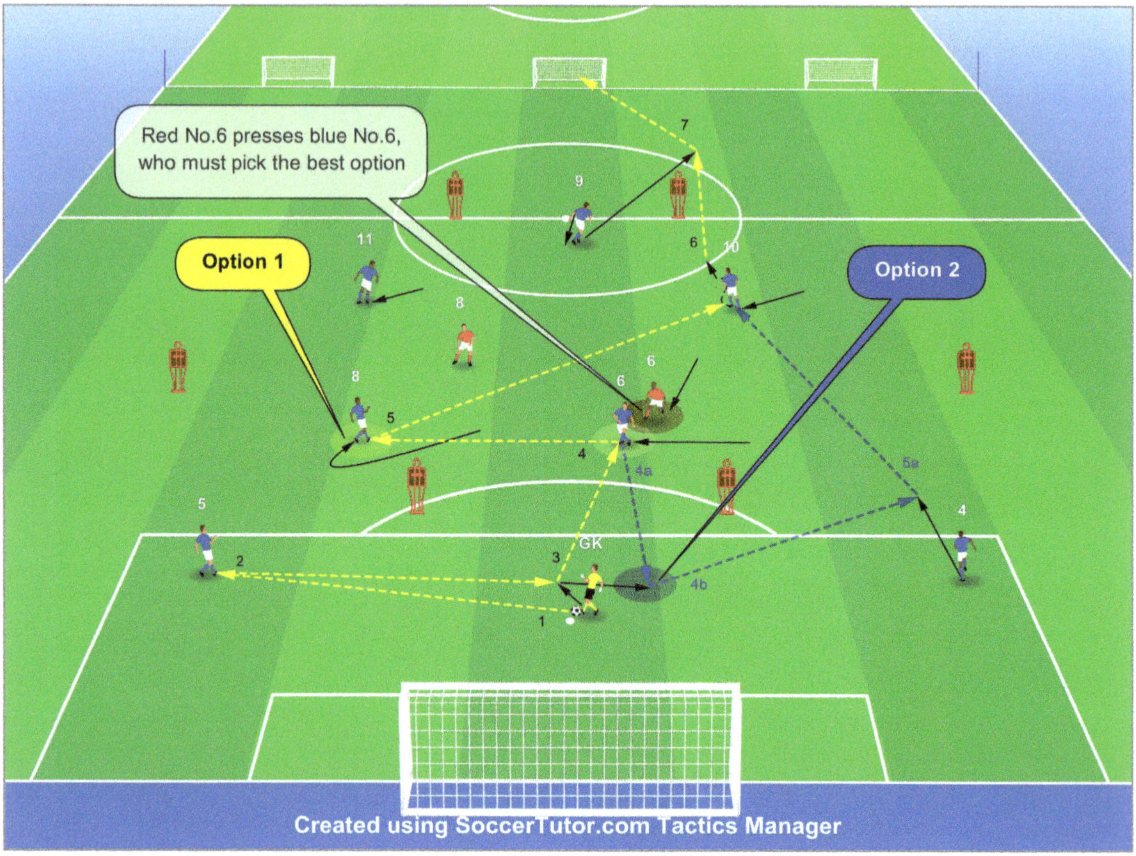

Red No.6 presses blue No.6, who must pick the best option

Option 1

Option 2

Practice Description (Variation 2)

- In **Variation 2, the red midfielder presses blue N°6** as soon as the goalkeeper plays the pass. This means turning is not a good option as in Variation 1.

- N°6 must make a **quick decision whether to pass to the other defensive midfielder (N°8), back to the GK, or possibly back to a centre back**.

- Quick ball circulation is used to **exploit the space behind red N°6 and move the ball to the blue attacking midfielder (N°10)** behind the second pressing line. **Option 1** (yellow arrows) uses **N°8** as the link player. **Option 2** uses **N°4** as the link player.

- **N°10** plays in behind for the **forward (N°9)** to score.

- **Note: Adapt for a 2-at-the-back box midfield** by positioning the **GK** wider and **N°5** more central.

Coaching Points

1. **Recognise pressing early** and decide quickly whether to turn or pass.
2. **Communicate clearly** using prompts like "turn" or "pass."
3. **Move the ball quickly** to exploit space behind the press.
4. **Use sharp combinations** to break through pressing lines.

Box Midfield Session 1: Break Lines vs High Press Zonal Defending

PROGRESSION

3. Breaking Lines Against a High Press in a 9 (+GK) v 6 Positional Game

Variation 1: Draw Press to Create Space Behind Second Pressing Line

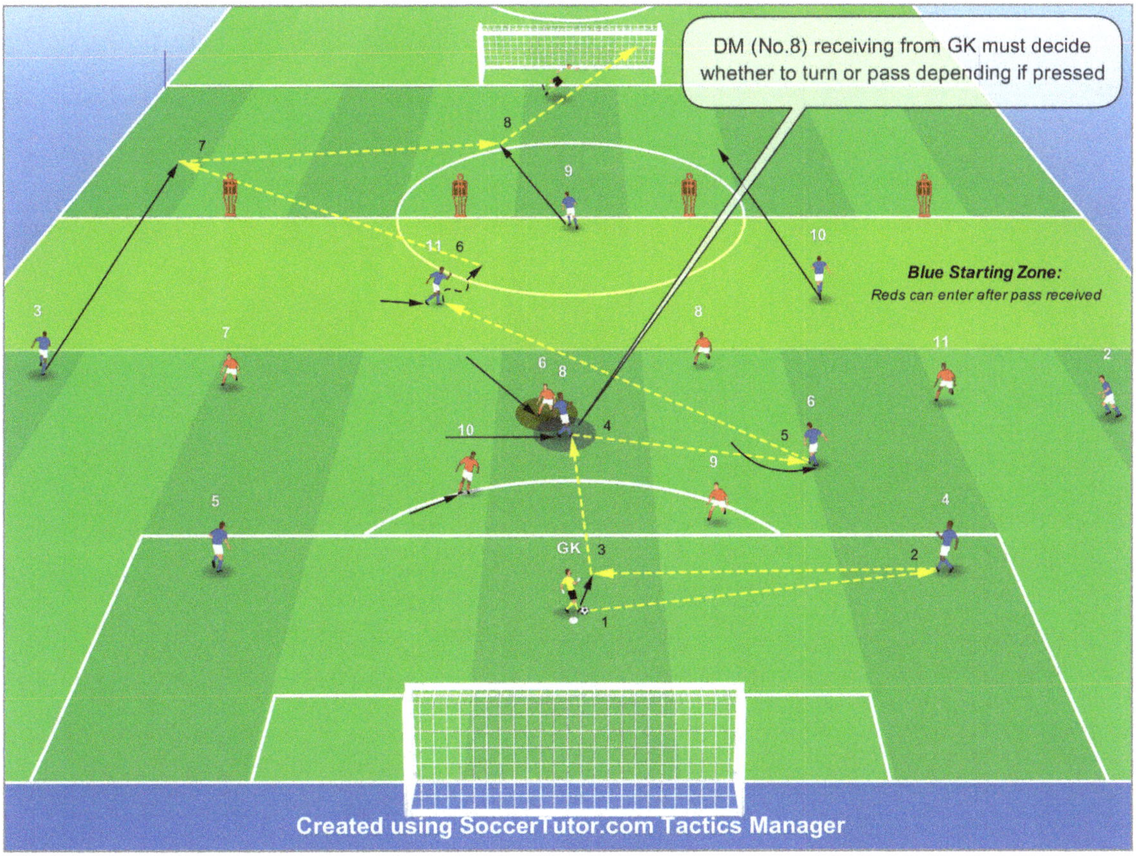

![diagram]

DM (No.8) receiving from GK must decide whether to turn or pass depending if pressed

Blue Starting Zone: Reds can enter after pass received

Practice Description (Variation 1)

- The yellow zone marks where the 3 blue attackers (**Nº11, Nº9,** and **Nº10**) start. The reds can only enter once a blue player receives inside it.

- The goalkeeper (**GK**) starts and circulates the ball with the **centre backs** (**Nº5 and Nº4**) before passing to a **defensive midfielder** (**Nº8 in diagram**) behind the first pressing line. The reds are in a 4-2 defensive shape

- **Nº8 must decide to turn or pass** based on whether the closest red midfielder (Nº6) moves to press or not.

- *Refer to the previous practice for more detail*.

- **Blue Objective:** Build up from back, break through the second line, and then the third line (mannequins) to score.

- **Red Objective:** Press to win the ball and counter to score within 8–12 seconds.

Box Midfield Session 1: Break Lines vs High Press Zonal Defending

Variation 2: Goalkeeper Draws Press to Create Space for Centre Back

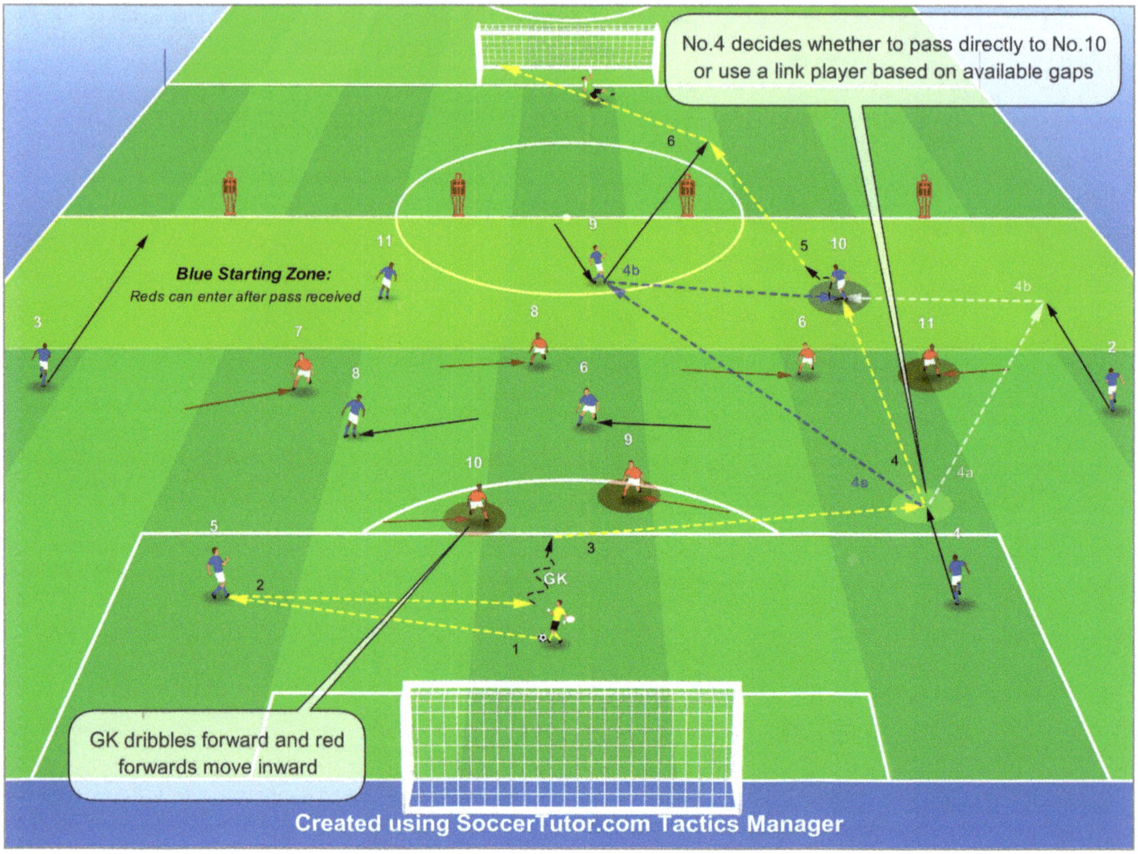

No.4 decides whether to pass directly to No.10 or use a link player based on available gaps

Blue Starting Zone: Reds can enter after pass received

GK dribbles forward and red forwards move inward

Practice Description (Variation 2)

- In this variation, the **goalkeeper** (**GK**) moves forward with he ball and the red forwards (N°10 and N°9) block the central passing lane. **GK** passes wide to a **centre back** (**N°4**). The blue **full backs** (**N°3 and N°2**) advance to support.

- **Blue Objective:** N°4 must read the red midfielders' reactions, such as whether the red winger (N°11) shifts inside.

- Based on the available passing lanes, **N°4** plays directly to the **attacking midfielder N°10** (yellow arrow) or uses link players (blue and white arrows). Once **N°10** receives, the aim is to play in behind and finish.

- **Red Objective:** Press to win the ball and counter to score within 8–12 seconds.

- **Note:** This can be adapted from a 3-at-the-back to a 2-at-the-back box midfield build up play practice by positioning the **GK** wider and **centre back** (**N°5**) more centrally. However, the **GK** will lose the option to dribble the ball forward.

Coaching Points

1. **Recognise pressure** and decide whether to turn, pass back, or switch play.
2. **Circulate the ball quickly** to exploit space behind pressing lines.

BEAT THE PRESS WITH A BOX MIDFIELD

Box Midfield Session 1: Break Lines vs High Press Zonal Defending

PROGRESSION

4. Break Lines Through Turning, Recycling the Ball, or Dribbling Forward 3 Zone Conditioned Game

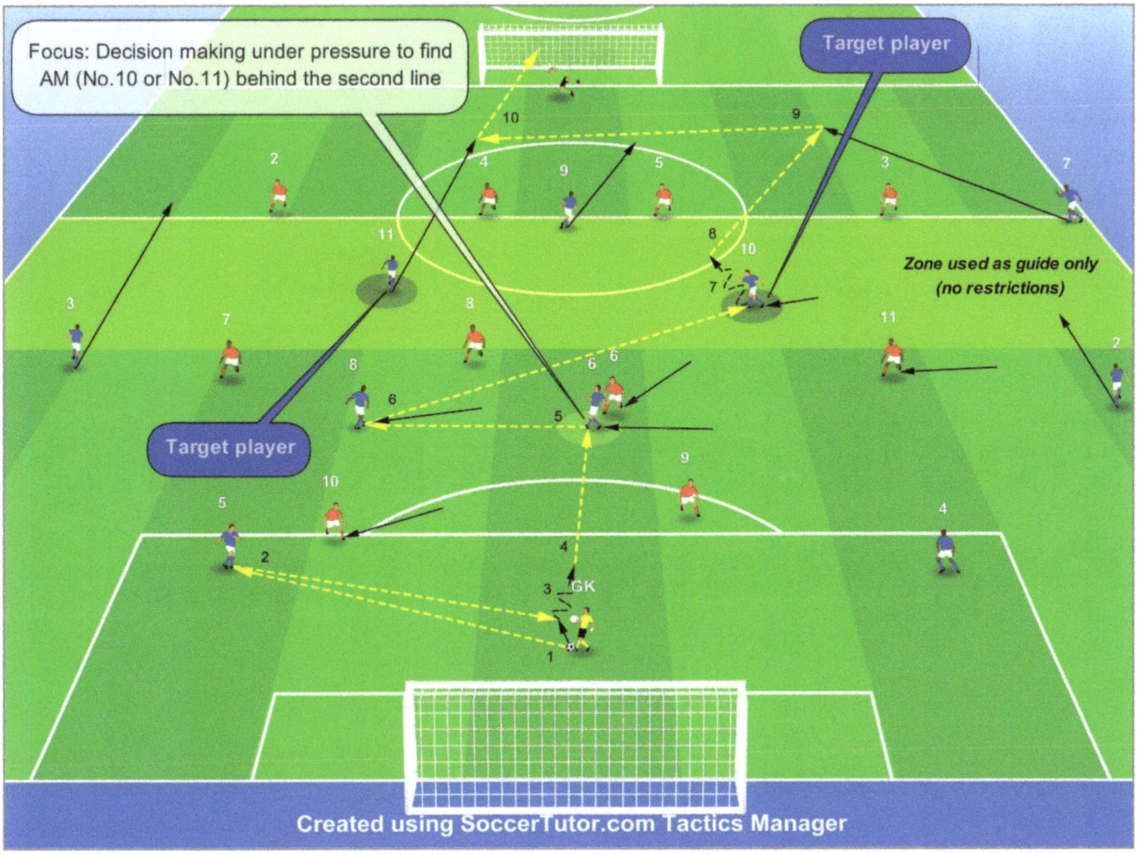

Focus: Decision making under pressure to find AM (No.10 or No.11) behind the second line

Zone used as guide only (no restrictions)

Practice Description

- This final progression of this session is a conditioned 11v11 game in 3/4 of a full pitch. The yellow zone represents space between the lines but has no restrictions.
- **Blue Objective:** Focus on decision making when receiving under pressure to **find an attacking midfielder (N°11 or N°10) behind the second pressing line**, then progress beyond the third line to score. Also, awareness is needed if the goalkeeper dribbles forward and creates space for the centre backs to receive.

- Players must **read the reds' defensive actions** and decide to turn, recycle the ball, or dribble forward into space.
- **Red Objective:** The red team **press high immediately after the GK's first pass**. If they win the ball, they counter to try and score within 12 seconds.
- **Note:** This can be adapted from a 3-at-the-back to a 2-at-the-back box midfield build up play practice by positioning the **GK** wider and **centre back** (**N°5**) more centrally. However, the **GK** will lose the option to dribble the ball forward.

BOX MIDFIELD BUILD UP

Tactical Analysis

Goalkeeper's Passing Over Pressing Lines

Build up play patterns from Guardiola, Alonso, and Arteta's teams

Goalkeeper's Passing Over Second Pressing Line

The goalkeeper can play the ball directly to the players positioned behind the second line of pressing, **bypassing the opposition's midfield press in a single pass**. This method allows the team to **progress quickly while avoiding the risks associated with building up through shorter passes under pressure**. However, for this approach to be successful, 3 key elements must be present:

1. The **receiver must be positioned effectively between lines and opponents**, ensuring they have enough space to control and progress the ball. The **ability to receive on the half-turn and scan the pitch before receiving is crucial**, as it allows them to make a quick decision on the next action.

2. Nearby **teammates must position themselves strategically to challenge the defenders' decision making, and make it difficult for them to press without leaving gaps**. By stretching the defensive line and adjusting their positioning, they can force defenders into reactive decision making, which can be exploited with quick ball movement.

3. **Awareness and communication** between the receiver and nearby teammates is essential. The **receiver must anticipate pressure from opponents and recognise when to release the ball quickly or dribble the ball forward into space**. Teammates must also signal their availability and adjust their movements to ensure they provide the best possible passing options, continually adapting to the opposition's positioning, pressing actions, and the overall flow of play.

The ability to play over the second line with the 2-at-the-back box midfield shape is similar to that of the 4-3-3, as the positioning of players behind the second pressing line is nearly identical in both. This structural similarity allows for a **seamless transition between short build up play and more direct progression**, giving the team multiple options to break through the press depending on the defensive setup they face.

Note: The goalkeeper plays a vital role in recognising when to build up play through short passes and when to play directly over the lines. A well-timed long pass can bypass multiple defenders in one action, **quickly advancing the team into the attacking phase**.

Box Midfield Build Up: Goalkeeper's Passing Over Pressing Lines

Goalkeeper's Passing Over Second Pressing Line (2 at Back)

1. Attacking Midfielder Receives Goalkeeper's Aerial Pass in Space Behind the Second Pressing Line

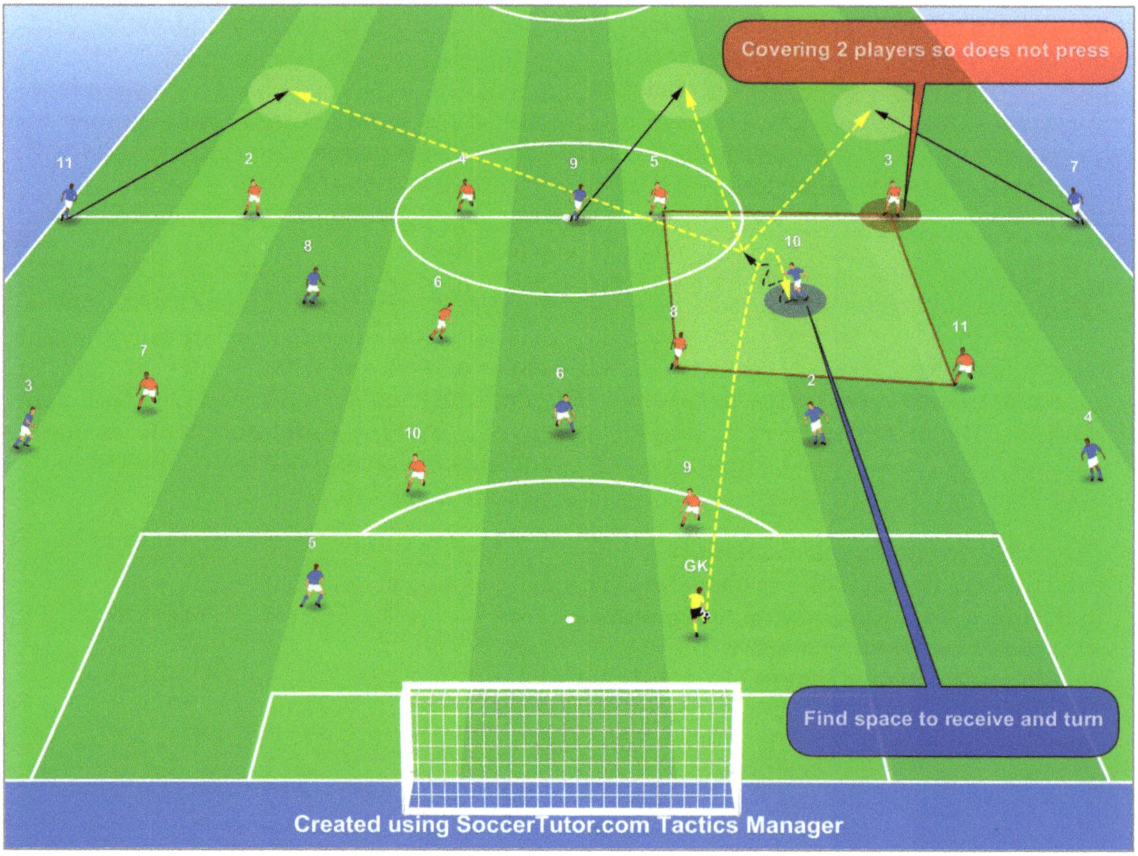

In the diagram, the **goalkeeper (GK)** plays into the **attacking midfielder (N°10)**, who finds space between the lines.

The red full back (N°3) is caught in an in-between position, having to cover the **right winger (N°7)** and **N°10**.

By not stepping forward to press, **red N°3 leaves N°10 unmarked**, allowing him to receive freely and turn.

This positioning opens a clear opportunity to progress the attack. Once turned, **N°10** can play a through pass in behind the red defensive line to find a teammate making a run in behind - 3 options are shown in the diagram.

BEAT THE PRESS WITH A BOX MIDFIELD

Box Midfield Build Up: Goalkeeper's Passing Over Pressing Lines

2. Exploiting Space Created in Behind by the Opposing Full Back Moving Forward to Press Receiver

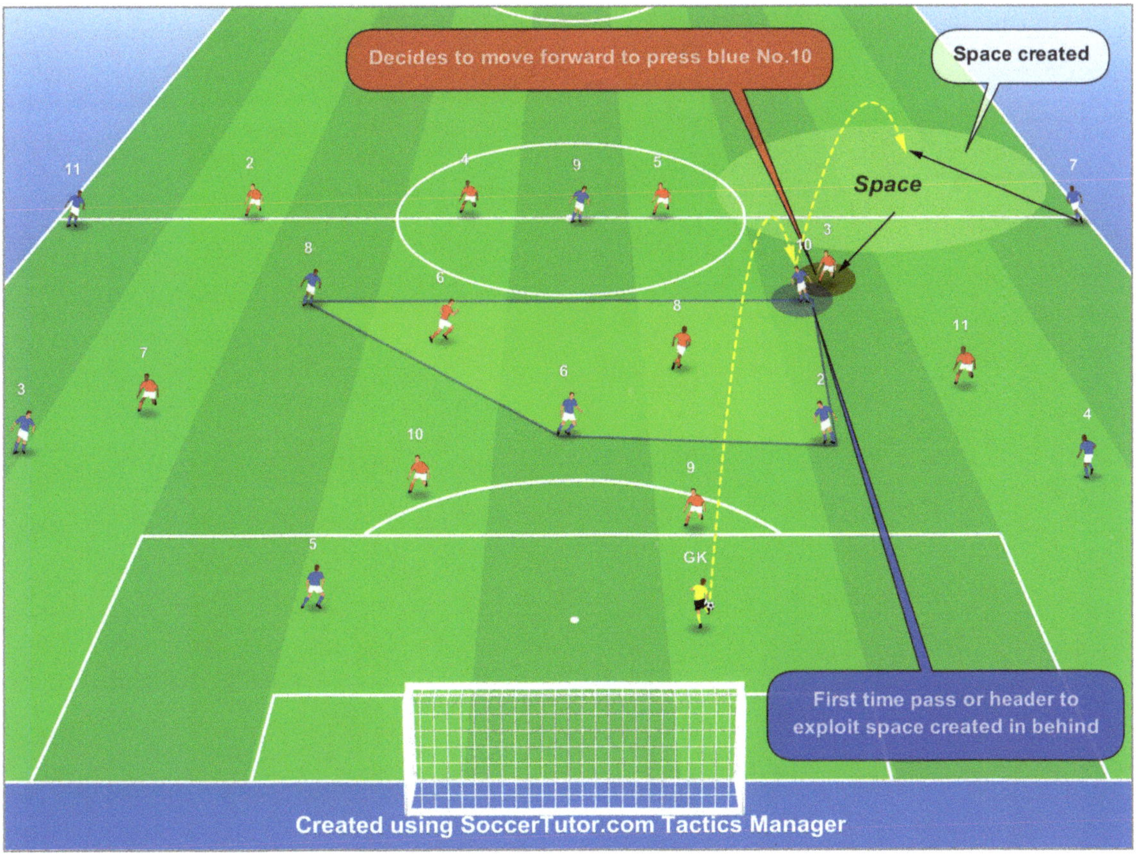

In this variation of the previous example, the **opposing red full back (N°3) decides to step forward and press the receiving blue attacking midfielder (N°10)**, attempting to prevent him from turning between the lines.

However, this pressing action by red N°3 **creates available space in behind which can be exploited**.

If N°10 recognises the movement early through scanning or is alerted by a teammate (**N°7** or **N°9**), he **can play a first-time pass or header into the space** left by red N°3.

This allows the **right winger (N°7)** to run in behind and receive in an advanced position.

The success of this move relies on **N°10's** awareness, the timing of **N°7's** run, and clear communication between teammates. If executed well, the **team can bypass the pressing lines and progress quickly into the attacking phase**.

BEAT THE PRESS WITH A BOX MIDFIELD

Box Midfield Build Up: Goalkeeper's Passing Over Pressing Lines

3. Exploiting Space Created in Behind by the Opposing Centre Back Moving Forward to Press Receiver

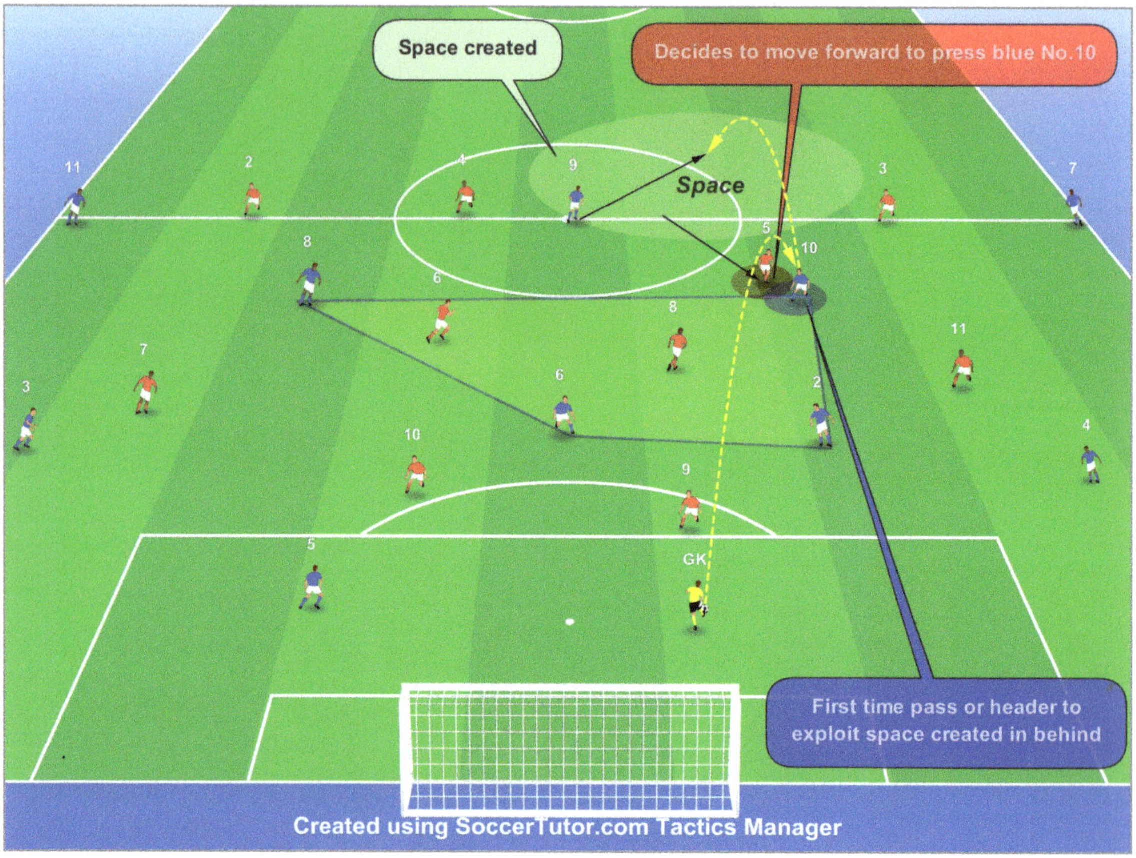

If an **opposing centre back** (red N°5 in the diagram) **steps out to press the blue attacking midfielder** (**N°10**), it leaves a gap in the centre of the defence, disrupts the shape of the back line, and creates space behind that can be exploited.

The **blue forward** (**N°9**) is positioned effectively between the 2 red centre backs, allowing him to remain unmarked, ready to move into the open space as soon as the opportunity arises.

If **N°10** sees red N°5's movement or is alerted by a teammate (**N°7** or **N°9**), he can play a **first-time pass or header** into the created space.

N°9 then has a clear chance to receive and carry the ball towards goal for a scoring opportunity.

©SOCCERTUTOR.COM

BEAT THE PRESS WITH A BOX MIDFIELD

Box Midfield Build Up: Goalkeeper's Passing Over Pressing Lines

Goalkeeper's Passing Over Second Pressing Line (3 at Back)

1. Positioning of Opposing Defenders when Building Up Play with the 3-at-the-Back Box Midfield Shape

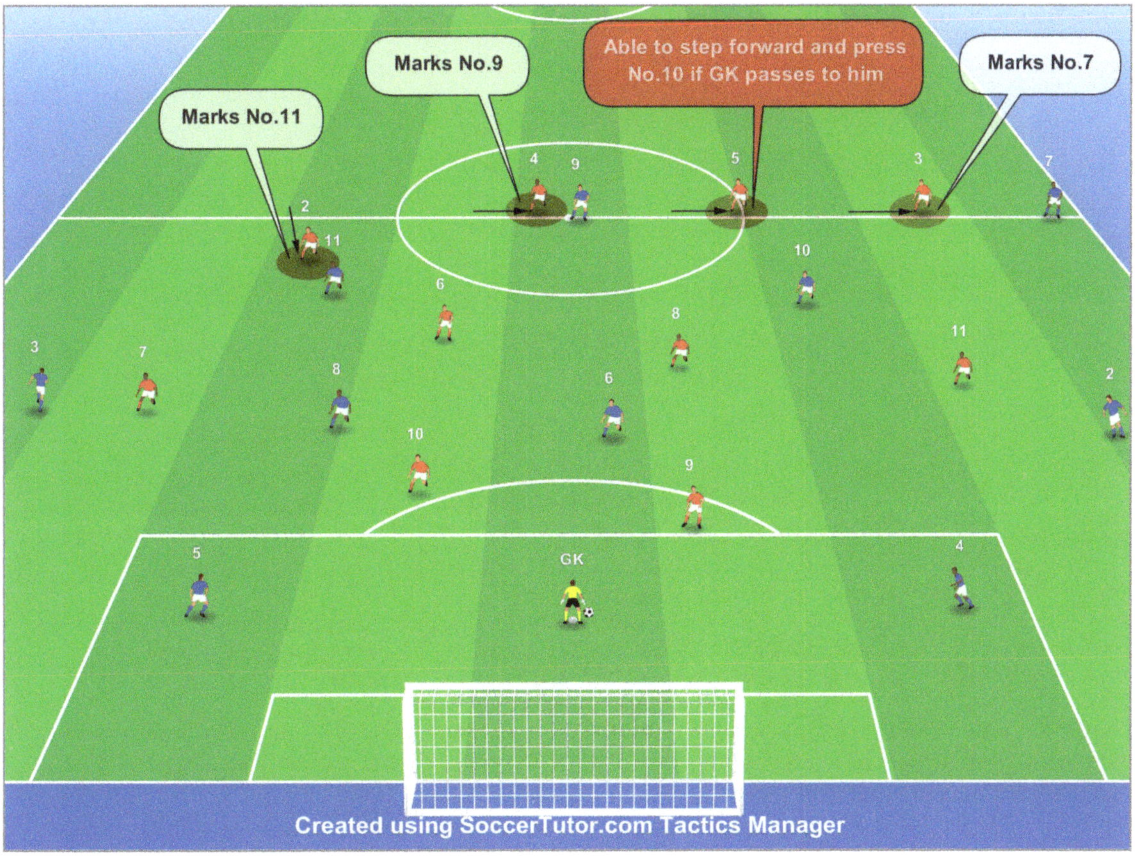

Marks No.11 — *Marks No.9* — *Able to step forward and press No.10 if GK passes to him* — *Marks No.7*

Created using SoccerTutor.com Tactics Manager

The **3-at-the-back box midfield is easier for the opposition to manage** when the ball is played over the second pressing line compared to the 2-at-the-back shape. This is because **only 2 attacking players (N°9 and N°7) are in advanced positions** against the 4 red defenders.

In this example, the **goalkeeper (GK)** has the ball and both **attacking midfielders (N°11 and N°10)** position themselves well.

N°11 is marked by the red right back (N°2), as there is no other player in an advanced position on that side.

The remaining 3 red defenders (N°4, N°5, and N°3) can shift across to the right to cover **blue N°9** and **N°7** without being overloaded.

©SOCCERTUTOR.COM BEAT THE PRESS WITH A BOX MIDFIELD

Box Midfield Build Up: Goalkeeper's Passing Over Pressing Lines

2. Full Back's Forward Movement Forces Opponents' Quick Decisions: Goalkeeper Plays Long Pass Over Second Pressing Line

A key way to break play beyond the second pressing line is through the forward movement of the left back (N°3).

This movement happens simultaneously with the **defensive midfielder (N°8)** shifting left to maintain defensive balance, while the **forward (N°9)** shifts right to occupy both centre backs.

Red Winger - Track or Hold Position?

1. **If the red winger (N°7) does not track blue N°3 (as shown in diagram)**, the red full back (N°2) must decide whether to step forward and block a pass to **blue N°11** or hold his position.

2. **If red N°7 tracks blue N°3's movement, space opens up on that side**. This can be exploited by **N°8** moving wider to receive from the **GK** or via the centre back (**N°5**) before dribbling forward.

Red Full Back - Press or Hold Position?

1. **If the red full back (N°2) moves forward as GK plays the ball, space opens up for blue N°3**, who can be reached with a first-time pass or header.

2. **If red N°2 stays deep (as in diagram), blue N°11 can receive and turn** unmarked behind the second line of pressure.

BOX MIDFIELD SESSION

Training Session 2 (4 Practices)

Goalkeeper's Passing Over Pressing Lines

Based on Guardiola, Alonso, and Arteta build up patterns

BEAT THE PRESS WITH A BOX MIDFIELD

Box Midfield Session 2: Goalkeeper's Passing Over Pressing Lines

TRAINING SESSION (4 PRACTICES)
1. Goalkeeper's Passing Over Pressing Lines and Decisions to Play in Behind

Variation 1: First-time Pass to Exploit Space when Pressed by Full Back

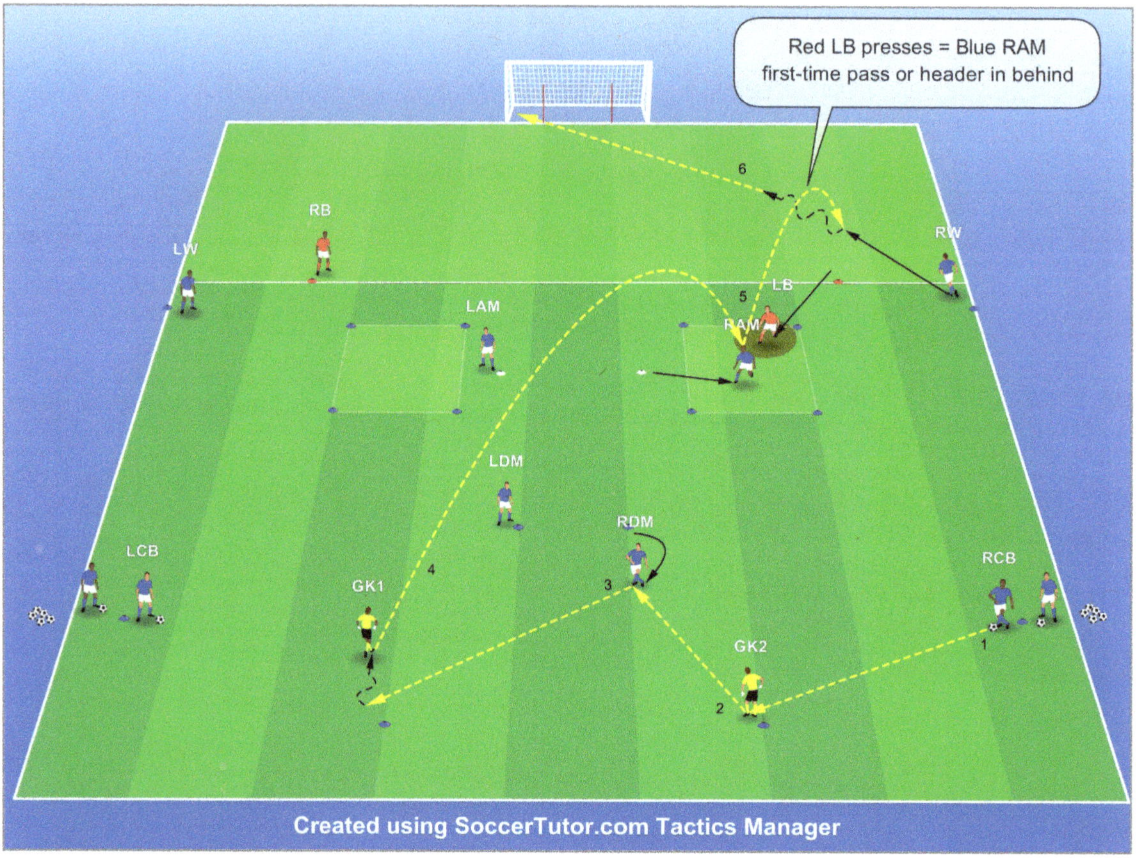

Red LB presses = Blue RAM first-time pass or header in behind

Practice Description (Variation 1)

- **Objective:** Improve decision making for receiving, turning, or playing a first-time pass to exploit space effectively.
- The practice starts with **RCB** passing to the goalkeeper (**GK2**).
- **GK2** then passes to **RDM**, who plays back to the other goalkeeper (**GK1**).
- **GK1** plays a long diagonal pass to **RAM** in the target area (25-35 metre distance).
- **If the red full back (LB) presses RAM as the ball travels, RAM must play a first-time pass into space for RW**, who runs to receive in behind and score (aiming for the corners marked by poles).
- This quick action prevents the red full back from recovering and maintains attacking momentum.
- After each repetition, the blue outfield players rotate positions e.g. **RCB → RDM → RAM → RW → LCB**.

©SOCCERTUTOR.COM   BEAT THE PRESS WITH A BOX MIDFIELD

Box Midfield Session 2: Goalkeeper's Passing Over Pressing Lines

Variation 2: Receive, Turn, and Play Forward when Full Back Does Not Press

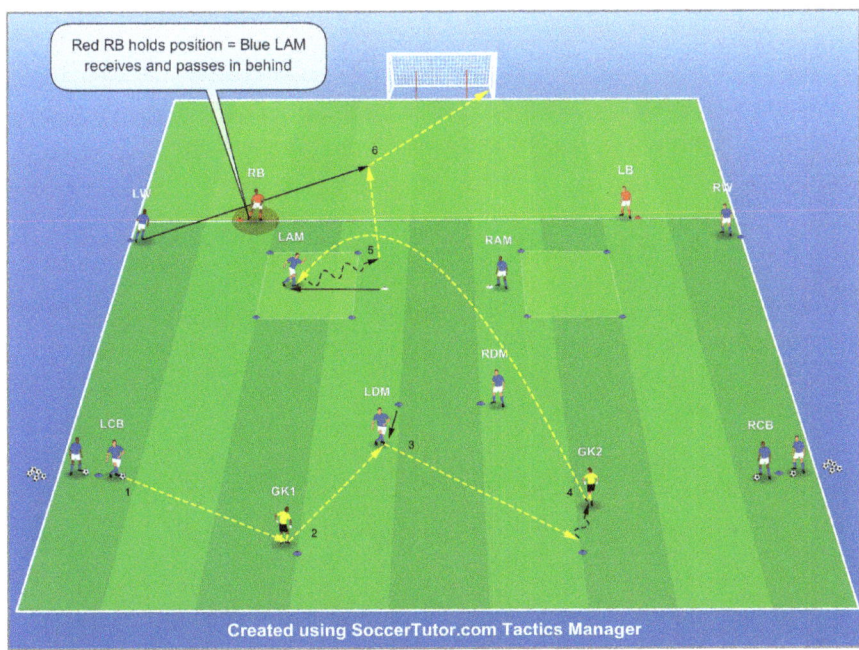

In this variation, we start on the left side with **LCB**.

If the red full back (RB) holds their position instead of moving to press, **LAM** receives in the target area, turns, and plays forward to **LW**, who times a run in behind to score.

Note: When the red defender does not press, it allows for more control and a high quality pass.

Variation 3: First-time Pass to Exploit Space when Pressed by Centre Back

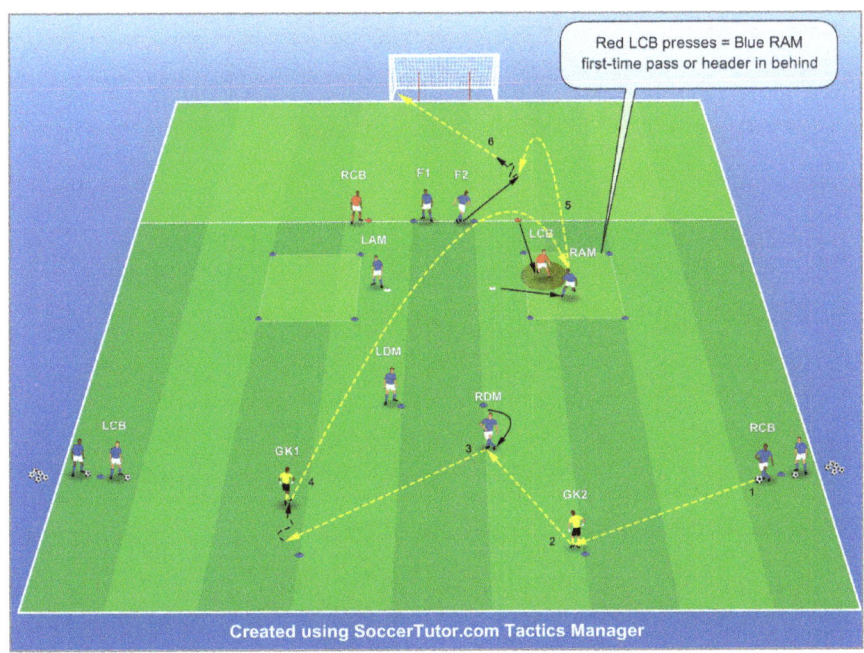

In this variation, the red defenders are now centre backs instead of full backs.

If the red centre back (LCB) presses **RAM**, he plays a first-time pass in behind for the run of the **forward (F2)**, who tries to score.

Note: Shots should be aimed in the corners of the goal, which are marked out with poles.

Box Midfield Session 2: Goalkeeper's Passing Over Pressing Lines

Variation 4: Receive, Turn, and Play Forward when Centre Back Does Not Press

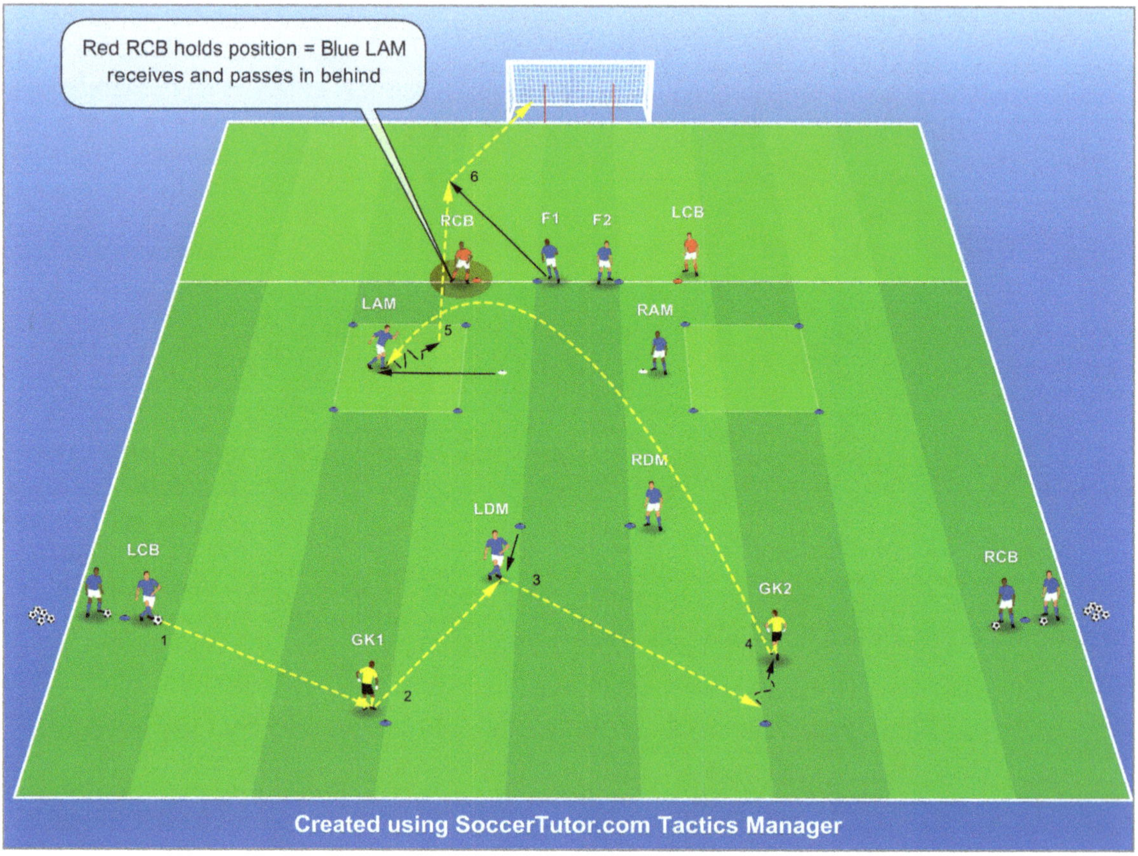

Red RCB holds position = Blue LAM receives and passes in behind

Practice Description (Variation 4)

- In this variation, we start on the left side with **LCB**.
- If the red centre back (RCB) holds their position instead of moving to press, **LAM** receives in the target area.
- From there, **LAM** turns and plays forward to **F1**, who times a run in behind to score (aiming for the corners of the goal marked out by the poles).
- After each repetition, the blue outfield players rotate positions e.g. **LCB → LDM → LAM → F1 → RCB**.
- **Note:** The red defender roles can be played by coaches if needed.

Coaching Points

1. **Pass accuracy:** The goalkeepers must deliver precise passes into target areas.
2. **Shot accuracy:** The wingers or forwards focus on finishing in the corners.
3. **Decision making:** Players must react quickly under pressure to maintain fluidity.
4. **Communication:** Clear verbal cues enhance movement, timing, and support play.
5. **High tempo:** Smooth transitions between positions ensure intensity and result in match realistic training.

BEAT THE PRESS WITH A BOX MIDFIELD

Box Midfield Session 2: Goalkeeper's Passing Over Pressing Lines

PROGRESSION

2. Goalkeeper's Passing Over Second Pressing Line Functional Practice with Target Zones

Variation 1: Box Midfield with 3-at-the-Back (7+GK v 4+GK)

AM: Scan to see if there is pressure from a red defender

Practice Description (Variation 1)

- The practice starts with the coach and 3 players circulating the ball until the **goalkeeper (GK)** plays forward.
- **GK's aim is to find an attacking midfielder** arriving in one of the 5x5m target zones at the right moment.
- **Main Blue Objective:** The attacking midfielder's decision to turn or pass first-time in behind depends on whether a red defender moves forward to press.
- If **RAM is free to turn (in diagram)**, it triggers a **5v4 attack** with the aim to **score within 8 seconds**.
- **Red Objective:** Win the ball and counter to score in the 2 small goals within 8 seconds.
- *On the following page, the second variation shows the same situation with a 2-at-the-back box midfield shape.*

BEAT THE PRESS WITH A BOX MIDFIELD

Box Midfield Session 2: Goalkeeper's Passing Over Pressing Lines

Variation 2: Box Midfield with 2-at-the-Back (6+GK v 4+GK)

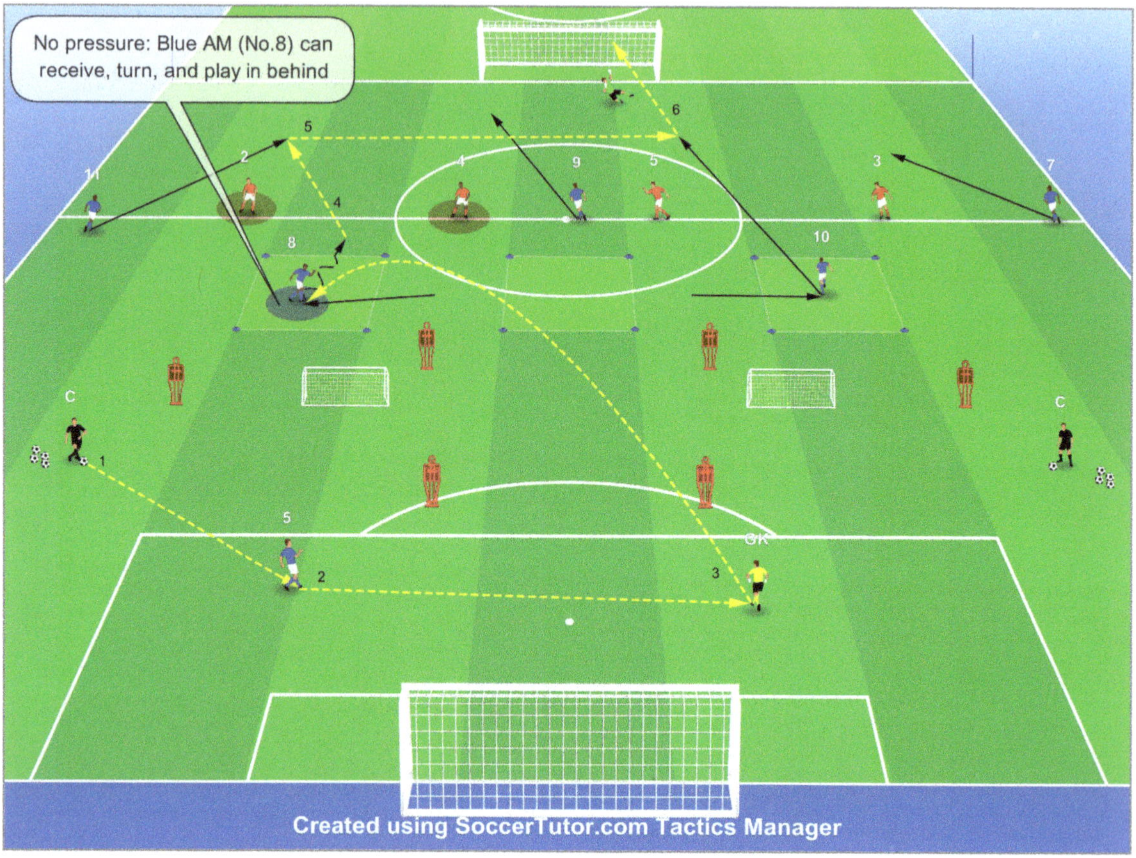

[Diagram note: "No pressure: Blue AM (No.8) can receive, turn, and play in behind"]

Practice Description (Variation 2)

- In this variation, the **shape is adjusted to a 2-at-the-back box midfield** with the **goalkeeper (GK)** and **centre back (N°5)** forming the deepest line.

- The left back and 1 centre back area removed. A **left winger (N°11) is added**.

- Apart from the blue team's shape with 1 less player, the practice setup remains identical to the previous variation.

- **Refer to the analysis on pages 64–66** for the correct build up tactics, positioning, and combinations when using a 2-at-the-back box midfield.

Coaching Points

1. The **goalkeeper must play accurately** into the target zones.
2. **Quick decision making** when receiving.
3. **Scanning before receiving** and communication are key to deciding whether to turn or play first-time.
4. Fast and **accurate finishing**.

BEAT THE PRESS WITH A BOX MIDFIELD

Box Midfield Session 2: Goalkeeper's Passing Over Pressing Lines

PROGRESSION

3. Goalkeeper's Passing Over Second Pressing Line 10 (+GK) v 8 Functional Practice with Target Zones

Variation 1: Box Midfield with 3-at-the-Back

Red CB (4) presses, so blue AM (11) uses first-time header into created space

Practice Description (Variation 1)

- This progression has the same main objective as the previous practice (**see page 73**). The blues build up from the **goalkeeper (GK)** against 4 red defenders and 4 pressing midfielders.

- The 3 players at the back circulate the ball until the **GK** plays forward. If the ball is passed short behind the first pressing line (2 mannequins), the players turn, pass forward, or recycle possession.

- If **GK plays an aerial pass over the second pressing line (diagram example)** into a target zone to an attacking midfielder, the **receiver (N°11) must read the situation and either receive and turn or pass first-time in behind** for a runner (for **N°9** in diagram example).

- **Red Objective:** Press to win the ball and counter to score by dribbling through the red line, receiving beyond it, or by scoring in the goal.

BEAT THE PRESS WITH A BOX MIDFIELD

Box Midfield Session 2: Goalkeeper's Passing Over Pressing Lines

Variation 2: Box Midfield with 2-at-the-Back

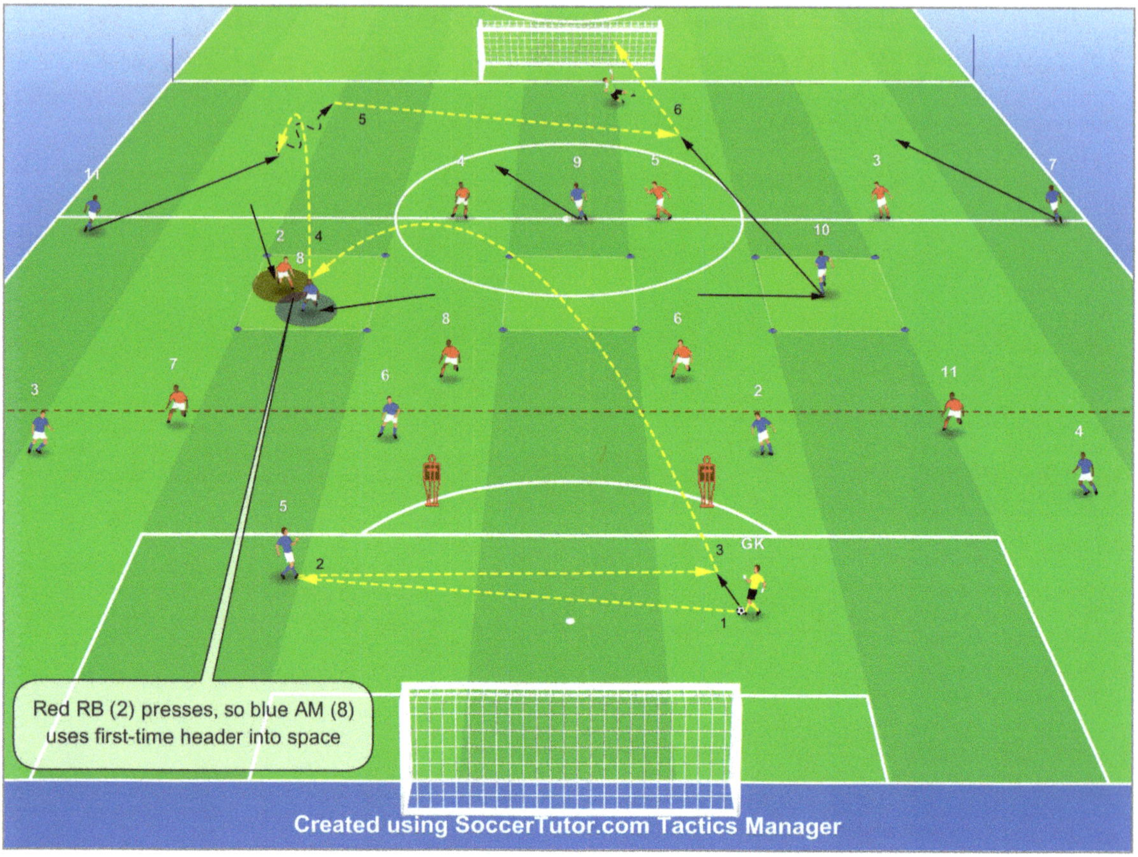

Red RB (2) presses, so blue AM (8) uses first-time header into space

Practice Description (Variation 2)

- In this variation, the **shape is adjusted to a 2-at-the-back box midfield** with the **goalkeeper (GK)** and **centre back (N°5)** forming the deepest line.

- The **left back (N°3)** is no longer required in an advanced position as the **left winger (N°11)** is in a normal position.

- Apart from the blue team's shape, the practice setup remains identical.

- The **main objective of the practice still focuses on the attacking midfielder's decision** to turn or pass first-time in behind, depending on if a red defender moves forward to press.

- In the diagram example, **N°8 is pressed by the red right back (N°2)**, so heads the ball in behind for the run of **N°11**.

- **N°11** passes the ball across for the run of the other **attacking midfielder (N°10)** to score at the back post.

- **Coaching Points:** Same as previous practices in this session.

BEAT THE PRESS WITH A BOX MIDFIELD

Box Midfield Session 2: Goalkeeper's Passing Over Pressing Lines

PROGRESSION

4. Goalkeeper's Passing Over Second Pressing Line Conditioned Tactical Game

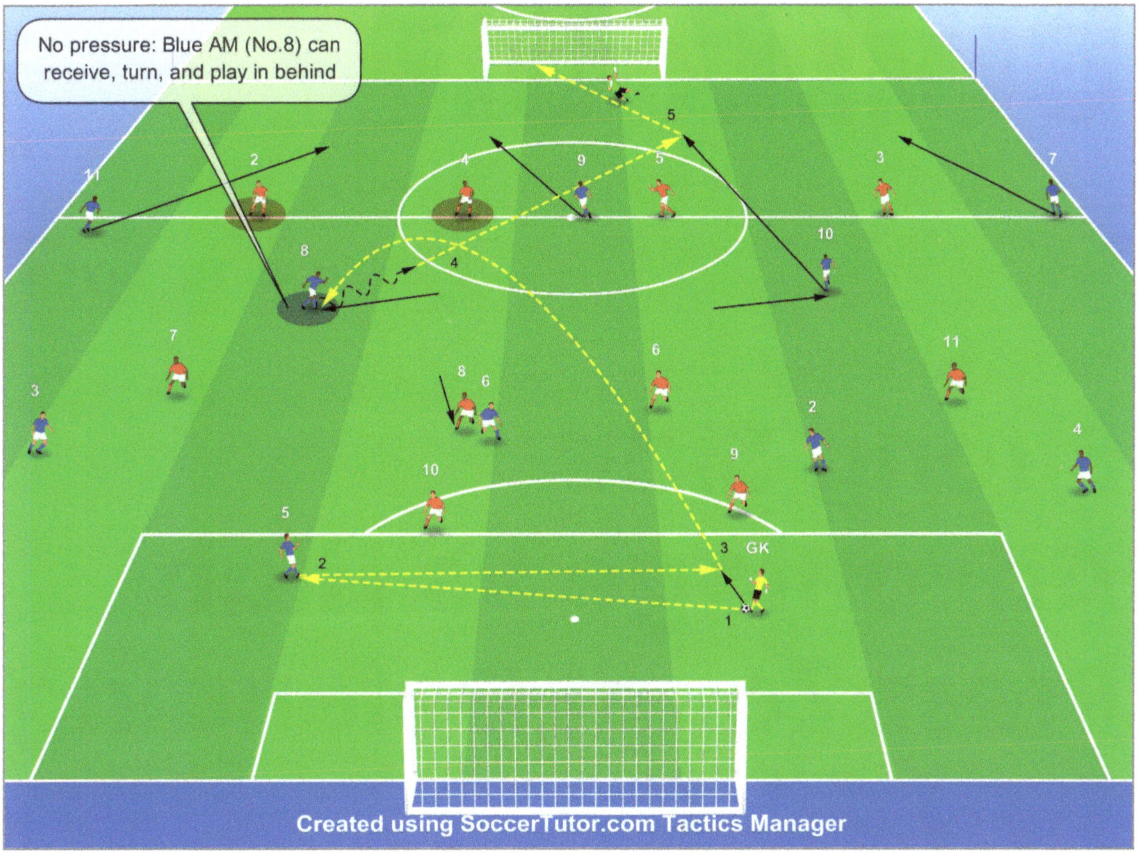

No pressure: Blue AM (No.8) can receive, turn, and play in behind

Practice Description

- **Main Blue Objective:** Attacking midfielder's decision to turn or pass first-time in behind, depending on if a red defender moves forward to press.

- This final practice of this session is an 11v11 game. Starting with the blue **goalkeeper** (**GK**), **the reds press aggressively after the first pass** and the blues build up play from the back.

- **GK decides how to progress play** by passing behind the first pressing line, over, or through the second line.

- *If a goal is scored after a long pass to an attacking midfielder, it counts double.*

- In the diagram example, **N°8 is not pressed and is able to receive**, turn, and play in behind for **N°10** to score.

- **Red Objective:** Press to win the ball and counter to score within 10–12 seconds.

- **Coaching Points:** Same as previous practices in this session.

- **Note:** The practice is presented with a 2-at-the-back box midfield shape but can easily be adapted to 3-at-the-back.

BEAT THE PRESS WITH A BOX MIDFIELD

BOX MIDFIELD BUILD UP

Tactical Analysis

Strong Side Advantage vs High Press Zonal Defending

Build up play patterns from Guardiola, Alonso, and Arteta's teams

Box Midfield Build Up: Strong Side Advantage vs High Press Zonal Defending

Numerical Situations vs High Pressing with Zonal Defending (2 at Back)

1. Numerical Advantage in Defence and Midfield Areas when Building Up Play from the Back

With the GK, the blues have 8 v 6 for build up in defence and midfield = +2 players

7 (+GK) v 6

Numerical superiority is a key principle of positional play, especially when building up play from the back.

Creating and exploiting advantages is a foundational objective of positional play.

Against a 4-4-2 zonal defensive shape, the 2-at-the-back box midfield shape creates a **7 (+GK) v 6 situation in defence and midfield** (highlighted).

The **blue team have 2 additional players** (**8 v 6**), enabling control of possession and potential for good ball progression.

BEAT THE PRESS WITH A BOX MIDFIELD

Box Midfield Build Up: Strong Side Advantage vs High Press Zonal Defending

2. Numerical Advantages with 2-at-the-Back Box Midfield Shape Against 4-4-2 Zonal Defending

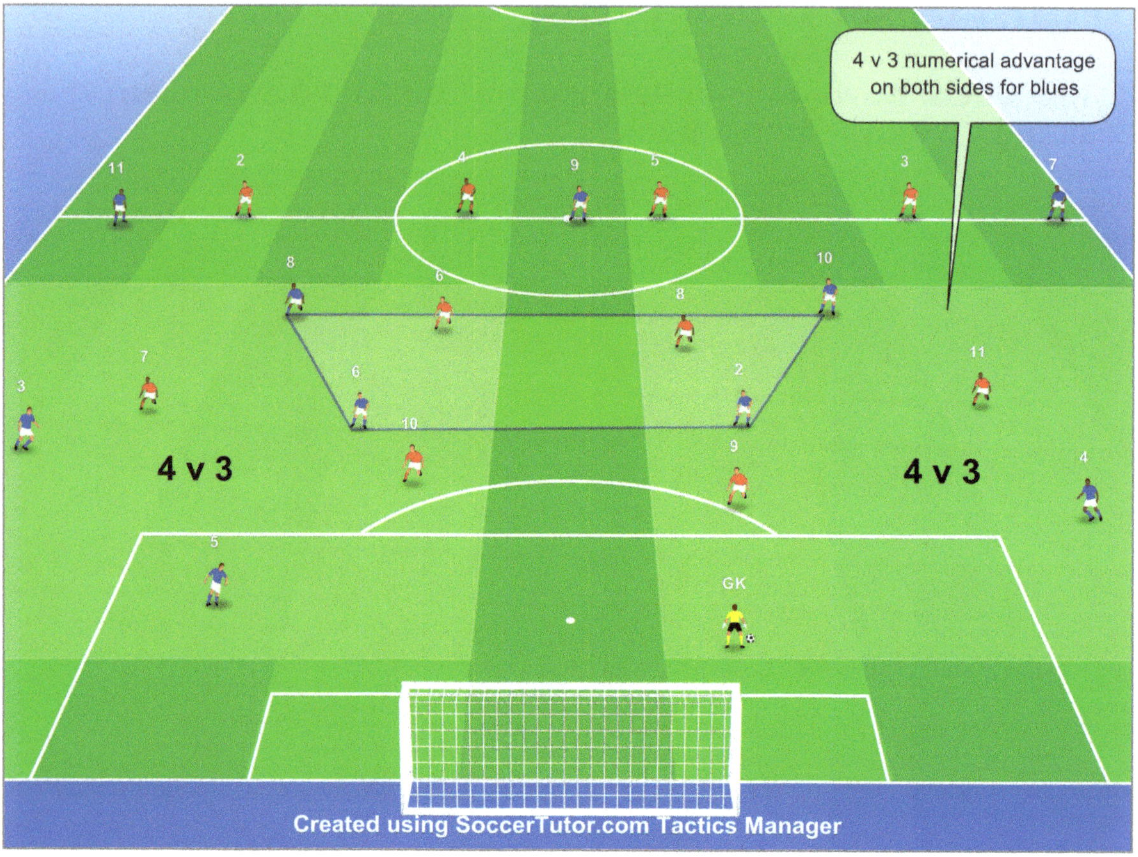

The box midfield shape with 2-at-the-back (goalkeeper and centre back) naturally creates a **4 v 3 numerical advantage on both sides** without requiring additional movement. This is because the goalkeeper shifts into a centre back role, which enables an extra outfield player to be higher.

When the defence and midfield areas are divided into left and right (highlighted in diagram), the numerical advantages become even clearer.

The **goalkeeper's positioning ensures an extra player is available on both sides**, allowing for efficient progression of play while maintaining defensive balance.

Note: The existing structure of the 2-at-the-back box midfield ensures multiple passing options are available, reduces the need for unnecessary adjustments, and allows for a smoother build up phase.

Box Midfield Build Up: Strong Side Advantage vs High Press Zonal Defending

3. Using Midfielder Positioning to Unbalance the Opposition's Defensive Zones of Responsibility

To prevent the red midfielders from covering both players at once, the blue midfielders increase the distance between themselves

Red No.8's zone of responsibility

Red No.6's zone of responsibility

4 v 3   **4 v 3**

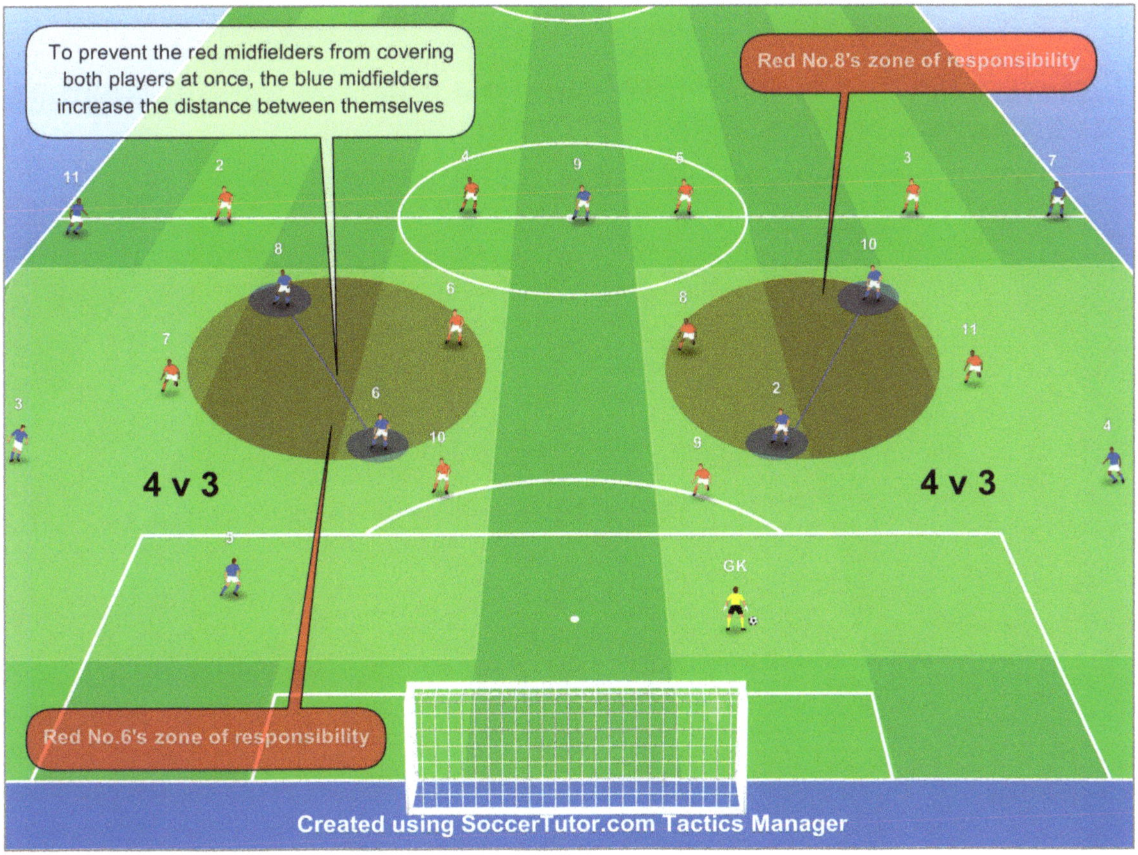

Numerical advantages are essential when building up play from the back. The attacking team must focus on 2 main objectives:

1. **Creating overloads near the ball**.
2. **Identifying and using the free player**.

As explained on the previous page, a 4v3 numerical advantage exists on both sides. When the **goalkeeper (GK)** or **centre back (N°5)** have the ball, the next step is to **identify the free player in that area**.

Achieving this relies heavily on the positioning of the 2 midfielders on each side.

As shown in the diagram, these players are positioned within the defensive zones of responsibility of the red midfielders:

1. **On the left**, blue N°6 and N°8 are in red N°6's zone of responsibility
2. **On the right**, blue N°2 and N°10 are in red N°8's zone of responsibility.

To prevent red midfielders from covering 2 players at once, the blue midfielders must increase the distance between themselves. **By stretching the space, they force their opponents into difficult decisions**, but they must also avoid drifting too close to other defending players.

BEAT THE PRESS WITH A BOX MIDFIELD

Box Midfield Build Up: Strong Side Advantage vs High Press Zonal Defending

Finding the Free Player Around the Ball Area (2 at Back)

1. Moving the Ball to Free Player Near the Ball from the Goalkeeper (4v3 Situation on Right Side)

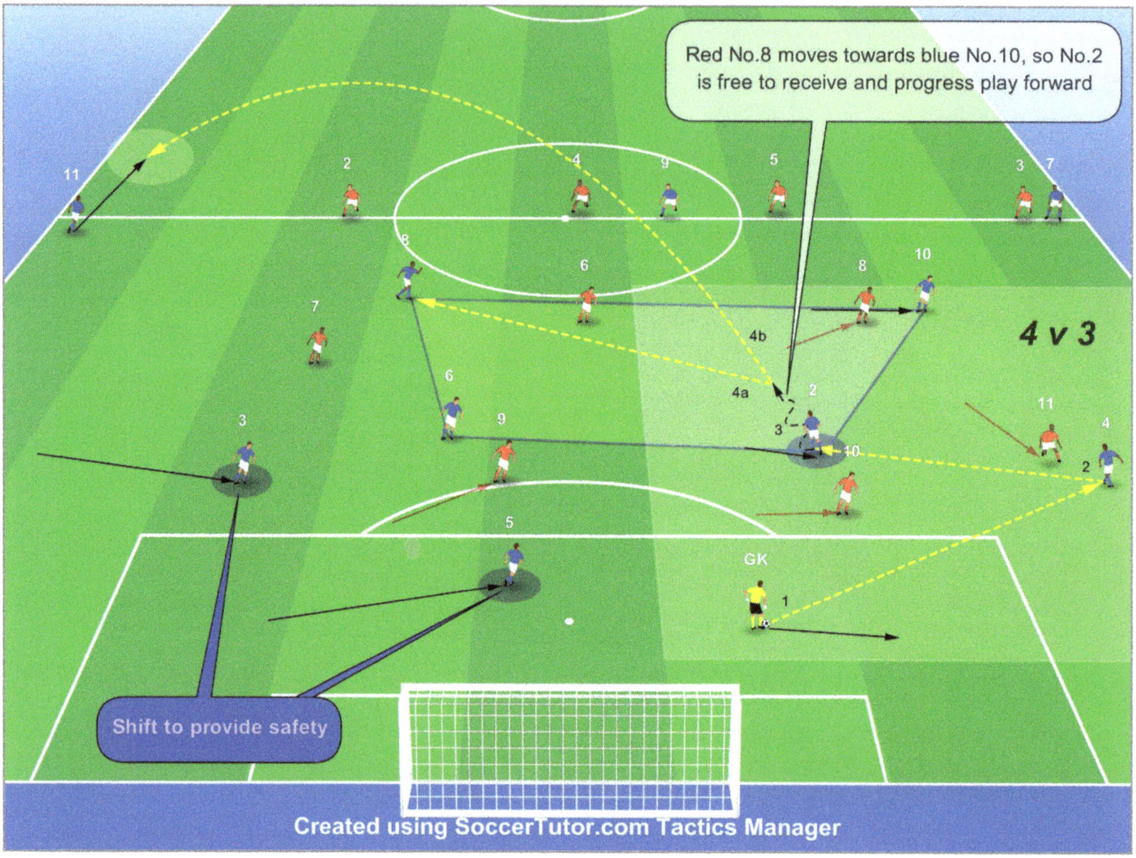

Red No.8 moves towards blue No.10, so No.2 is free to receive and progress play forward

4 v 3

Shift to provide safety

Created using SoccerTutor.com Tactics Manager

With a 4v3 numerical advantage, the **next step is to quickly identify and find the free player**. As explained, the **defensive midfielders (N°6 and N°2) and attacking midfielders (N°8 and N°10)** position themselves to prevent red N°6 and N°8 from marking 2 players at the same time.

In this example, red N°8 moves towards **blue N°10, so N°2 is free to receive from (N°4)** and progress the play forward.

When the build up is on the **goalkeeper's (GK)** side, the **left back (N°3)** and weak side **centre back (N°5)** must shift towards the strong side to provide defensive stability. This ensures **N°5** is ready to defend if possession is lost, as there is no extra defender behind the ball at this stage.

As the ball moves further forward, the team naturally transitions into a 3-2-2-3 possession phase outfield player shape.

©SOCCERTUTOR.COM

BEAT THE PRESS WITH A BOX MIDFIELD

Box Midfield Build Up: Strong Side Advantage vs High Press Zonal Defending

2. Switching Play via the Goalkeeper when Forward Passing Lanes are Blocked

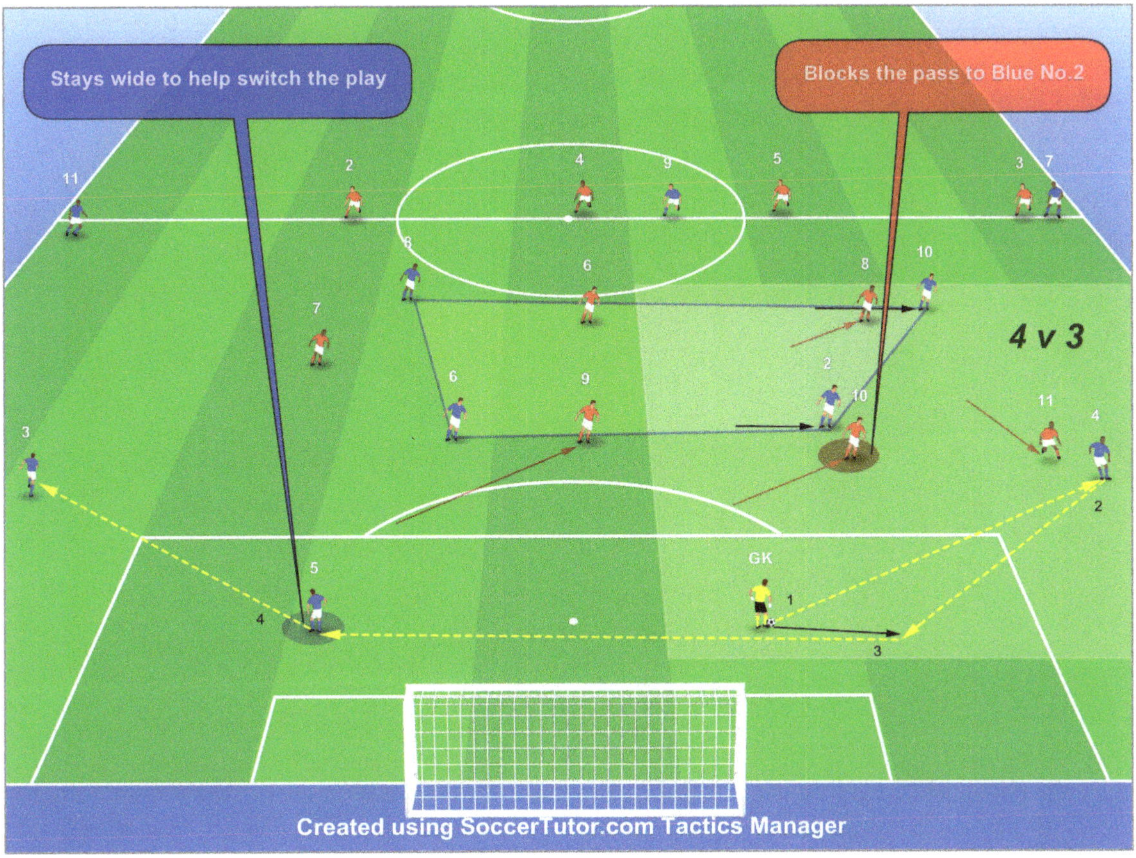

In this variation, we have the same 4v3 situation on the right side. However, this time the red Nº10 moves to block the inside pass while red Nº8 marks the **blue attacking midfielder (Nº10)**.

The **goalkeeper (GK)** is available for a back pass and becomes the best option.

The blues must recognise the numerical situations and adjust their positioning to maintain control and create passing options. The **players on the weak side must position themselves wider to prepare for a switch of play**. This allows the ball to be moved to an area where a numerical advantage exists, helping **bypass pressure and force the opposition to reposition themselves very quickly**.

In the diagram example, the **right centre back (Nº4)** passes back to **GK**, who then plays across to the **left centre back (Nº5)**. **Nº5** passes to the left back (**Nº3**) to complete the switch and the blues have space to progress the ball on the left side.

Note: A well-timed switch of play creates space and passing lanes, making progression easier. Quick ball circulation and precise movements are essential for executing it effectively.

Box Midfield Build Up: Strong Side Advantage vs High Press Zonal Defending

3. Build Up to Bypass Press on the Side with the Centre Back (4v3 Situation on Left Side)

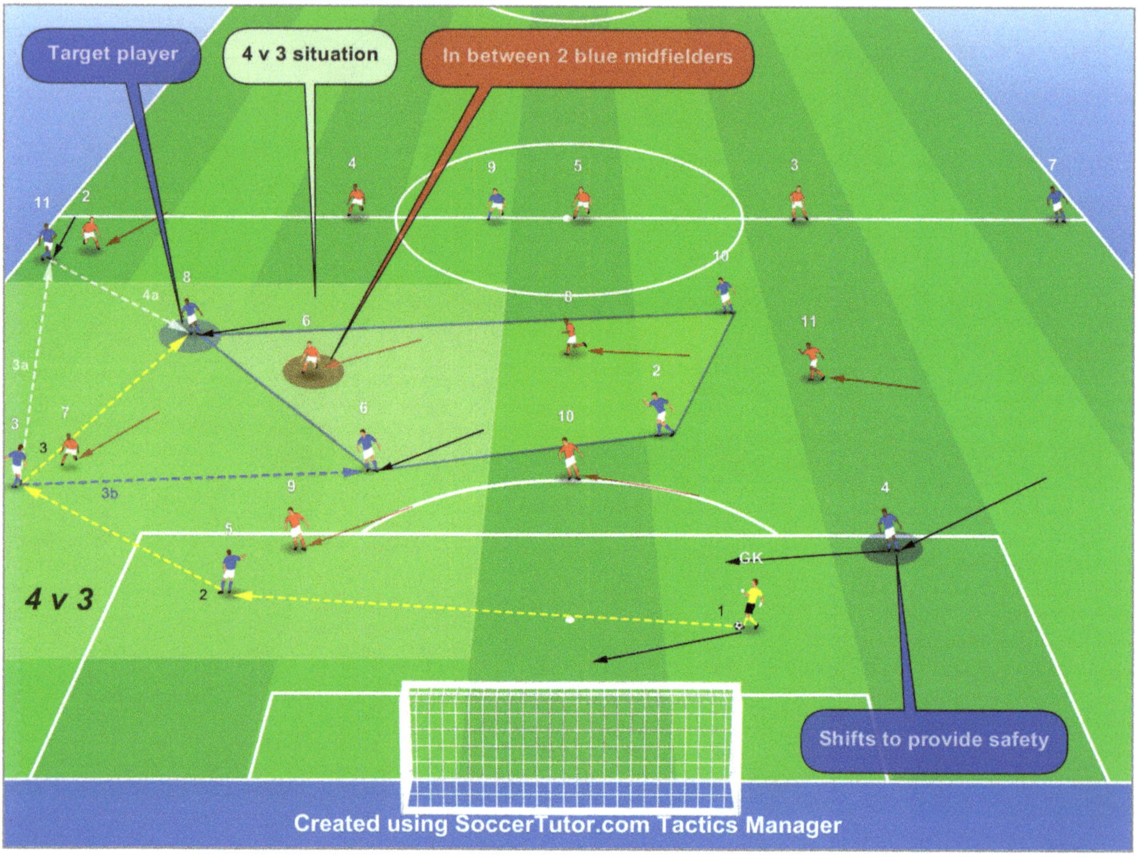

When building up with the **left centre back** (**N°5**) as the deepest player and the same 4v3 advantage, the **right centre back** (**N°4**) shifts toward the strong side to maintain defensive compactness and prevent the opposition from exploiting space.

The **goalkeeper** (**GK**) passes to **N°5**, who passes to the **left back** (**N°3**). As the reds shift across, **N°3 tries to find a forward passing lane to the attacking midfielder (N°8) - yellow arrow**, which would bypass 2 pressing lines and neutralise 6 red opponents.

The alternative options using link players are shown with the blue and white arrows.

The team transitions into a 3-2-2-3 shape, ensuring progression and stability.

Note 1: If **N°4** moves too wide, adjustments are needed. **N°2** drops into a centre back role, while **N°4** shifts slightly inside into a central midfield position. This stops the team being vulnerable to counter attacks and makes sure they retain balance.

Note 2: When building up with a numerical superiority and available space, a good option is to **play the first pass towards one side, draw the press, and switch play**. The ideal situation is to start on the **GK's** side and switch to **N°5**, so that more safety exists at the back.

Box Midfield Build Up: Strong Side Advantage vs High Press Zonal Defending

Numerical Situations vs High Pressing with Zonal Defending (3 at Back)

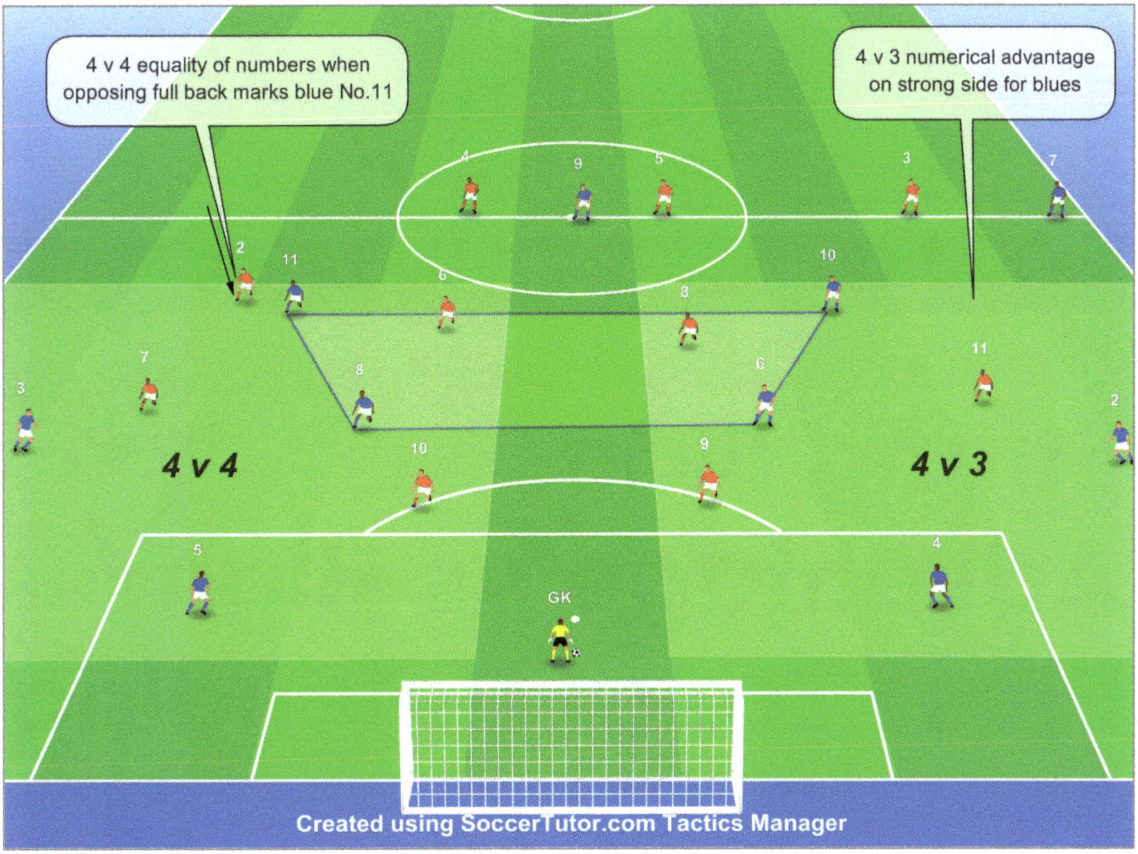

4 v 4 equality of numbers when opposing full back marks blue No.11

4 v 3 numerical advantage on strong side for blues

When using a 3-at-the-back box midfield, the opposition adjust their defensive setup. Here we show the **numerical situations with a 3-at-the-back box midfield against 4-4-2 zonal defending**.

The **red full back may track the winger (blue N°11) moving inside to create a box midfield**, altering the numerical situation.

There is a 4v4 equality on the left side and a 4v3 advantage on the right. The **goalkeeper (GK) must recognise the situation and play to the stronger side**.

Once the ball reaches the strong side, the next step is to find the free player. Quick decisions maximise this advantage.

Note: The 3-at-the-back shape ensures a numerical advantage on one side while maintaining defensive security if possession is lost. As the ball progresses, the shape transitions into an outfield player 3-2-3-2 shape, with N°4, N° 5, and N° 2 forming the back line, while N°3 pushes into a wing back role.

BEAT THE PRESS WITH A BOX MIDFIELD

BOX MIDFIELD SESSION

Training Session 3 (5 Practices)

Strong Side Advantage vs High Press Zonal Defending

Based on Guardiola, Alonso, and Arteta build up patterns

Box Midfield Session 3: Strong Side Advantage vs High Press Zonal Defending

TRAINING SESSION (5 PRACTICES)
1. Exploiting Numerical Advantage to Find the Free Player Continuous Possession Game

1/2: Start to Create and Exploit a Numerical Advantage

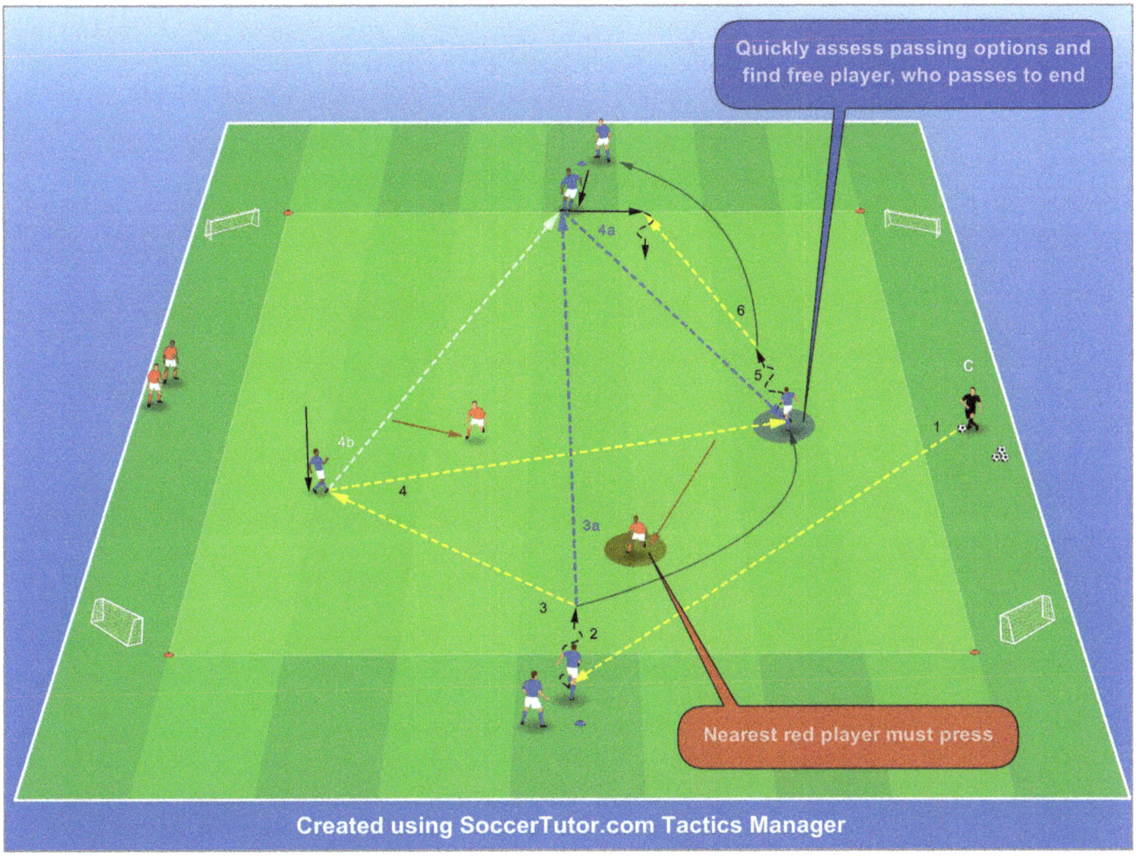

Quickly assess passing options and find free player, who passes to end

Nearest red player must press

Practice Description (1/2)

- The practice takes place in a 12 x 18m area, but you can adjust it based on player age or level. Inside the area, there is a 2v2 situation, with 2 additional blue players on the outside at each end.
- The practice begins with the coach passing to an outside player, who enters the area to create an overload.
- The nearest red defender must move forward to press, forcing the blue team

to **quickly assess passing options and find the free player**.

- The ball can be moved directly to the free player (yellow arrow) or via the link player at the top (blue and white arrows).
- Once the free player receives the ball, they pass to the player at the opposite end, ensuring **quick ball circulation and continuous positional adjustments**, before rotating to the outside (top).

BEAT THE PRESS WITH A BOX MIDFIELD

Box Midfield Session 3: Strong Side Advantage vs High Press Zonal Defending

2/2: Continuous Practice with Opposite End Rotations

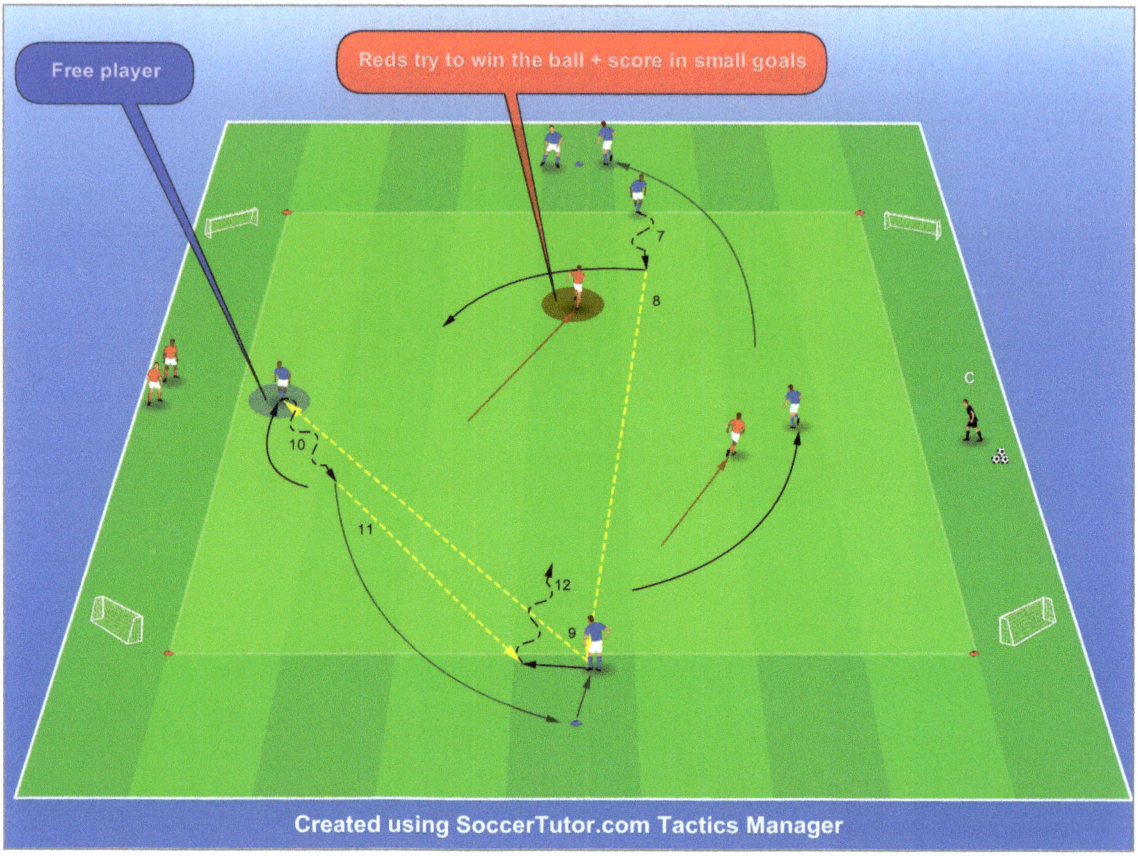

Free player

Reds try to win the ball + score in small goals

Created using SoccerTutor.com Tactics Manager

Practice Description (2/2)

- This second diagram shows how the practice continues with the same aims and objectives.
- The outside player (at the top) enters the area to repeat in the opposite direction while the previous starting player remains inside the area.
- Again, the nearest red defender must move forward to press, forcing the blue team to quickly assess passing options and find the free player.
- The **objectives remain the same for the blue team**, trying to find the free player and pass forward.

- **Defending Objective:** Win the ball and score in either of the 2 small goals at the same end you win the ball.

Coaching Points

1. **Assess the situation quickly** and identify passing options.
2. **Adjust positioning** to create passing lanes (diamond shape).
3. **Make intelligent decisions** to move the ball efficiently to the free player.
4. **Use quick combination play** to maintain fluid ball circulation.
5. **Keep a high tempo** to apply continuous pressure on the opposition.

BEAT THE PRESS WITH A BOX MIDFIELD

Box Midfield Session 3: Strong Side Advantage vs High Press Zonal Defending

PROGRESSION

2. Exploiting 4v3 Numerical Advantage 3-Team Small Sided Game

ZONE 3: Score vs goalkeeper

ZONE 2: 2 v 1 Overload

ZONE 1: 3 v 2 Overload

Practice Description

- **ZONE 1** = 25 x 42m (divided into halves).
- **ZONE 2** = 25 x 10m.
- **ZONE 3** = 25 x 7m.
- There are 2 attacking teams (blue and yellow) and 1 defending team (red).
- The blues and reds start inside the area and the yellows start outside.
- The **initial setup is 1v1 in each half of Zone 1 and 1v1 in Zone 2**. A yellow player enters by dribbling the ball, creating a 2v1 overload in the first half of Zone 1.

Attacking Objective:

1. **Find the free player in Zone 1.**
2. **Free player dribbles into Zone 2.**
3. **Pass into Zone 3 and score.**

Defending Objective: Win the ball and score in either of the 2 small goals.

Rules/Restrictions: After the first pass, all players move freely. Defenders cannot enter Zone 3. After each attack, the player who finishes moves out and the other players move one position forward (new player enters). After a set time, the defending team switch roles.

Box Midfield Session 3: Strong Side Advantage vs High Press Zonal Defending

PROGRESSION

3. Build Up with Numerical Advantage on Strong Side with Box Midfield Dynamic Game (2 at Back)

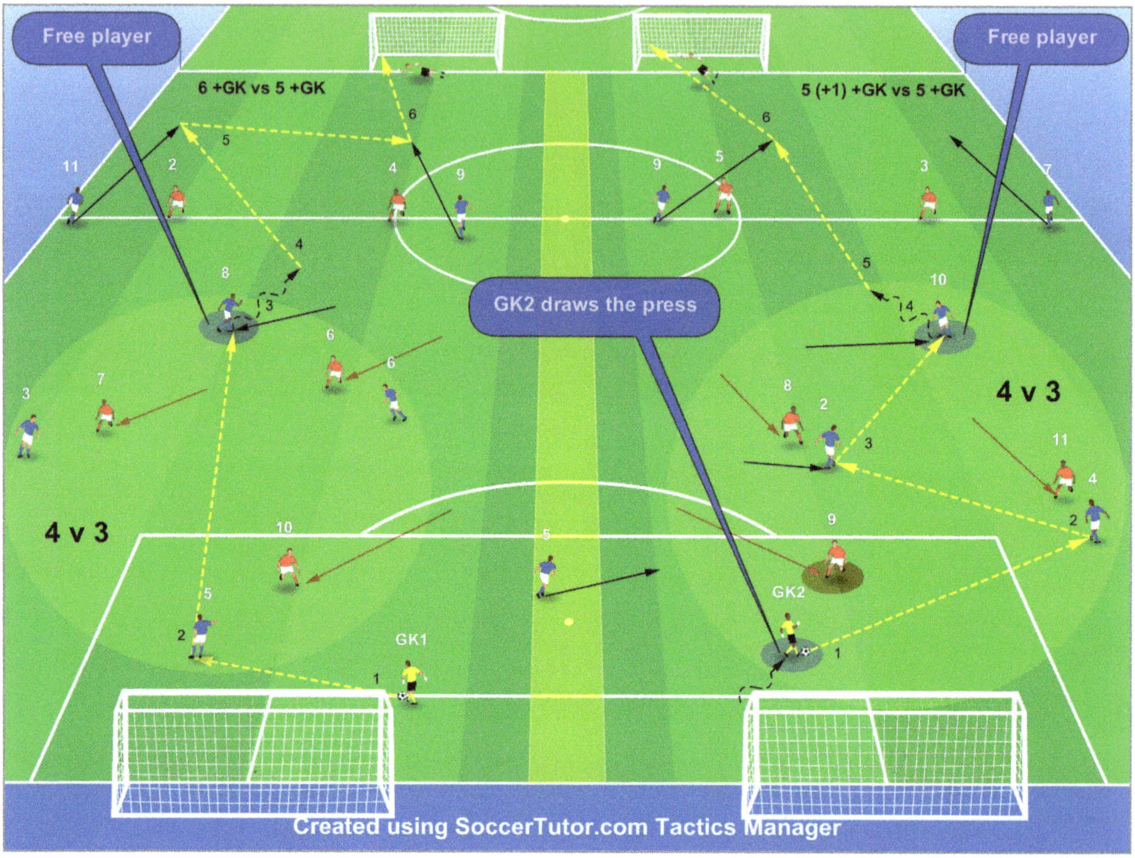

Practice Description

- The playing area is 3/4 of a full pitch split into 2 halves by a 5-metre vertical zone. In each half, the red team are in a 2-2-1 defensive shape (4-4-2 combined).
- **On the left**, the blues build up with **6+GK vs 5+GK**, so have an overload. The **aim is to find the free player, which is the attacking midfielder (Nº8)**, then score.
- **On the right**, it starts with **5 (+GK) vs 5 (+GK)**, with **GK2** acting as a centre back to create a **4v3 numerical superiority for the build up**.
- The **left centre back (Nº5) enters (+1) after the first pass** to provide balance in case possession is lost.
- **GK2 draws the red forward's press (Nº9)** to open up forward passing lanes.
- **Defending Objective:** If the reds win the ball (either side), they counter to score within 10-12 seconds.
- After each phase, all players reset to their starting positions for the next repetition.

Box Midfield Session 3: Strong Side Advantage vs High Press Zonal Defending

VARIATION

4. Build Up with Numerical Advantage on Strong Side with Box Midfield Split-Pitch Game (3 at Back)

Variation 1: Overload on Right with Attacking Midfielder on that Side

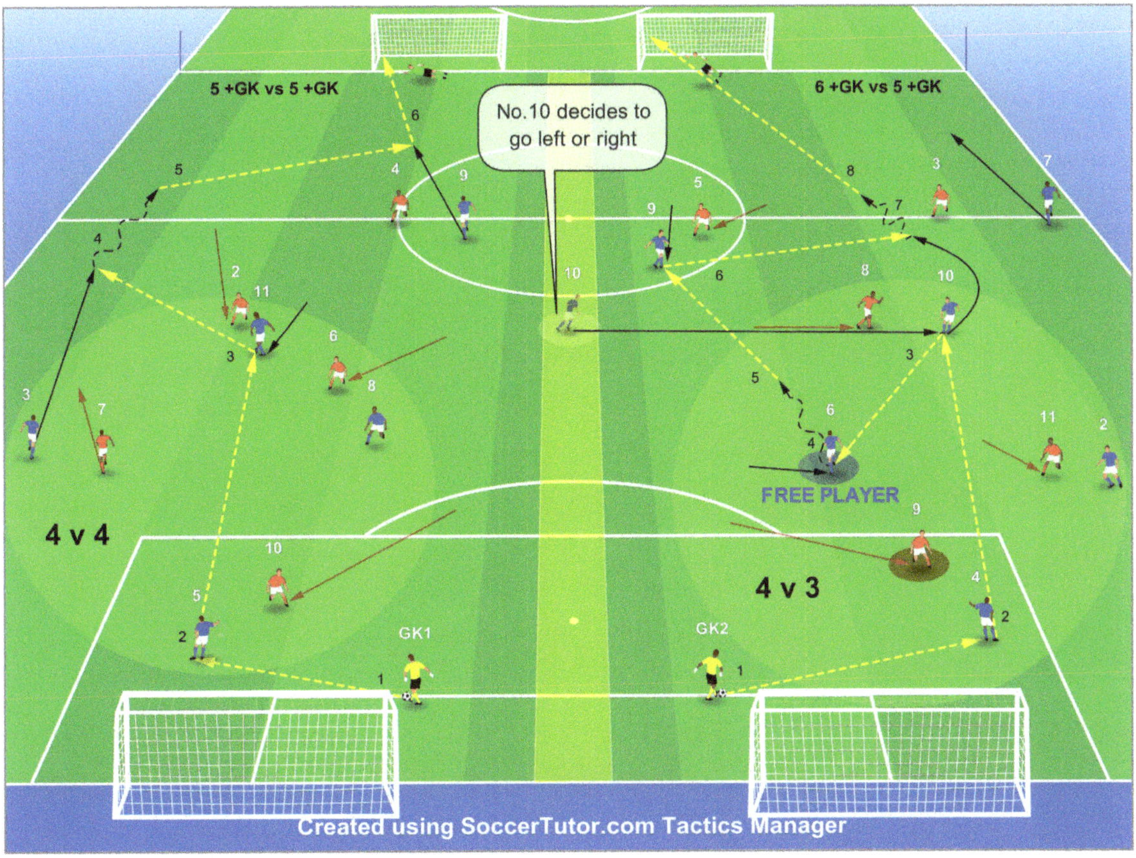

Practice Description (Variation 1)

- The **5 metre yellow vertical middle zone splits the 2 sides** and first the attacking midfielder (**N°10**) moves either left or right from there to determine which side has the overload and if the winger stays wide or moves inside. In this example, **N°10** moves to the right side.

- **On the left**, it is **5 (+GK) vs 5 (+GK)**, so the blues **build up with a 4 v 4 numerical equality**. The aim is to **play through the press and score**.

- Without a left winger (because they are acting as an attacking midfielder - **N°11**), the **emphasis is on the left back** (**N°3**) **to provide an attacking option** on the flank.

- **On the right**, it is **6 (+GK) vs 5 (+GK)**, so the blues **build up with a 4 v 3 overload**. The aim is to **find the free player** (**N°6**) **and score**.

- **Defending Objective:** If the reds win the ball (either side), they counter and try to score within 10-12 seconds.

©SOCCERTUTOR.COM   BEAT THE PRESS WITH A BOX MIDFIELD

Box Midfield Session 3: Strong Side Advantage vs High Press Zonal Defending

Variation 2: Overload on Left with Attacking Midfielder on that Side

[Diagram showing: 6 +GK vs 5 +GK on left side with "4 v 3" overload, 5 +GK vs 5 +GK on right side with "4 v 4", FREE PLAYER indicated on left, and note "No.10 decides to go left or right"]

Practice Description (Variation 2)

- Once variation 1 (overload on right) is complete, the **attacking midfielder (Nº10)** shifts to the left side of the pitch. All other players reset to their original positions, and the next phase begins.
- **On the left**, it is now **6 (+GK)** vs **5 (+GK)** and there is an **overload**.
- **On the right**, it is **5 (+GK)** vs **5 (+GK)** and there is **numerical equality**.
- The objective remains the same, which is to identify the free player, progress the ball, and finish the attack.
- The same rules and restrictions from variation 1 still apply.

- **Note:** *You can use 2 attacking midfielders (Nº10's) and one of them rests during each repetition*.

Coaching Points

1. **Quick reading of the situation:** Players must recognise defensive movements and react accordingly.
2. **Support play:** Positioning in passing lanes to provide progressive options.
3. **Fast combination play:** Using quick, sharp passes to break defensive lines.
4. **High tempo execution:** Keeping intensity high to replicate match situations.

Box Midfield Session 3: Strong Side Advantage vs High Press Zonal Defending

PROGRESSION

5. Build Up with Numerical Advantage on Strong Side with Box Midfield 11v11 Conditioned Game

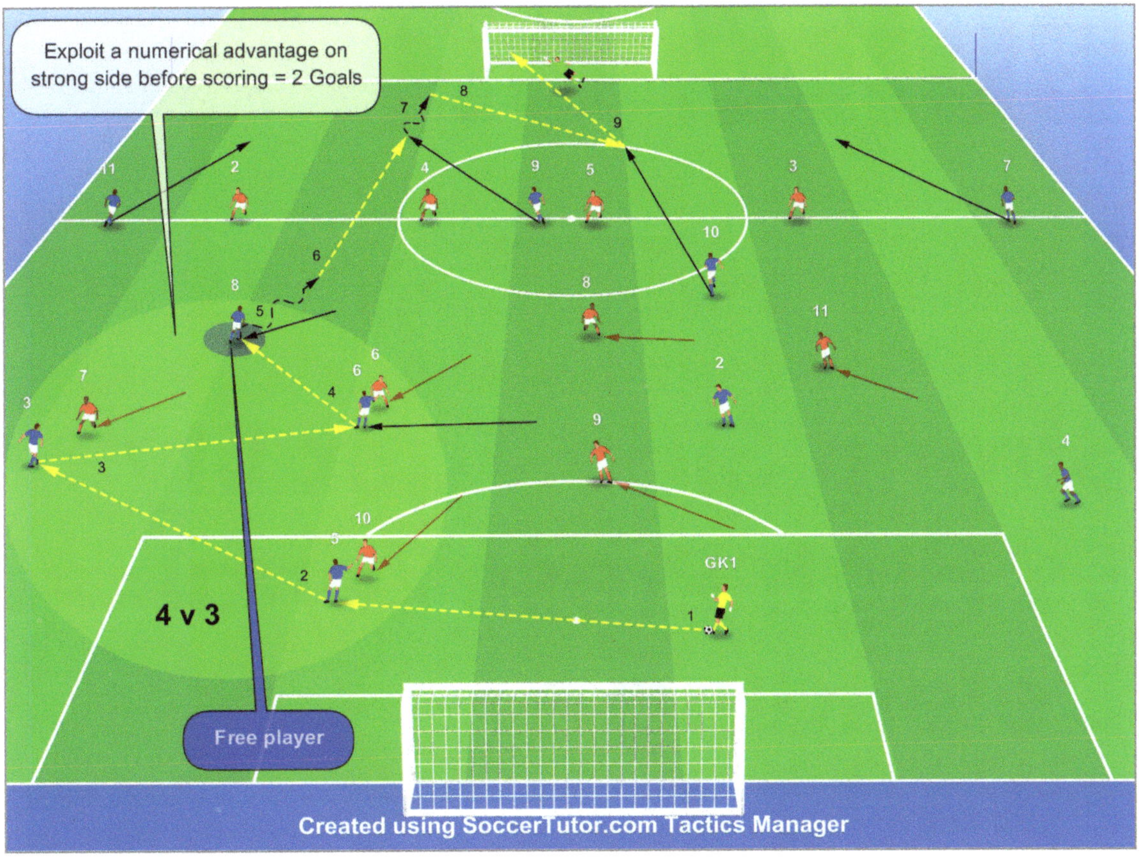

Exploit a numerical advantage on strong side before scoring = 2 Goals

4 v 3

Free player

Practice Description

- To complete the session, we play an 11v11 game in 3/4 of a full pitch.
- **Note:** *See previous practices (+ analysis) for different tactics to be applied.*
- **Blue Objective 1:** Build up play from GK and score (1 goal).
- **Blue Objective 2:** Build up play and successfully exploit a numerical advantage on the strong side before scoring (2 goals).
- **Red Objective:** Win ball and counter.
- Play always restarts with the blue **GK**. Switch the team roles after a set time.

Coaching Points

1. **Quickly assess the situation** to identify passing options and position effectively to create and maintain passing lanes.
2. **Make intelligent decisions** to exploit numerical superiority.
3. **Execute fast combination play** to break defensive lines.
4. **Maintain a high tempo** to sustain attacking momentum.

BEAT THE PRESS WITH A BOX MIDFIELD

BOX MIDFIELD BUILD UP

Tactical Analysis

Strong Side Equality vs High Press Zonal Defending

Build up play patterns from Guardiola, Alonso, and Arteta's teams

Box Midfield Build Up: Strong Side Equality vs High Press Zonal Defending

Switching Play from Strong to Weak Side (2 at Back)

1. Equality in Numbers on the Strong Side Creates a Numerical Advantage and Available Space on the Weak Side

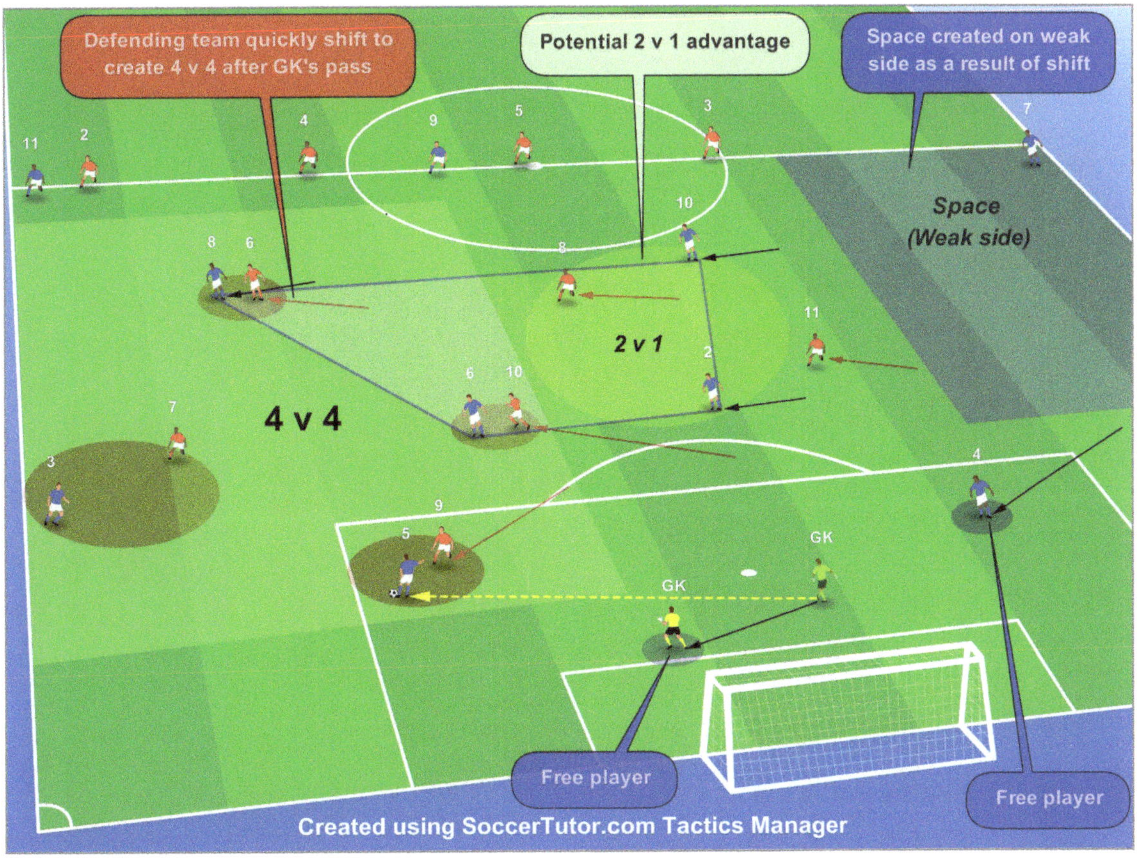

The **red defending team quickly shifts to the strong side after the first pass from the goalkeeper (GK)**. This can result in **equal numbers and no overload on the strong side**. However, this **creates space elsewhere** on the pitch.

In the example, when the ball is played to the **blue left centre back (N°5)**, the red N°10 quickly moves to mark the **defensive midfielder (N°6)**, preventing a numerical advantage around the ball.

This leaves the **right centre back (N°4)** and **GK** as the free players. The **right winger (N°7) has significant space available on the weak side** (highlighted blue in diagram).

In midfield, **N°10 and N°2 can also exploit space**. Red N°8 is unable to cover both of them and red N°11 would struggle to shift across in time. This creates a potential 2v1 advantage in the centre. If red N°11 does shift across to cover **N°2**, even more space opens up out wide.

BEAT THE PRESS WITH A BOX MIDFIELD

Box Midfield Build Up: Strong Side Equality vs High Press Zonal Defending

2. Exploit 2v1 Advantage in the Centre to Switch Play to the Free Winger on the Weak Side

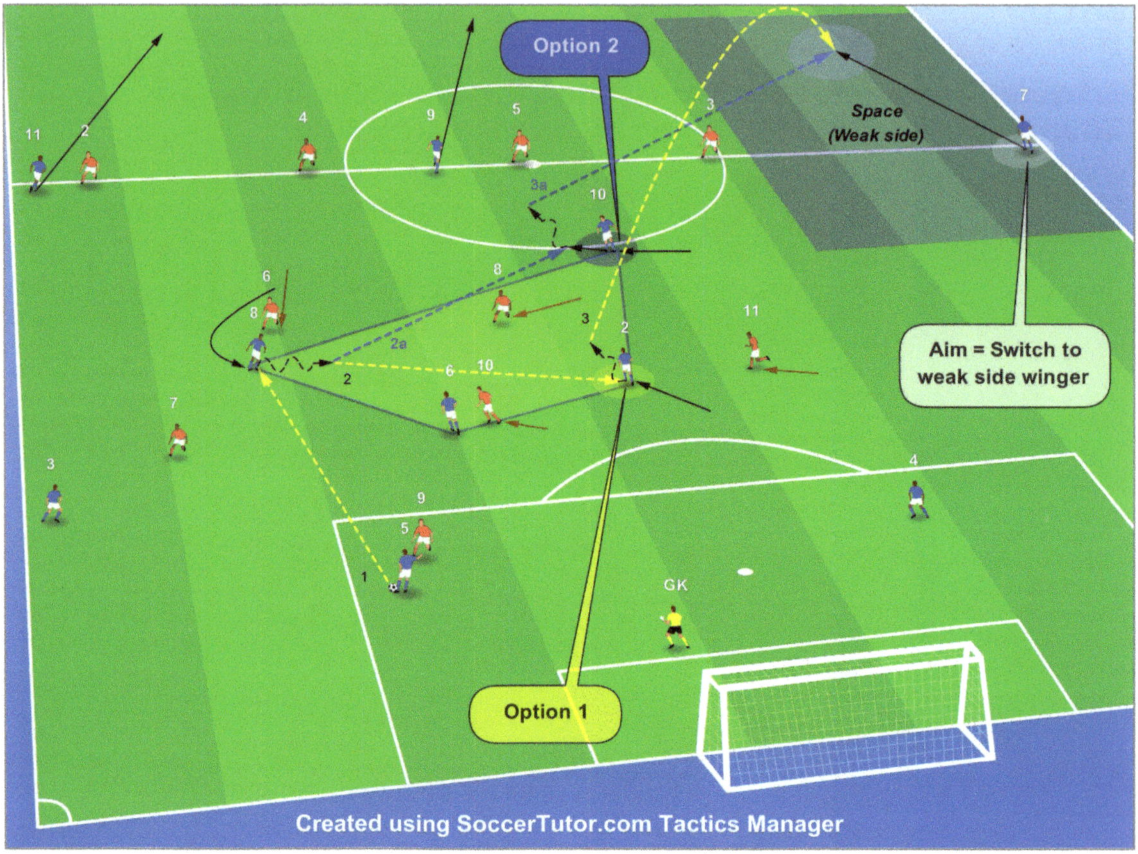

Although the strong side does not offer a clear overload, the blue attacking team must identify where the advantage lies.

A **numerical advantage can be found either in the centre (2v1) or on the weak side** (highlighted area).

The team should:

A. **Beat the press on the strong side** and find a teammate with time and space to switch the play.

B. **If this is not possible directly**, use the nearby free players to reset and move the ball across.

In the diagram example, the **attacking midfielder (Nº8)** receives, carries the ball inside to find space, and can then either pass to:

1. The **defensive midfielder** in the centre (**Nº2** - yellow arrow).

2. The other **attacking midfielder** (**Nº10** - blue arrow).

From there, the **ball can be switched to the free winger (Nº7)** on the weak side, who has time and space to attack.

BEAT THE PRESS WITH A BOX MIDFIELD

Box Midfield Build Up: Strong Side Equality vs High Press Zonal Defending

3. Reset through the Goalkeeper or Centre Back to Switch Play to the Weak Side

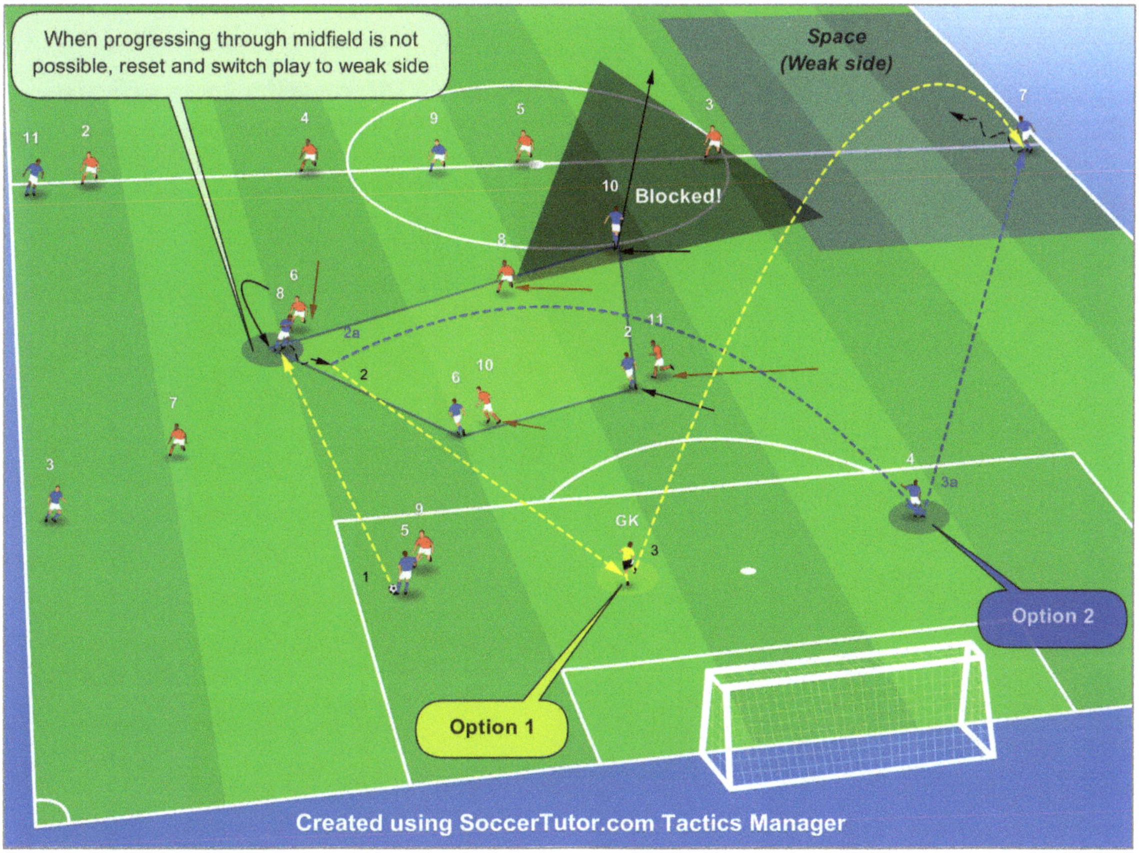

If the **red team manage to eliminate the numerical advantage in the centre** by shifting their winger (red N°11) towards the blue **defensive midfielder (N°2)** and positioning their central midfielder (N°8) to **block the path towards the attacking midfielder (N°10)**, the other attacking midfielder in possession (**N°8**) is unable to switch play directly.

In this situation, **N°8 uses the free players to move the ball to the weak side (GK and centre back N°4).**

N°8 receives the ball from the **centre back (N°5)** and plays to the **GK** (yellow arrow) or the other **centre back** (**N°4** - blue arrow).

The next step is to move the ball to the **weak side winger (N°7)**, who can receive in space, move forward, and attack in behind the opposition's defensive line.

Note: As the switch is from a deeper position, it gives the opposition more time to shift back and across and reduce the winger's (**N°7**) available space. **Switching from deeper is less effective** than progressing through midfield and then finding **N°7** on the weak side (example on previous page).

BEAT THE PRESS WITH A BOX MIDFIELD

Box Midfield Build Up: Strong Side Equality vs High Press Zonal Defending

Strong Side Build Up with Numerical Equality (2 at Back)

1. Centre Back's Aerial Pass to Forward or Winger with Immediate Support Play

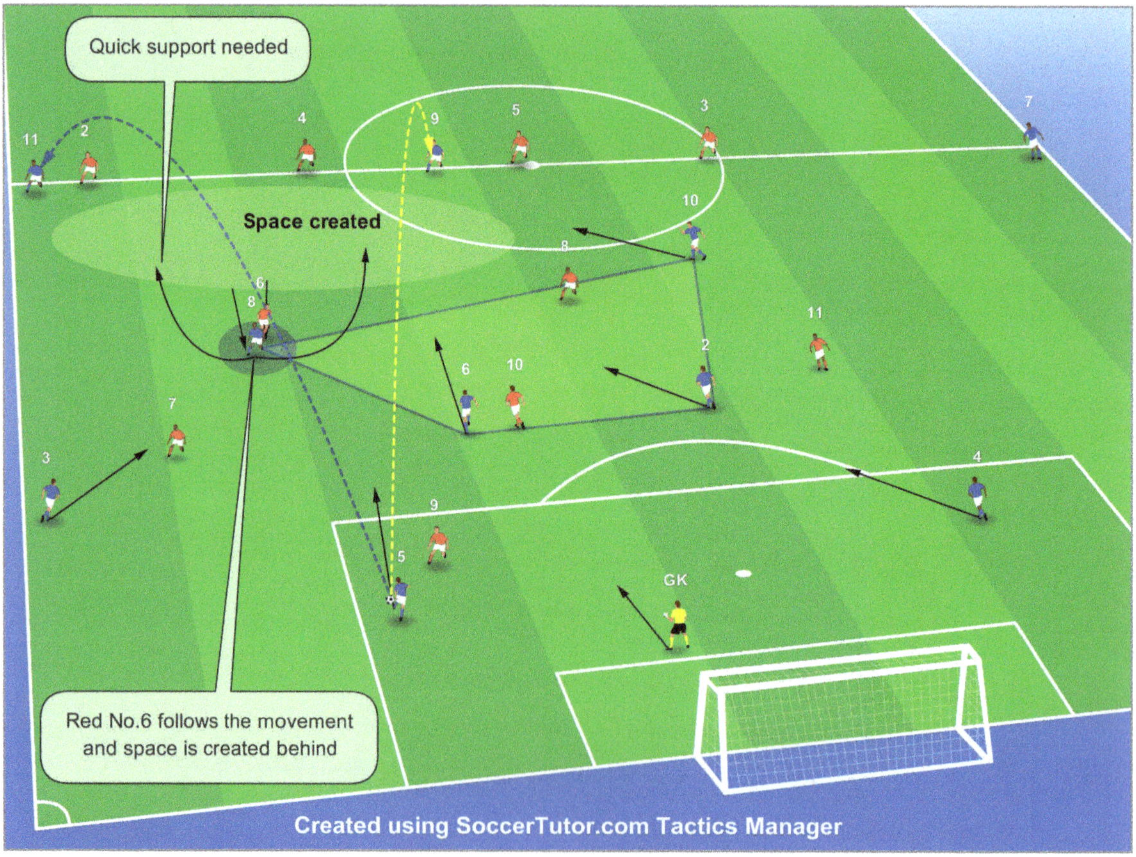

Although building up play on the strong side is less favourable due to equal numbers, it can still be effective with quality execution. For example, with Pep Guardiola's Manchester City, a forward like Haaland with strong hold-up play can play a key role when well supported.

As the **centre back (Nº5)** receives under pressure, the **attacking midfielder on that side (Nº8) drops back to escape his marker**.

The red central midfielder (Nº6) follows, **leaving space behind for the winger (Nº11) or forward (Nº9) to exploit**.

If Nº11 or Nº9 receive a long pass and hold up the ball, **quick support from teammates can secure possession** (or win the second ball). The **centre backs' (Nº4 and Nº5)** moving forward also helps by leaving the red forward (Nº9) offside, protecting against a quick counter attack.

Box Midfield Build Up: Strong Side Equality vs High Press Zonal Defending

2. Full Back's Aerial Pass to Exploit Space Behind the Pressing Full Back who Follows the Winger's Movement

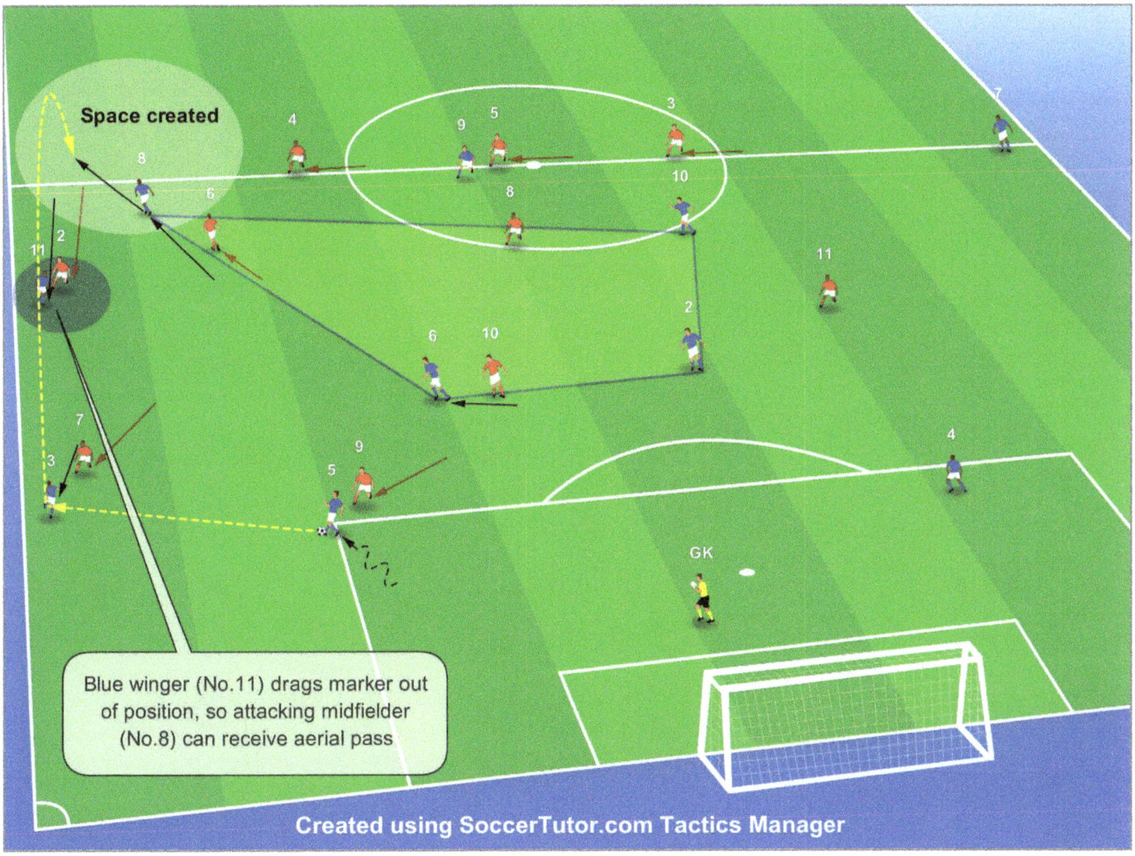

Blue winger (No.11) drags marker out of position, so attacking midfielder (No.8) can receive aerial pass

When numbers are equal, off-the-ball movement becomes essential. Attacking players must **move intelligently to open up space and create passing options**.

In this example, the **left back (N°3)** drops back to receive from the **centre back (N°5)** and turns forward.

At the same time, the **left winger (N°11) drops back and drags the opposing right back (red N°2) out of position**.

This opens up space behind red N°2, so the **blue attacking midfielder (N°8) makes a well-timed forward run into the created space**.

If the red central midfielder (N°6) does not track **blue N°8's** run quickly enough, **N°3** can exploit this by playing an aerial pass, as shown.

Note: This sequence has the potential to eliminate 7 opposing players and move the ball into a dangerous attacking area.

BEAT THE PRESS WITH A BOX MIDFIELD

Box Midfield Build Up: Strong Side Equality vs High Press Zonal Defending

3. Combination Play and Movements to Create Space for Switch to Weak Side Winger

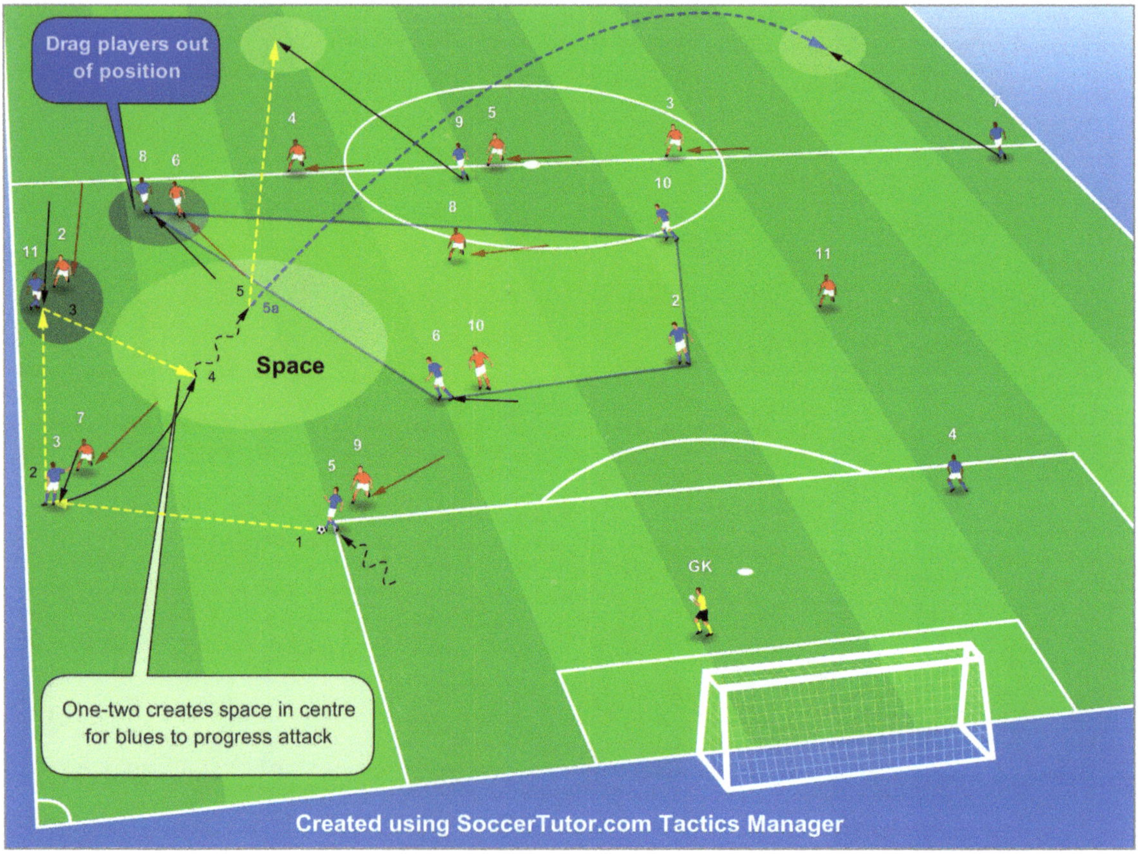

In a variation of the previous example, we show what happens if the **red central midfielder (N°6) follows the blue attacking midfielder (N°8) tightly** and prevents the opening for the left back (**N°3**) to play an effective aerial pass to **N°8**.

In this situation, **space is instead created in the central area (highlighted), which can be exploited by playing a one-two combination with the left winger (N°11)**.

As soon as **N°3** receives in the centre, passes towards the **forward (N°9 - yellow arrow)** or the **weak side winger (N°7 - blue arrow)** open up. Both options get the team in behind the opposition's defensive line.

Note 1: This combination allows the blue team to bypass at least 4 opponents, but its success relies on good decision making, communication, awareness, and technical quality under pressure to move the ball accurately and at speed.

Note 2: For the situation to be effective, the **defensive midfielder (N°6) must avoid being positioned too close to the strong side**, as it may drag red N°10 across, reducing the space available and limiting the impact of the attacking move.

BEAT THE PRESS WITH A BOX MIDFIELD

Box Midfield Build Up: Strong Side Equality vs High Press Zonal Defending

4. Using the Forward to Link Play to Create and Exploit a Wide Overload

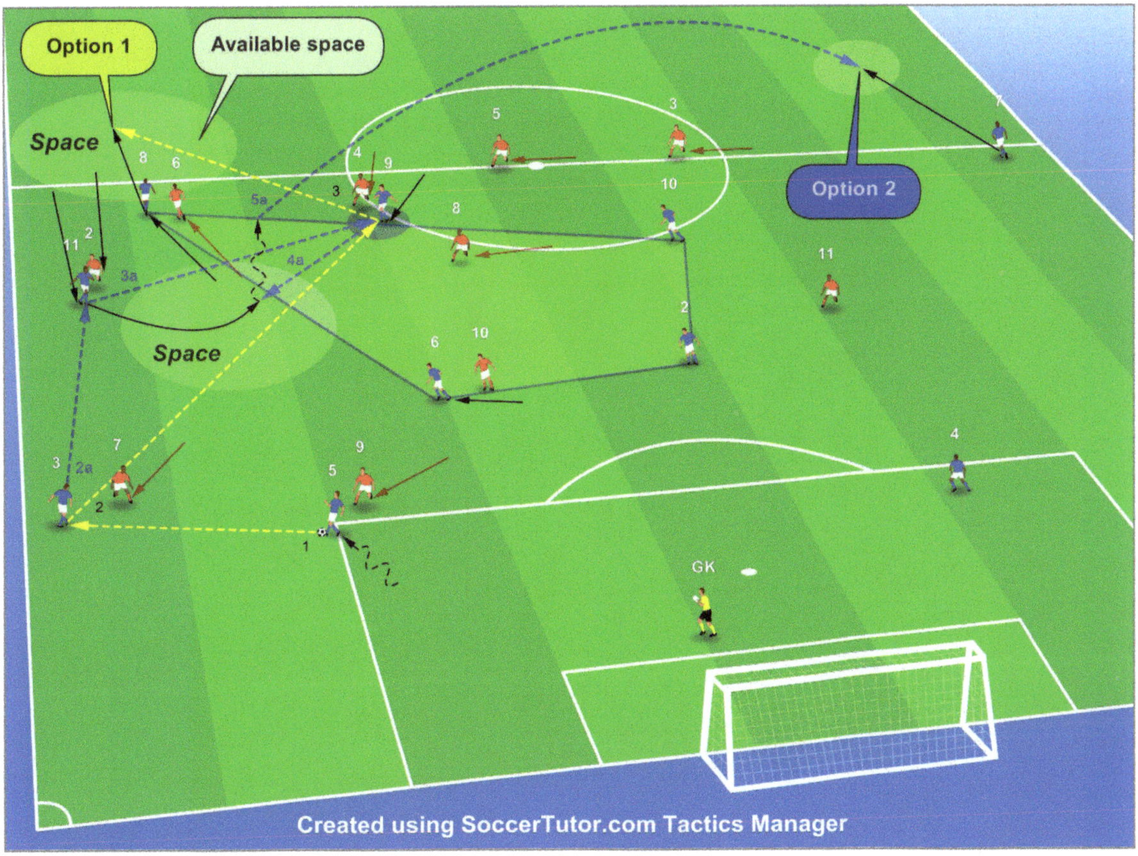

Combination play on the strong side can also involve the **forward** (**N°9**) dropping back to link up play.

In this example, as the **left back** (**N°3**) receives, the **left winger** (**N°11**) and the **left attacking midfielder** (**N°8**) move together, as **N°9** drops back to offer support.

Option 1: N°3 can play directly to **N°9** (yellow arrow), who has 2 options:

1. **Play forward and in behind for the run of N°8** (yellow arrow 3).
2. **Lay the ball back into space for N°11 to receive** (blue arrow 4a).

Option 2: If the direct pass to **N°9** is not available, **N°3** can pass to **N°11**, who then plays first-time to **N°9** before moving to receive a return pass in the available space immediately.

The next step is to **switch the play to the winger on the weak side** (**N°7 - blue arrow 5a**), where space is available.

BEAT THE PRESS WITH A BOX MIDFIELD

Box Midfield Build Up: Strong Side Equality vs High Press Zonal Defending

Strong Side Build Up with Numerical Equality (3 at Back)

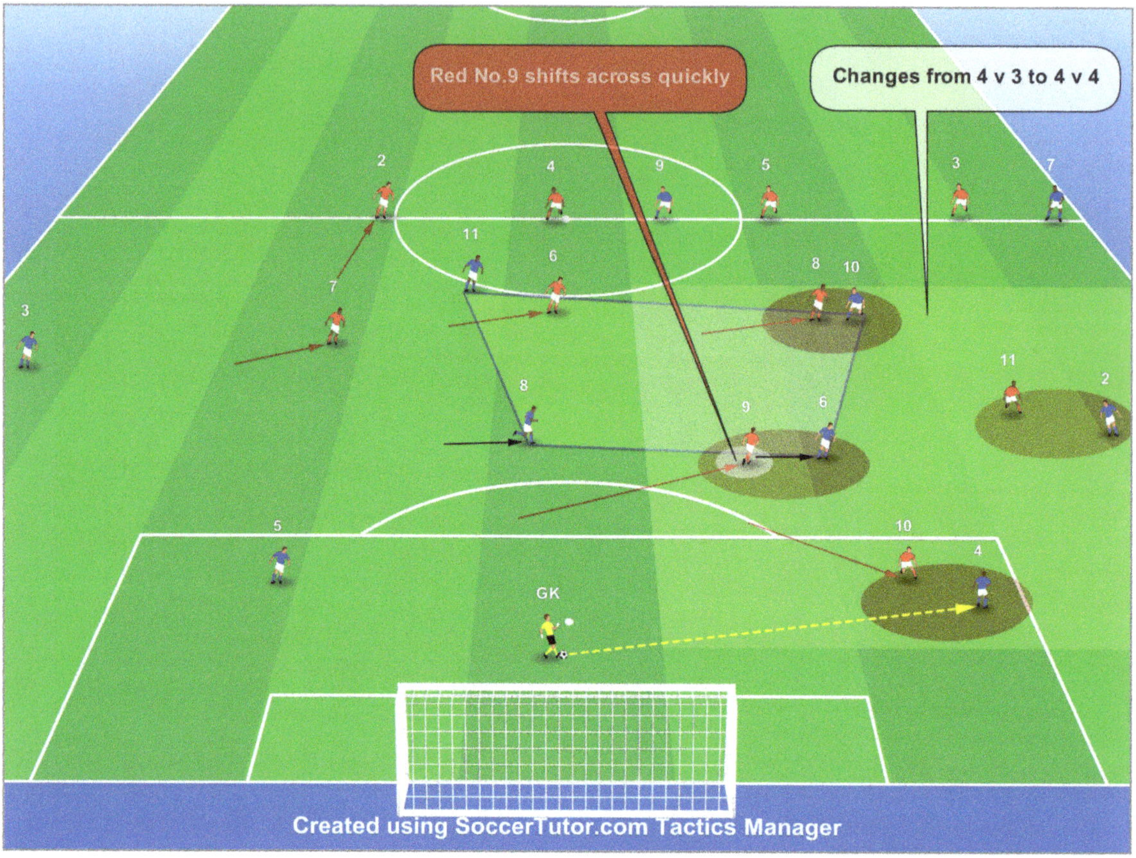

(Diagram: Red No.9 shifts across quickly — Changes from 4 v 3 to 4 v 4)

When the 3-at-the-back box midfield is used to build up play from the back, there is a strong side with a 4v3 numerical advantage for build up play, but a **weak side is created with a 4v4 equality**.

If the ball is moved to the side of the pitch where there is a numerical advantage and the opposing team shift across quickly, specifically the opposing forward (red N°9), then there is equality on that side.

After these movements, there is now a similar situation as when we looked at the 2-at-the-back box midfield.

The **same options previously described (see pages 98-101) can be applied** in this situation with a 3-at-the back box midfield:

1. Centre back's aerial pass to forward or winger with immediate support play.

2. Full back's aerial pass to exploit space behind the pressing full back who follows the winger's movement.

3. Combination play/movements to create space for switch to weak side winger.

4. Using the forward to link play to create and exploit a wide overload.

BEAT THE PRESS WITH A BOX MIDFIELD

Box Midfield Build Up: Strong Side Equality vs High Press Zonal Defending

Weak Side Build Up with Numerical Equality (3 at Back)

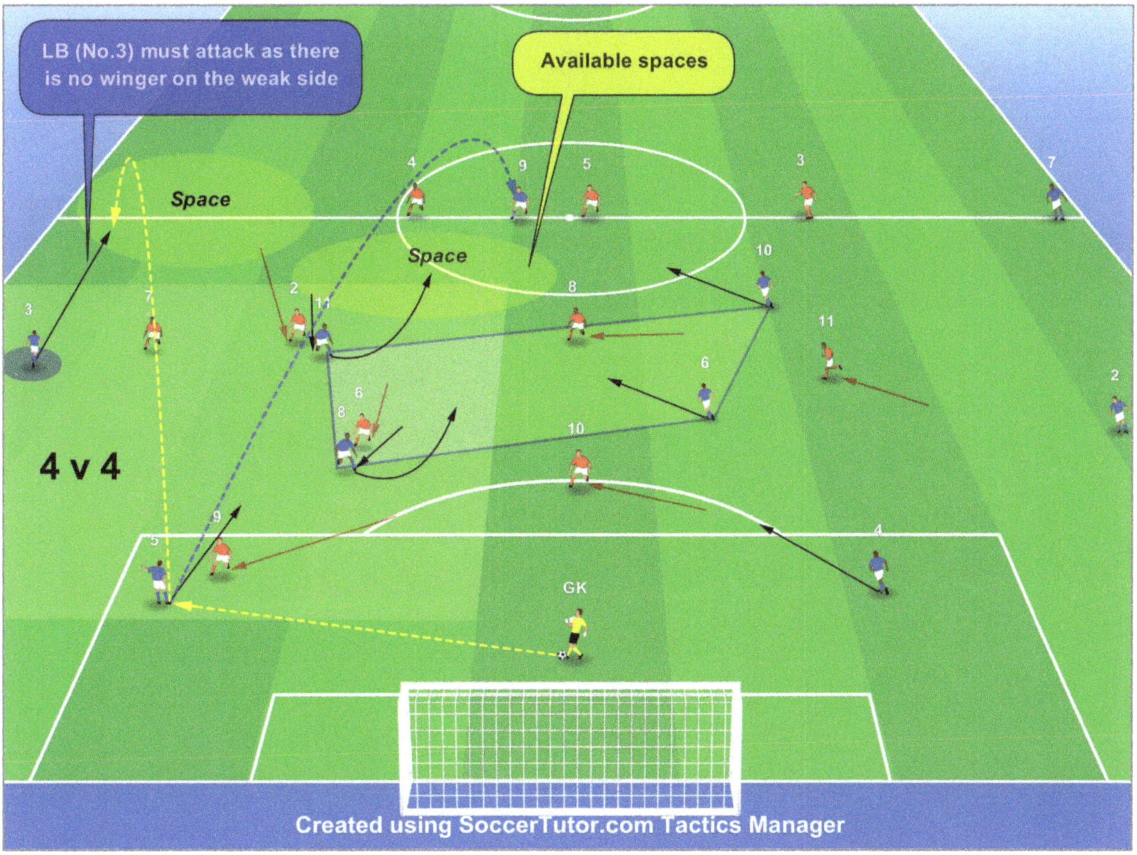

Diagram labels: LB (No.3) must attack as there is no winger on the weak side; Available spaces; Space; Space; 4 v 4

If the ball is played to the weak side (left), a 4v4 situation exists and options are more limited due to the lack of a winger.

The **centre back (N°5)** has fewer passing options but more space to work with. The best option is for the **left back (N°3)** to make a forward run.

The **attacking midfielder (blue N°11) drops back to pull the red right back (N°2) out of position** and create space. This movement also reduces the chances of the **forward (N°9)** being double-marked.

At the same time, the **defensive midfielder (blue N°8) drops back to drag the red central midfielder (N°6) forward**.

N°5 can play a long aerial pass for the run of N°3 or pass to N°9, who can hold the ball up and link play or rely on nearby supporting teammates to win the second ball.

BEAT THE PRESS WITH A BOX MIDFIELD

BOX MIDFIELD SESSION

Training Session 4 (4 Practices)

Strong Side Equality vs High Press Zonal Defending

Based on Guardiola, Alonso, and Arteta build up patterns

Box Midfield Session 4: Strong Side Equality vs High Press Zonal Defending

TRAINING SESSION (4 PRACTICES)
1. Box Midfield Build Up Combinations and Switching Play with Target Areas

Variation 1: Wide Support with Deep Switch

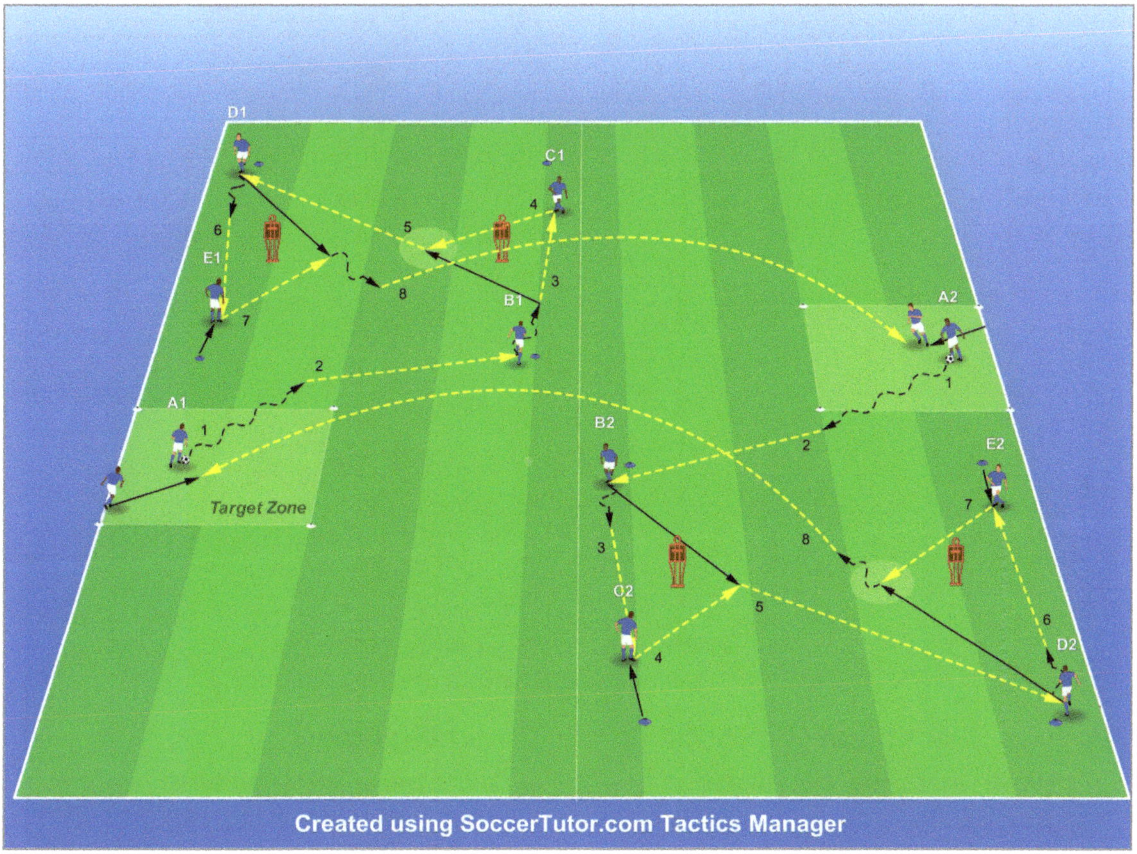

Practice Description (Variation 1)

The practice is set up in a 40x60m area divided vertically into 2 zones, with 8x5m target areas on each side. The combination runs simultaneously on both sides

1-2. **A** starts by dribbling out of the target zone and passing to **B**.

3-6. **B** combines with **C** and receives the return pass. **B** then finds **D**, who takes a forward touch and passes to **E**.

7-8. **D** receives a return pass from **E** and switches play to the opposite target zone for the next player waiting.

→ The practice continues.

→ **Player Rotations:** A1 → B1 → C1 → D1 → E1 → A2 → B2 → C2 → D2 → E2 → A1.

BEAT THE PRESS WITH A BOX MIDFIELD

Box Midfield Session 4: Strong Side Equality vs High Press Zonal Defending

Variation 2: Forward Combination with 2 Switch Options

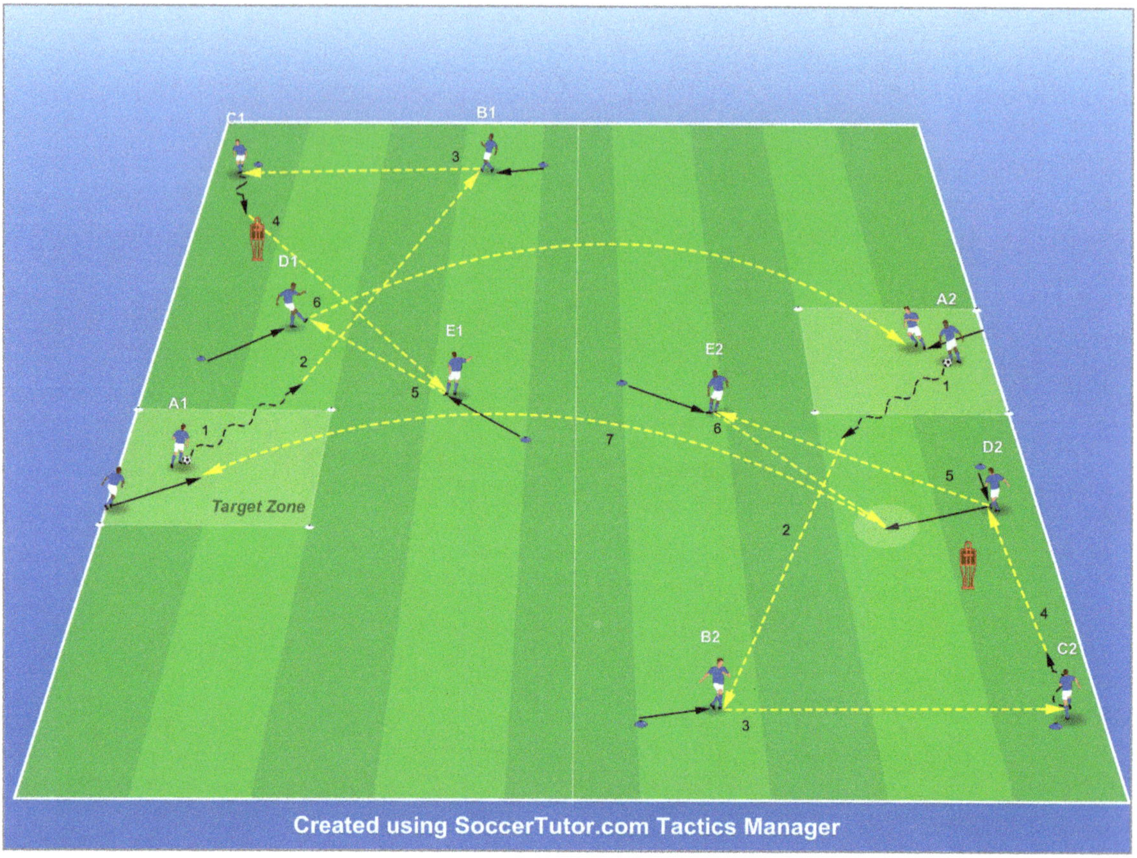

Practice Description (Variation 2)

- In this variation, the sequence changes.
- **A** starts by dribbling out of the target zone and passing to **B**, who passes to **C**.
- **C** moves forward and has 2 options: Pass to **E** (left side of diagram) or pass to **D** (right side).
- If **E** receives, they lay it off for **D**.
- **D** switches play to the opposite target zone for the next player waiting and the practice continues.
- → Player Rotations: **A1** → **B1** → **C1** → **D1** → **E1** → **A2** → **B2** → **C2** → **D2** → **E2** → **A1**.

Coaching Points

1. **Quick, purposeful combination play** to break lines and maintain control.
2. **Precision passing** (short and long) to support fluid ball movement.
3. **Consistent high tempo** with sharp movement and fast decision making.

BEAT THE PRESS WITH A BOX MIDFIELD

Box Midfield Session 4: Strong Side Equality vs High Press Zonal Defending

PROGRESSION
2. Box Midfield Build Up with Equal Numbers and Switch Play in a Dynamic 3-Team Game
1/2: 4v4 with Outside Support and Switching Objective

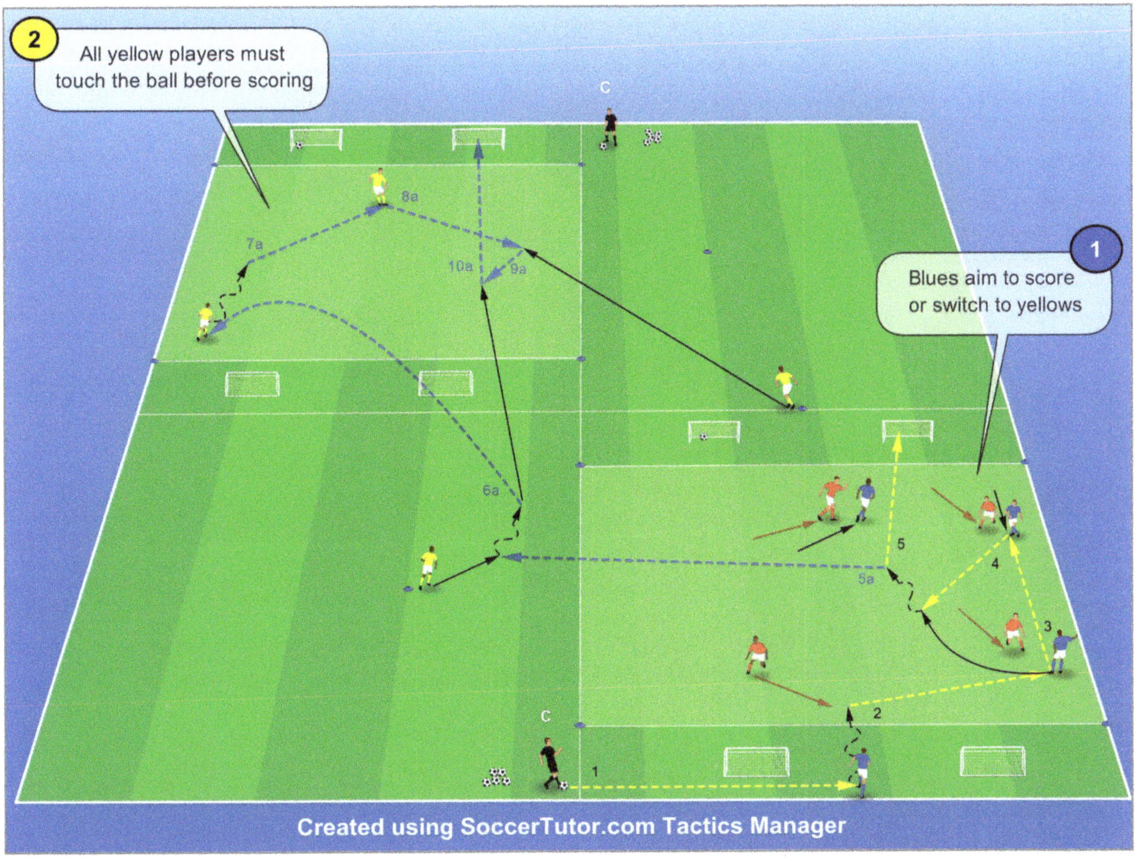

All yellow players must touch the ball before scoring

Blues aim to score or switch to yellows

Practice Description (1/2)

- We use two 25x15m areas with 3 teams of 4 (blue, red, and yellow).
- The coach passes to a blue player, who dribbles into the area. The **blues play 4v4 against the reds and aim to score in the 2 small goals or pass to a yellow outside support player**. The positioning replicates the centre back, full back, winger and attacking midfielder when building up play out wide.

- **Defending Objective:** The reds try to win the ball and counter to score in the other 2 small goals.
- If an outside yellow player receives (as shown in the diagram), they then **switch play to a teammate** in the other area. From there, the 2 outside players must sprint into the new area.
- **All yellow players must touch the ball before scoring a goal**.

BEAT THE PRESS WITH A BOX MIDFIELD

Box Midfield Session 4: Strong Side Equality vs High Press Zonal Defending

2/2: Transition and Rotation After Switch or Goal

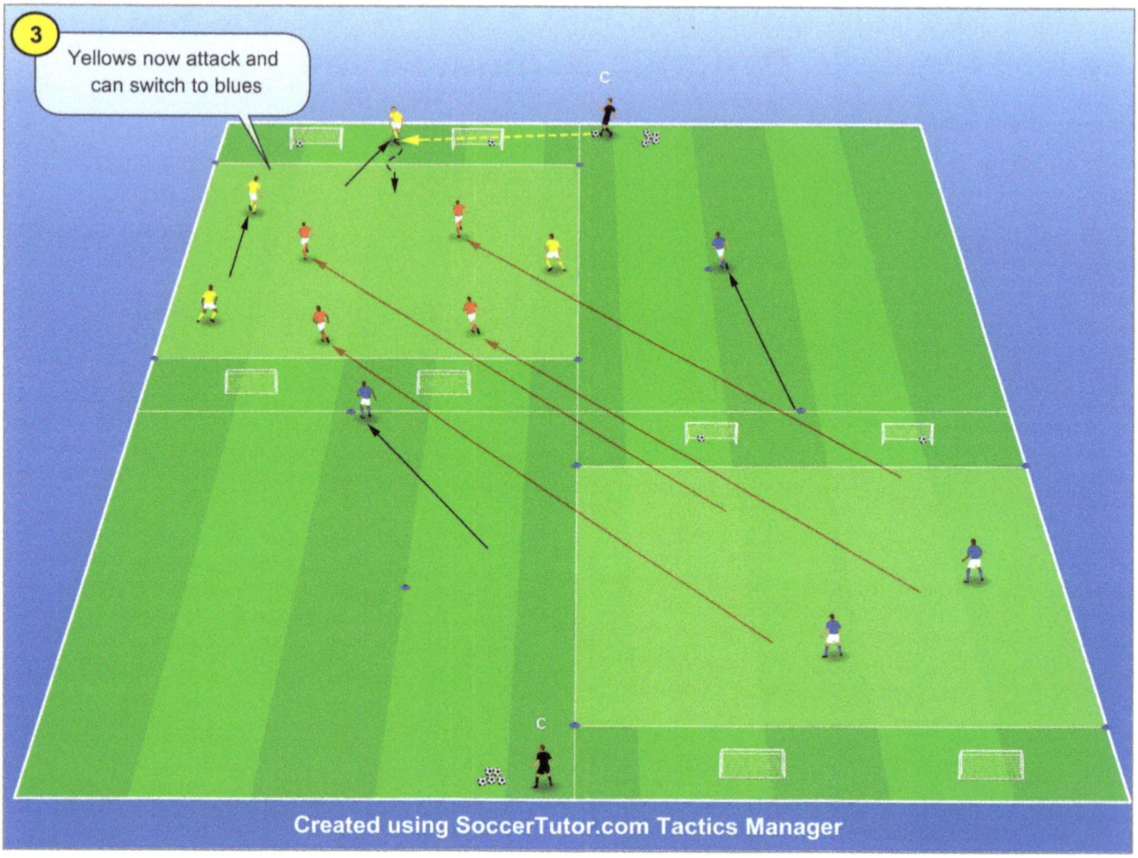

3 Yellows now attack and can switch to blues

Practice Description (2/2)

- After a goal or a completed switch, **all 4 red players quickly transition to defend in the second area**. 2 blue players move outside and 2 stay in the first area.

- The **coach passes a new ball in with the yellow team now aiming to score or switch play** to the blues back in the opposite direction.

- If the ball goes out at anytime, the practice restarts from the coach.

- **Rule:** The attacking team must complete their objective within a set time. If they fail, the coach blows the whistle and they become the defending team.

- Area dimensions can be adjusted based on the player level and/or age group.

Coaching Points

1. **Intelligent off-the-ball movement** to offer clear passing options.
2. **Supporting players adjust positions** to open new passing lanes.
3. **Fast, coordinated combination play**.
4. **Quality long passes** with immediate forward support.
5. **Sustain a high speed of play** under pressure.

BEAT THE PRESS WITH A BOX MIDFIELD

Box Midfield Session 4: Strong Side Equality vs High Press Zonal Defending

PROGRESSION

3. Split-Pitch Box Midfield Build Up Tactical Game with Equal Numbers

Variation 1: Box Midfield with 2-at-the-Back

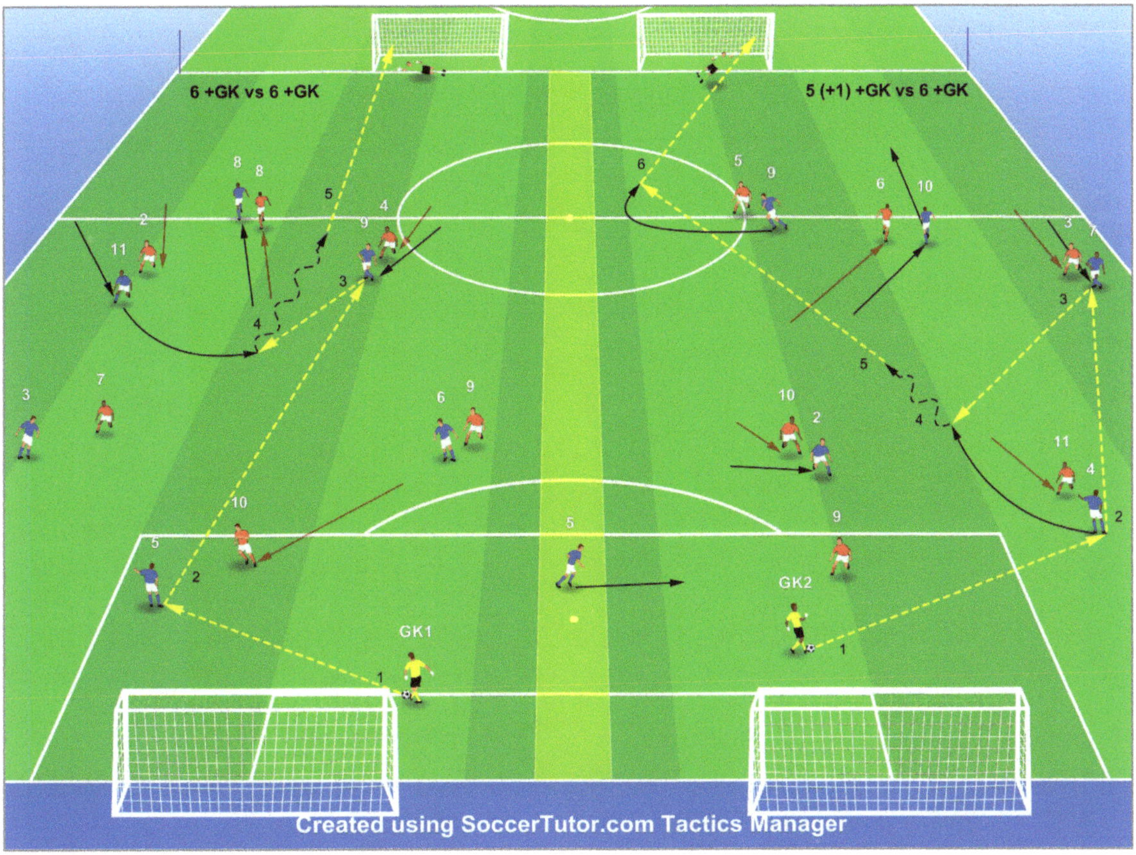

Practice Description (Variation 1)

- The pitch is split into 2 halves, with both active at the same time. This first variation focuses on the **2-at-the-back box midfield shape**.

- **On the right**, it starts with **5 (+GK) vs 6 (+GK)**, with the goalkeeper acting as a centre back. The **centre back (N°5) enters (+1) after the first pass** to support the build up and provide balance in case possession is lost.

- The blue team **build up play through short combinations or play long**, then support the second ball. The aim is to beat the press, play in behind, and score.

- *See analysis pages for all options*.

- **On the left**, it is **6 (+GK) vs 6 (+GK)** with the same objectives.

- **Defending Objective:** If the reds win the ball (either side), they counter to try and score within 10-12 seconds.

BEAT THE PRESS WITH A BOX MIDFIELD

Box Midfield Session 4: Strong Side Equality vs High Press Zonal Defending

Variation 2: Box Midfield with 3-at-the-Back

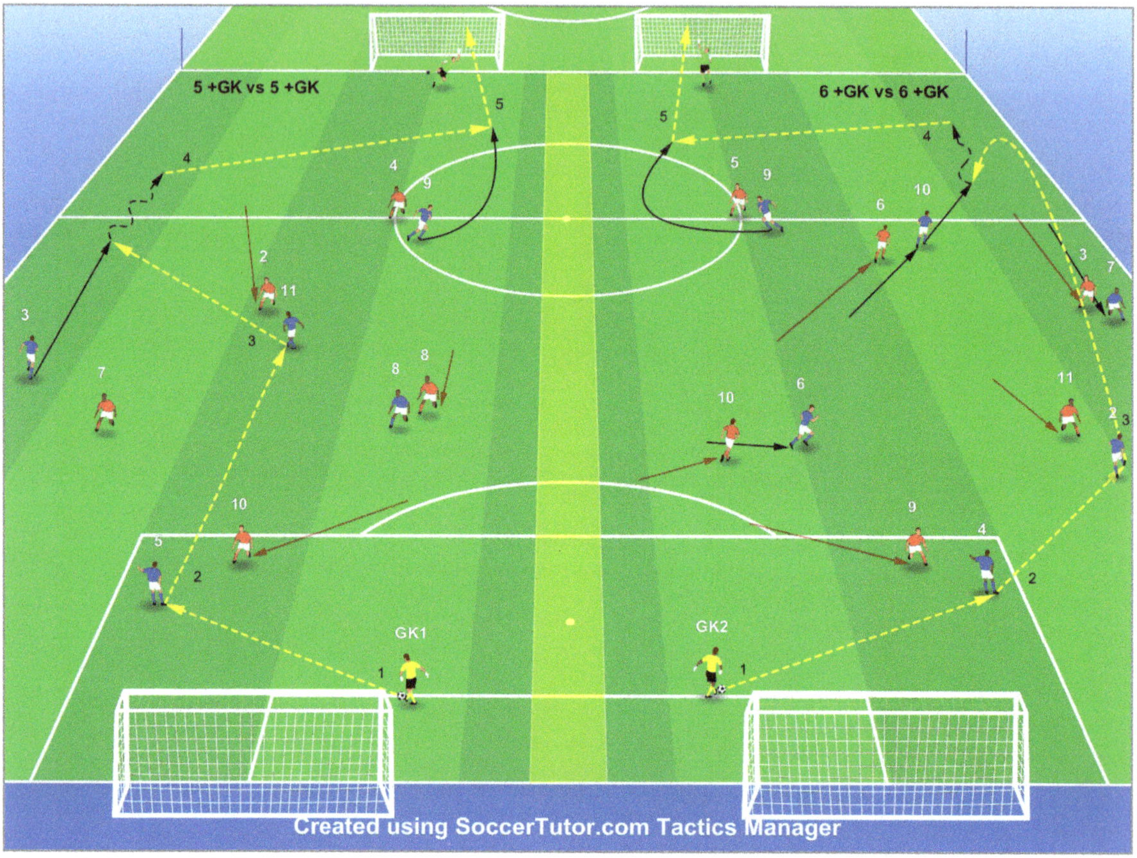

Practice Description (Variation 2)

- This second variation focuses on the **3-at-the-back box midfield shape**. There are equal numbers on both sides.
- This game replicates **realistic build up play situations with equal numbers using the box midfield** on both sides of the pitch.
- On the left, it is **5 (+GK) vs 5 (+GK)**.
- On the right, it is **6 (+GK) vs 6 (+GK)**.
- The blues use a more structured build up and the **reds apply an immediate high press after the first pass**.

Coaching Points

1. **Timed off-the-ball movement** to support progression.
2. **Create and adjust passing lanes** between and beyond lines.
3. **Quick, accurate combination play** under pressure.
4. **Use of long passes followed by quick support** (for second balls).
5. **Maintain high intensity and tempo** throughout on both sides of the pitch.

©SOCCERTUTOR.COM   BEAT THE PRESS WITH A BOX MIDFIELD

Box Midfield Session 4: Strong Side Equality vs High Press Zonal Defending

PROGRESSION

4. Box Midfield Build Up with Equal Numbers 11 v 11 Conditioned 3 Zone Game

Variation 1: Exploiting Strong Side Overloads

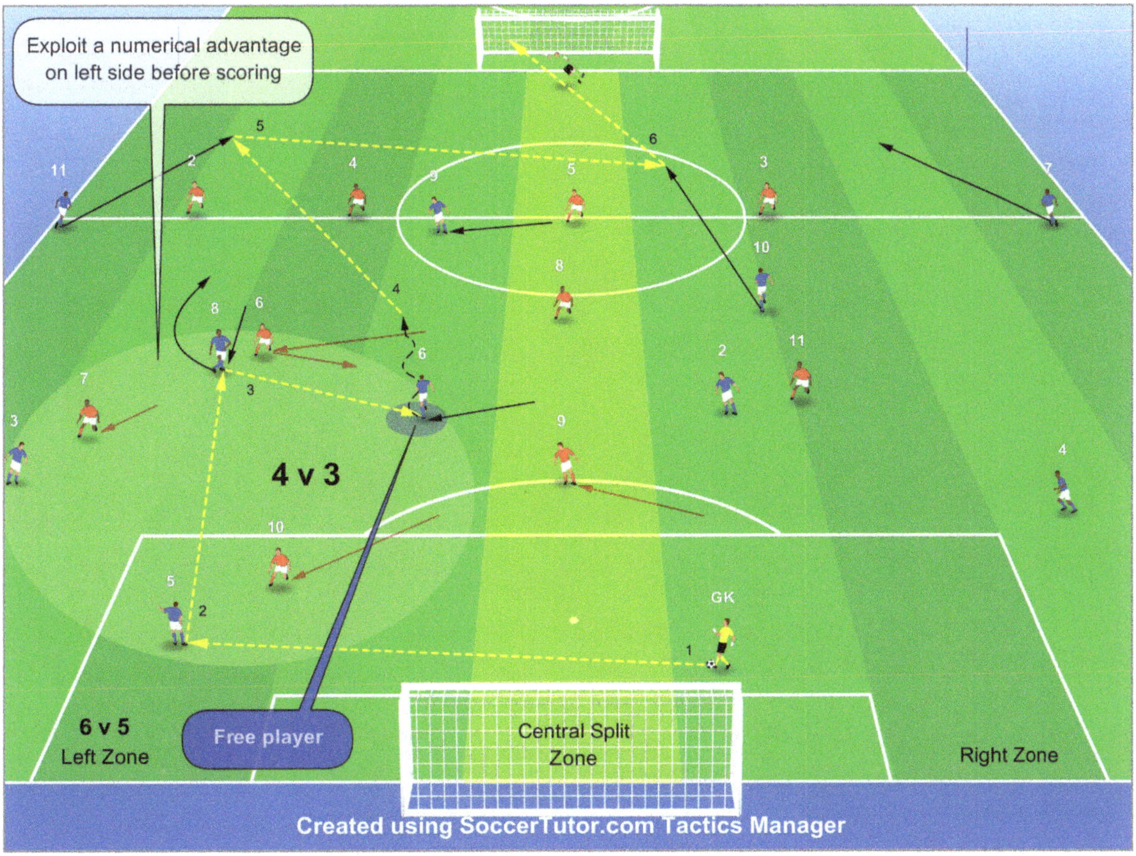

Exploit a numerical advantage on left side before scoring

4 v 3

6 v 5 Left Zone

Free player

Central Split Zone

Right Zone

Created using SoccerTutor.com Tactics Manager

Practice Description (Variation 1)

- Using 3/4 of a full pitch, the yellow 7 metre middle zone splits the pitch vertically.
- The **goalkeeper (GK)** starts by passing into either wide zone.
- When there is a **numerical advantage on that side (as in diagram), the blues aim to exploit it by using quick combination play before scoring**.

- There is a **4 v 3 advantage for the build up** (highlighted) and the **blues move the ball to the free player (defensive midfielder Nº6)**. Overall there is a 6 v 5 advantage on the left side.
- **Defending Objective:** If the reds win the ball, they counter attack and try to score within 10-12 seconds.
- **Note:** The example uses a 2-at-the-back box midfield shape but the practice can easily be adapted for 3-at-the-back.

BEAT THE PRESS WITH A BOX MIDFIELD

Box Midfield Session 4: Strong Side Equality vs High Press Zonal Defending

Variation 2: Switching from Equal Numbers to the Weak Side

Practice Description (Variation 2)

- In Variation 2, the **red players shift early to create a numerical equality** on the left side of the pitch.
- The **blues must decide the best option**:
  1. Continue using combination play.
  2. Pass long and provide support for the second ball.
  3. Switch to the weak side where space may be available (diagram example).
- Clear communication is essential to identify whether an overload, equality, or a switching opportunity exists.
- **Restriction:** The reds can only press after the first pass from **GK** is played.
- **Progression:** Remove the visual zones for players to play naturally.

Coaching Points

1. **Read and react quickly** to changing situations.
2. **Use verbal cues** to support team decision making.
3. **Offer passing options** through intelligent positioning.
4. **Switch play with accuracy and awareness**.
5. **Maintain a high tempo** throughout the practice.

BEAT THE PRESS WITH A BOX MIDFIELD

BOX MIDFIELD BUILD UP

Tactical Analysis

Against High Press with Zonal Defending and Man Marking

Build up play patterns from Guardiola, Alonso, and Arteta's teams

BEAT THE PRESS WITH A BOX MIDFIELD

Build Up Against High Press with Zonal Defending and Man Marking (Hybrid)

Another type of defending that can be used when applying a high press is a hybrid of zonal defending and man marking. Therefore, we must be prepared with tactical solutions to build up play with a box midfield against it.

In this situation, the defending players man mark opponents who are within their zone of responsibility in a more aggressive way of defending.

However, as there is a **big numerical advantage (4v2) in midfield**, it makes it impossible for 2 opposing midfielders to man mark 2 players, as it would leave the other 2 completely free. To deal with this situation, the **defending team will almost always move 1 player to join the midfielders, changing it to 4v3**.

When using a 2-at-the-back box midfield shape, the best choice for the opposing team (to compensate for the numerical disadvantage) is to move one of their 2 forwards back. This would preferably be the one who is positioned closest to the goalkeeper.

After this movement, the opposition have the following numerical situations to deal with:

1. **1v2 in the first pressing line**.
2. **3v4 in midfield**.

In midfield, 2 of the opposing players apply man marking but the other one will have to cover 2 players.

The principles and actions the possession team apply to be effective in building up against this type of defending are:

A. **Make it difficult for the opposing midfielder** to control 2 players at the same time.

B. **Move the ball to the midfielder who has the most available space**.

Note: The following pages outline the tactical solutions for building up play with a box midfield against a high press with zonal defending and man marking (hybrid), exploiting the player that has to cover 2 players in midfield to progress the play.

Build Up Against High Press with Zonal Defending and Man Marking (2 at Back)

1a. Opposition Positioning Adjustments (4-4-2 to 4-1-4-1) to Apply Marking Against a Box Midfield

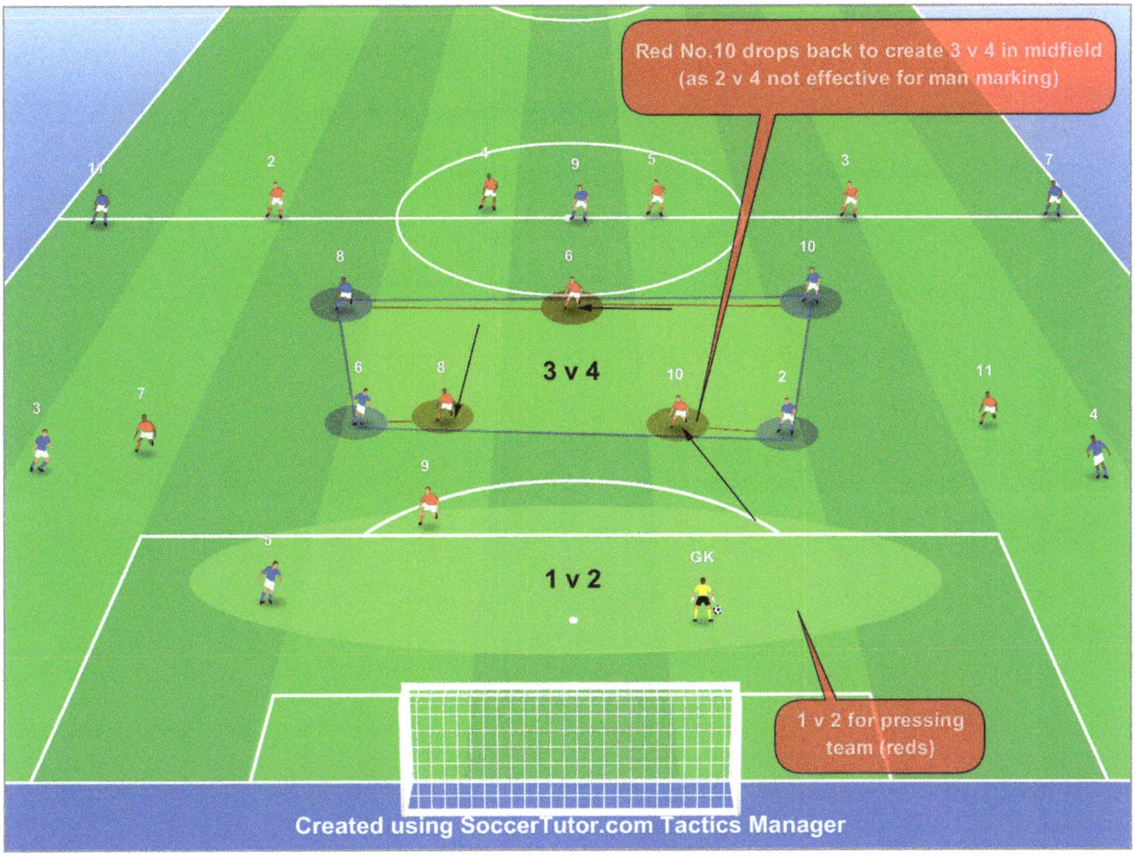

Against a 2-at-the-back box midfield (goalkeeper and centre back), the red defending team must adjust to apply man marking in midfield. A 2v4 disadvantage makes standard man marking ineffective, requiring an additional player to drop back. The **best solution is for the red N°10 to drop into midfield, while N°9 stays forward to mark the blue centre back (N°5)**. This reinforces defensive coverage while maintaining a 1v2 press in the first line.

Red N°10 marking blue N°2 triggers position shifts in midfield. Red N°6 moves centrally to cover both blue N°8 and N°10, while red N°8 pushes forward to mark blue N°6, ensuring defensive compactness and control in key areas.

Note: There is a **2v1 advantage in the centre of defence for the red team**, allowing them to press effectively while maintaining their defensive stability.

Box Midfield Build Up: Against High Press with Zonal Defending and Man Marking

1b. Reactions and Movements of Midfielders for Effective Build Up Play Against Man Marking Tactics

![Tactical diagram showing attacking midfielders (No.8 and No.10) increase the distance between each other; the red No.6 is forced to cover 2 players; defensive midfielders (No.6 and No.2) move to create space for No.8 and No.10. Passing lanes shown from GK.]

As shown on the previous page, both of the **defensive midfielders** (**N°6 and N°2**) are marked by red N°8 and N°10 but **red N°6 is left to cover both of the blue attacking midfielders** (**N°8 and N°10**).

N°8 and **N°10** apply the first principle action to **increase the distance between each other and make it difficult for red N°6 to control both of them**.

N°8 moves into a wider position while maintaining a distance away from nearby opponents (red N°2 and N°7).

N°10 also shifts wider at an equal distance from red N°3 and N°11.

N°10 can be available for a direct pass from the **goalkeeper** (**GK**) but this is not possible for **N°8** positioned on the weak side, who can only receive an aerial pass.

More space can be created for the attacking midfielders if **N°6 and N°2 drop back and shift towards the centre to drag their direct opponents (red N°8 and N°10) with them**. This action can also keep the passing lane to **N°10** open.

Note: The goalkeeper increases the chances of playing an accurate pass if the ball is carried forward first.

©SOCCERTUTOR.COM

BEAT THE PRESS WITH A BOX MIDFIELD

Box Midfield Build Up: Against High Press with Zonal Defending and Man Marking

2a. Opposition Positioning Adjustments (4-4-2 to 4-2-3-1) to Apply Marking Against a Box Midfield

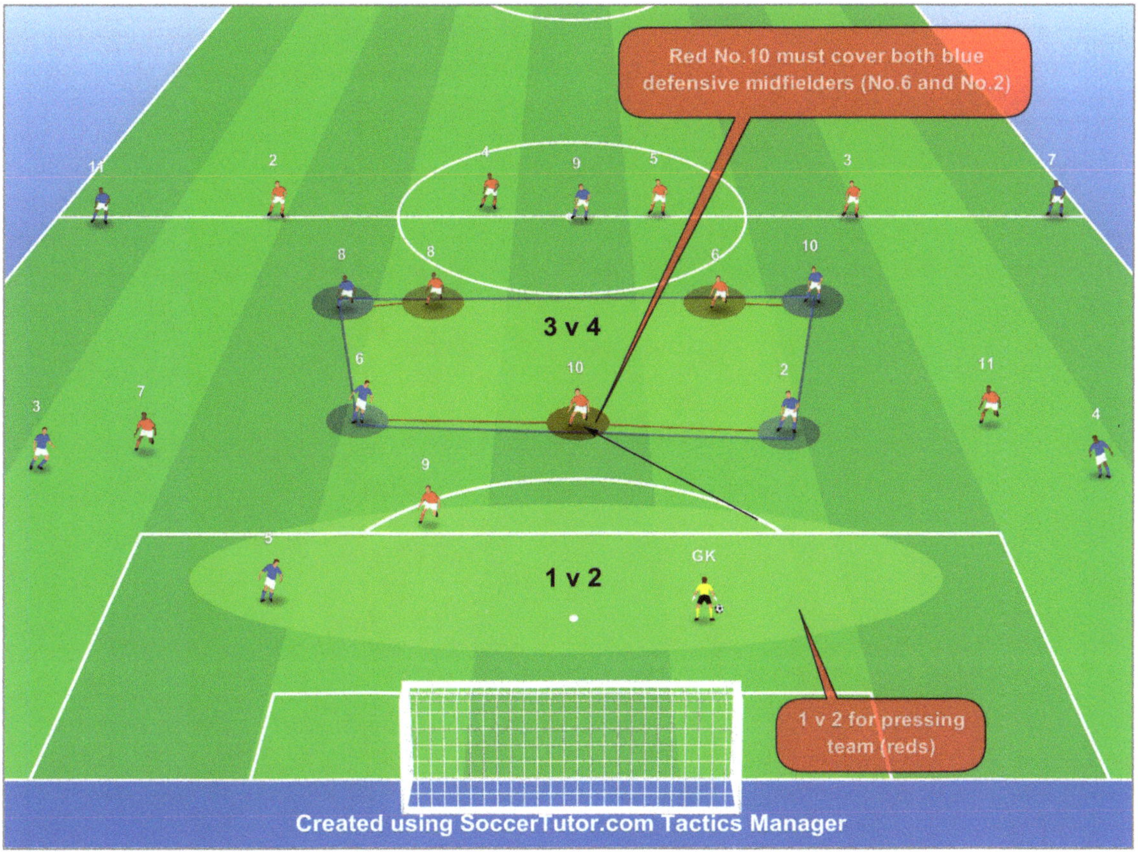

Here we show another way the opposition can apply **man marking in midfield while maintaining a 1v2 press in the forward line**.

The **2 red central midfielders (N°8 and N°6) stay back to mark the 2 blue attacking midfielders (N°8 and N°10)**. This ensures that both of them are under control and the blue team's potential to progress the play centrally is restricted.

The **red N°10 again drops into midfield, while N°9 stays forward to mark the centre back (blue N°5)**.

However, now **red N°10 must cover both blue defensive midfielders (N°6 and N°2)**.

Note: By maintaining defensive stability and compactness in midfield, this setup makes it more difficult to play through the press effectively.

Box Midfield Build Up: Against High Press with Zonal Defending and Man Marking

2b. Reactions and Movements of Midfielders for Effective Build Up Play Against Man Marking Tactics

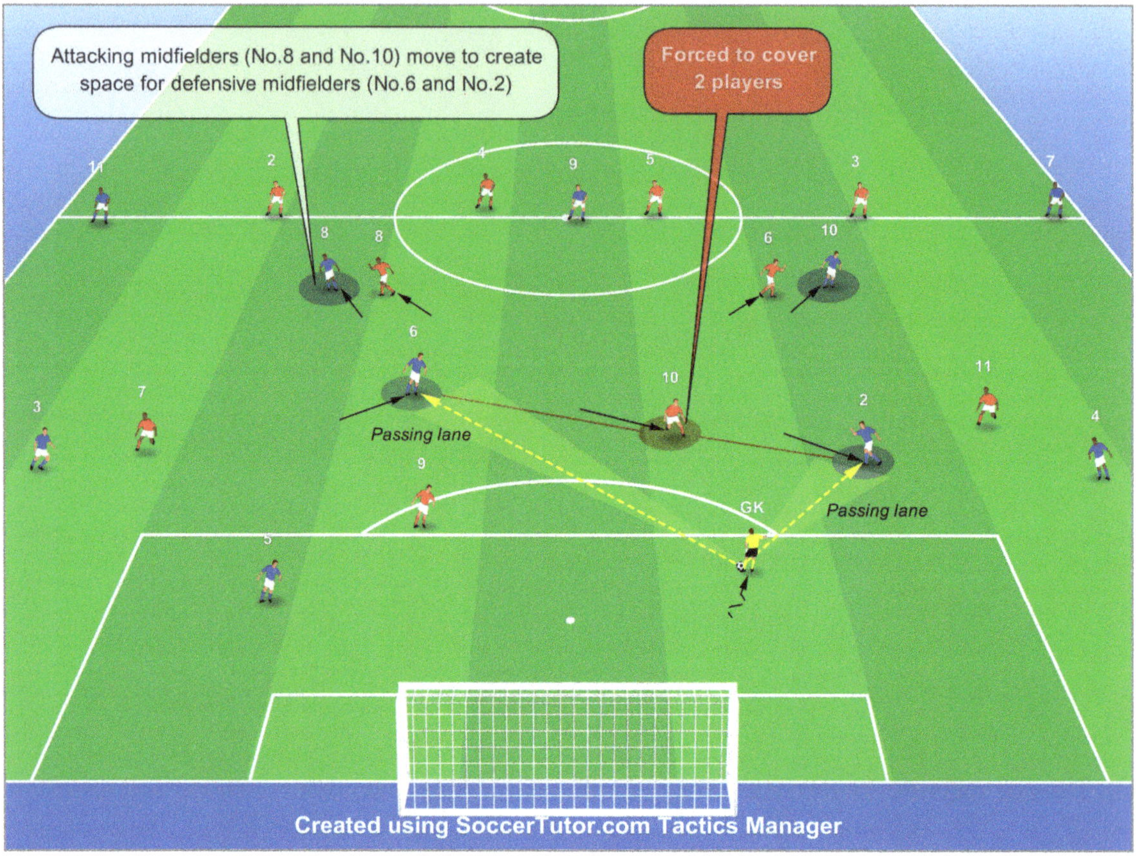

As the **blue defensive midfielders (N°6 and N°2) are not being marked tightly, they are able to receive directly from the goalkeeper (GK)**, as shown.

They look to retain a large distance between each other, stay an equal distance away from nearby opponents, and move towards available passing lanes.

Additionally, the **blue attacking midfielders (N°8 and N°10) create more space for N°6 and N°2 by moving a few metres wider and forward**, which forces their direct opponents (red N°8 and N°6) to shift close to them. This creates more space in the centre of the pitch.

Note: The goalkeeper increases the chances of playing an accurate pass if the ball is carried forward first.

BEAT THE PRESS WITH A BOX MIDFIELD

Box Midfield Build Up: Against High Press with Zonal Defending and Man Marking

2c. Options to Exploit the Numerical Superiority in Midfield if a Defensive Midfielder Receives

Blue No.2 draws press of red No.10, which leaves No.6 as the free player

Moving the ball to one of the 2 defensive midfielders (**inverted right back N°2 in diagram example**) enables the team to exploit the numerical superiority in midfield further. As **N°2 moves forward with the ball, the pressure of red N°10 is drawn, which leaves N°6 completely free of marking** in the centre of the pitch.

The **ball can be directed to the free player (N°6) via the attacking midfielder (N°10** - blue arrows) or the **forward (N°9** - yellow arrows), who act as link players.

The next step is to move the ball further forward depending on the reaction of the red N°8.

In the diagram example following the yellow arrows, the red N°8 is drawn to help close down **blue N°9**, which creates space for the **attacking midfielder (blue N°8)** to receive and carry the ball forward into the attacking half of the pitch.

BEAT THE PRESS WITH A BOX MIDFIELD

Build Up Against High Press with Zonal Defending and Man Marking (3 at Back)

1a. Opposition Positioning Adjustments (4-2-3-1 to 3-2-3-2) to Apply Marking Against a Box Midfield

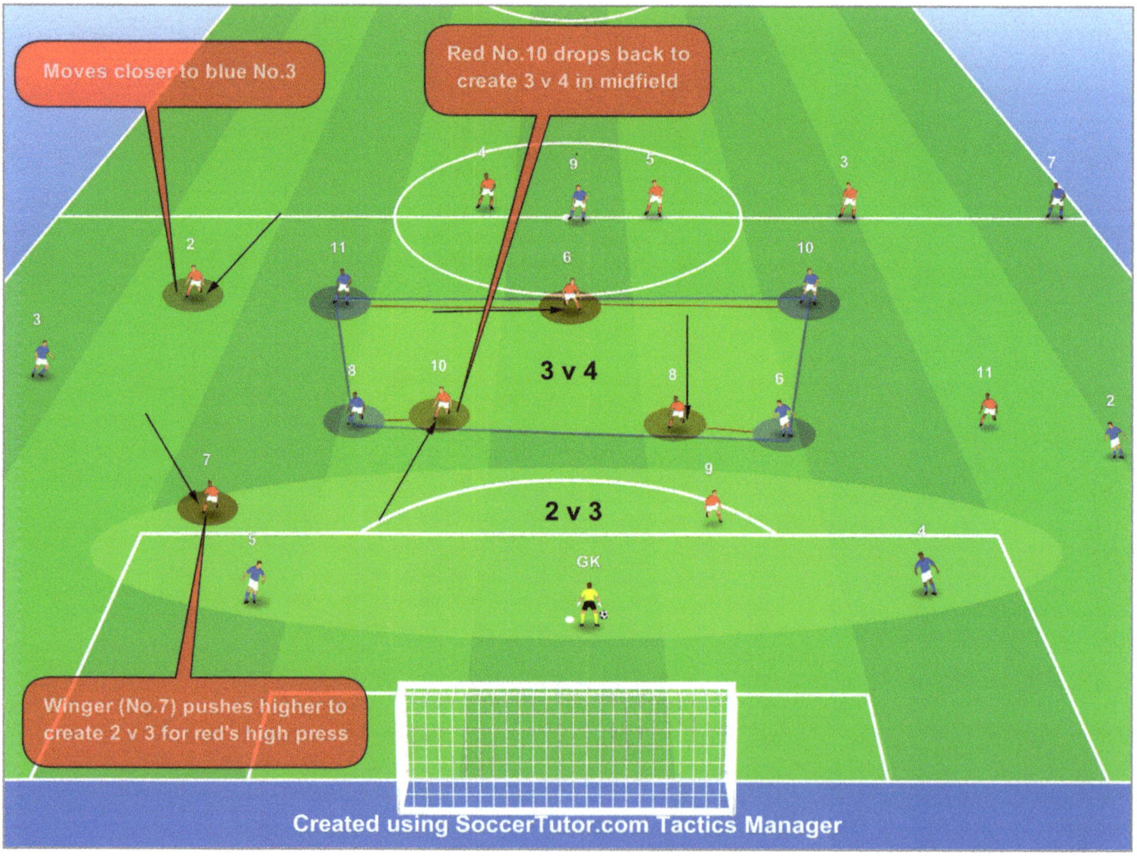

When using a 3-at-the-back box midfield (goalkeeper and 2 centre backs), the defending team must adjust accordingly.

A **red forward (N°10) drops back into midfield**, creating a 3v4 situation in the centre, which is easier to manage than a 2v4 disadvantage. This movement triggers the **winger on that side (N°7) to push higher**, to restore the 2v3 press in the forward line.

The **red full back on that side (N°2) steps forward** closer to the blue left back (N°3), **preventing an easy outlet pass**.

The midfielders adjust their positioning. **Red N°6** moves between blue N°11 and N°10, and **N°8** advances to mark blue N°6.

Note: All potential short passing options are marked, limiting the blue team's ability to play through the press.

Box Midfield Build Up: Against High Press with Zonal Defending and Man Marking

1b. Reactions and Movements of Midfielders to Create Space for Attacking Midfielders to Receive from Goalkeeper

As shown on the previous page, both of the **blue defensive midfielders (Nº8 and Nº6)** are marked by red Nº10 and Nº8 but red Nº6 is left to cover both blue attacking midfielders (Nº11 and Nº10). Their coordinated movements combined with off-the-ball adjustments, help create and exploit space effectively.

By moving away from each other and maintaining equal distances from nearby opponents, **Nº11 and Nº10 stretch the defensive shape**. At the same time, the **left back (Nº3)** moves forward and **Nº8** drops deeper, opening up more space for **Nº11** on the left side.

On the right, **Nº6** drops back and creates additional space for **Nº10**.

The **best solution for the goalkeeper (GK) is a direct aerial pass to Nº11 or Nº10**, as shown.

Note 1: After a successful pass, the blue team bypass the first pressing line and neutralise 5 red players to open up further attacking possibilities.

Note 2: If the goalkeeper steps forward a few metres, the angle to deliver an accurate medium-range pass to **Nº11** or **Nº10** improves.

Box Midfield Build Up: Against High Press with Zonal Defending and Man Marking

2a. Opposition Positioning Adjustments (4-4-2 to 3-3-2-2) to Prevent Ball Progression Through the Centre Against a Box Midfield

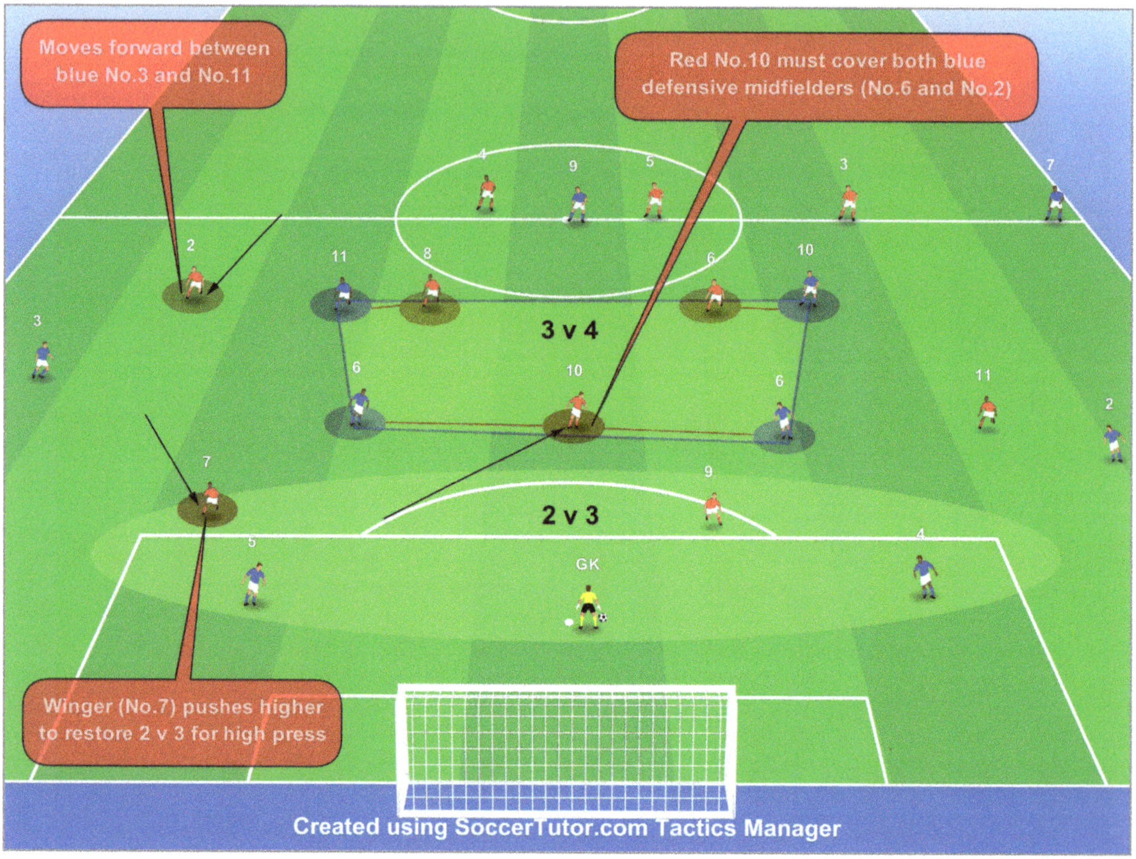

Moves forward between blue No.3 and No.11

Red No.10 must cover both blue defensive midfielders (No.6 and No.2)

3 v 4

2 v 3

Winger (No.7) pushes higher to restore 2 v 3 for high press

Created using SoccerTutor.com Tactics Manager

Another defensive approach against the 3-at-the-back box midfield shape is to **reposition a forward (N°10 drops back) between the 2 blue defensive midfielders (N°6 and N°8)**.

This adjustment, as shown in the diagram, helps **limit the blue team's central progression by adding an extra layer of defensive coverage**.

With **red N°8 marking blue N°11, the red right back (N°2) is free to push higher** up the pitch and engage the blue left back (N°3), reducing the ability to play through wide areas.

Note: These movements ensure that the red defending team remain compact while preventing easy build up through the midfield.

BEAT THE PRESS WITH A BOX MIDFIELD

Box Midfield Build Up: Against High Press with Zonal Defending and Man Marking

2b. Reactions and Movements of the Midfielders for Effective Build Up Play Against Man Marking Tactics

[Diagram: Attacking midfielders (No.11 and No.10) move to create space for defensive midfielders (No.8 and No.6). Forced to cover 2 players. Passing lane. Blocked! Link Player.]

To be effective in this situation, the 2 blue players at the base of the box midfield (**N°8 and N°6**) **increase their distance from red N°10** while keeping equal distances away from their nearby opponents.

To create more space for **N°8** and **N°6**, the 2 players a the top of the box midfield (**N°11** and **N°10**) move forward to force their direct opponents (red N°6 and N°8) to follow them.

N°8 and **N°6** want to be in available passing lanes to receive from the **goalkeeper** (**GK**). This can be achieved by **N°8** on the left but is not possible for **N°6** on the right.

As **GK** moves forward with the ball, he can pass directly to **N°8** (yellow arrow) or use the **centre back** (**N°4**) as a link player to move the ball to **N°6** (blue arrows).

Note 1: If the ball is successfully moved to either N°8 or N°6, 2 or 3 red players will be neutralised.

Note 2: If in any of these situations presented in this section, an opponent who is covering 2 players moves closer to one of them, the other one will be free of marking and become the target player.

BOX MIDFIELD SESSION

Training Session 5 (5 Practices)

Against High Press with Zonal Defending and Man Marking

Based on Guardiola, Alonso, and Arteta build up patterns

Box Midfield Session 5: Against High Press with Zonal Defending and Man Marking

TRAINING SESSION (5 PRACTICES)
1. Box Midfield Passing Combinations and Movements Against a Double Pivot

Practice Description

- The **3 red mannequins** represent an **opposing midfield** with a double pivot (e.g. 4-2-3-1). The **opposing Nº10 must cover both defensive midfielders** (**LDM** and **RDM**), so the aim is to build up play through one of them.

- *Yellow Arrows:* **A1** passes to **B1**, who plays to the goalkeeper (**GK**). **LDM** and **RDM** drop deeper and wider away from the mannequin. **LAM** and **RAM** push higher and wider. **GK** passes diagonally to **RDM**, who turns and finds **RAM**.

- **RAM** drops to receive, then plays back and across to **LDM**, who passes to **LAM**.

- **LAM** passes into the small goal.

- *The blue arrows show an alternative option.*

- **Player Rotations:** A1 → B1 → LDM → RDM → RAM → LAM → A2.

- The next sequence starts with **A2's** pass to **B2** on the opposite side, following the same pattern.

BEAT THE PRESS WITH A BOX MIDFIELD

©SOCCERTUTOR.COM

Box Midfield Session 5: Against High Press with Zonal Defending and Man Marking

VARIATION

2. Goalkeeper's Long Pass and Box Midfield Support Play Combinations Against a Single Pivot

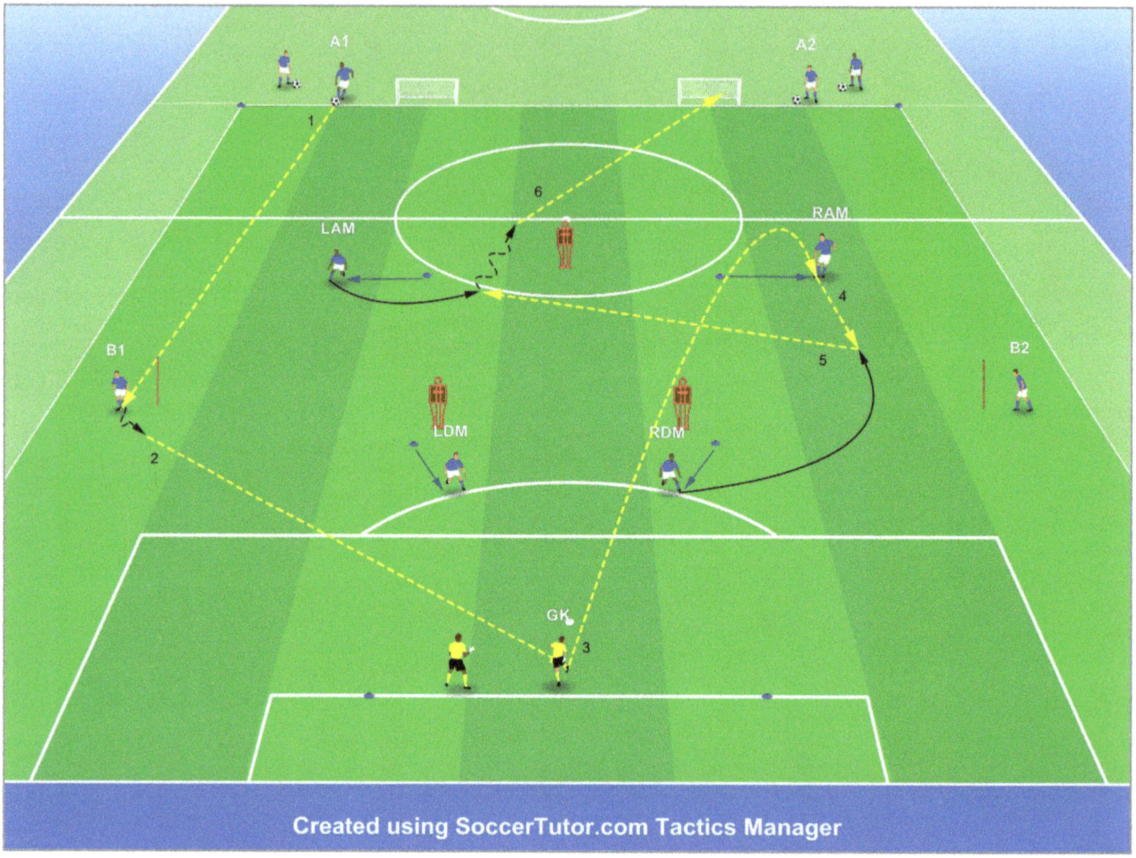

Practice Description

- In this variation, the mannequins represent a midfield with a single pivot (e.g. 4-3-3). The **opposing defensive midfielder must cover both attacking midfielders (LAM and RAM)**, so the aim is to build up play through one of them.

- **A1** passes to **B1**, who plays to **GK**. The **defensive midfielders** (**LDM** and **RDM**) drop back and the **attacking midfielders** (**LAM** and **RAM**) move wider.

- **GK** plays an aerial pass to **RAM**, who sets the ball back for the oncoming **RDM**.

- **RDM** passes diagonally forward to **LAM**, who receives, dribbles forward, and passes into the small goal.

- Player Rotations: **A1** → **B1** → **LDM** → **RDM** → **RAM** → **LAM** → **A2**.

- The next sequence starts with **A2**'s pass to **B2** on the opposite side.

Coaching Points

1. **Increase distance from the opponent (mannequin) covering 2 players.**

2. **Use synchronised off-the-ball movement** to create passing lanes in midfield.

Box Midfield Session 5: Against High Press with Zonal Defending and Man Marking

PROGRESSION

3. Find the Free Midfielder with 3-at-the-Back Box Midfield 6 (+GK) v 4 (+1) Positional Game

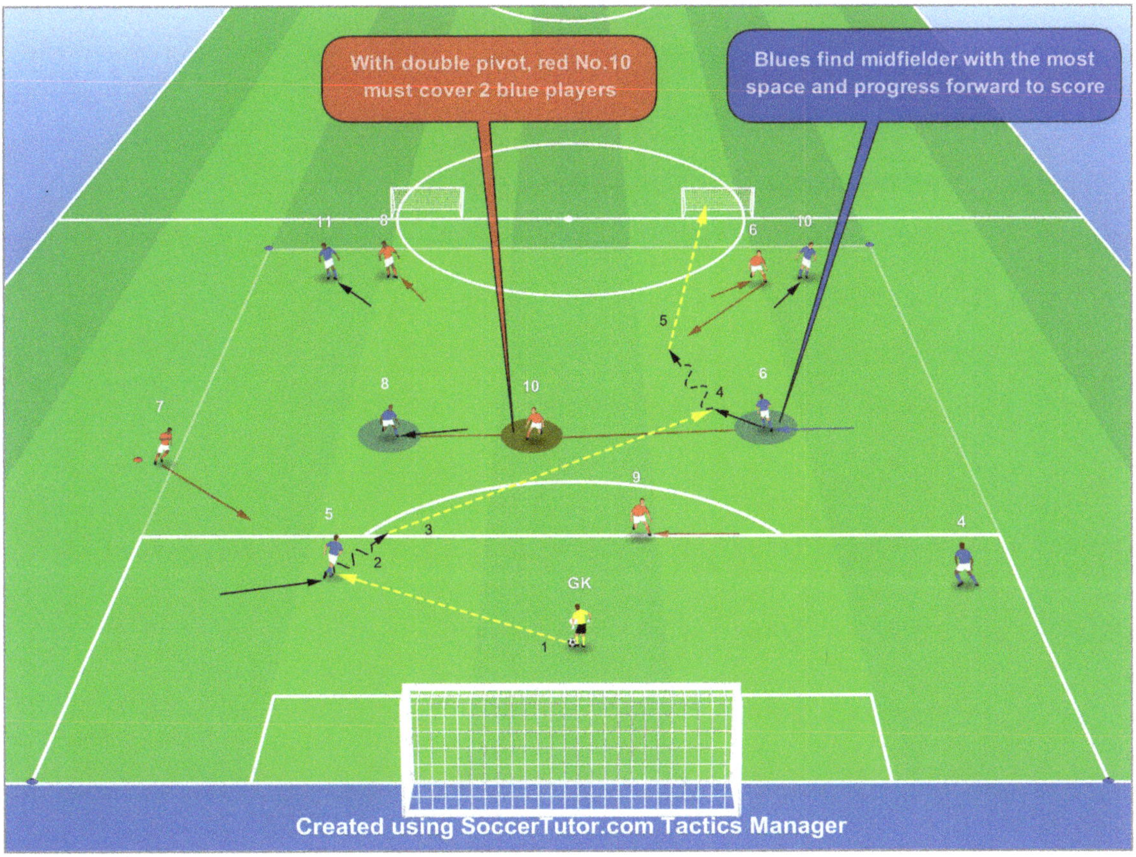

With double pivot, red No.10 must cover 2 blue players

Blues find midfielder with the most space and progress forward to score

Practice Description

- All players start inside the area except the red winger (N°7), who enters after the goalkeeper's (**GK**) first pass.
- The blues build up play in a 3-at-the-back box midfield shape, while the reds press high with man marking.
- **The reds use a double pivot**, so **N°10 must cover both defensive midfielders**. (**N°8 and N°6**) To exploit this, they take up wider positions, while the **attacking midfielders (N°10 and N°11)** push higher to stretch the play and create space.

- **Blue Objective:** Find the **free defensive midfielder (N°6 in diagram example)** and progress to score.
- **Red Objective:** Press to win the ball and counter to score within 8–12 seconds.
- **Coaching Points:** Movement and timing create passing lanes. Success depends on reading the press, the quickness of decision making, and the accuracy of line breaking passes.
- **Variation:** Adapt by alternating between a single or double pivot red midfield.

Box Midfield Session 5: Against High Press with Zonal Defending and Man Marking

VARIATION

4. Find the Free Midfielder with 2-at-the-Back Box Midfield 5 (+GK) v 4 Positional Game

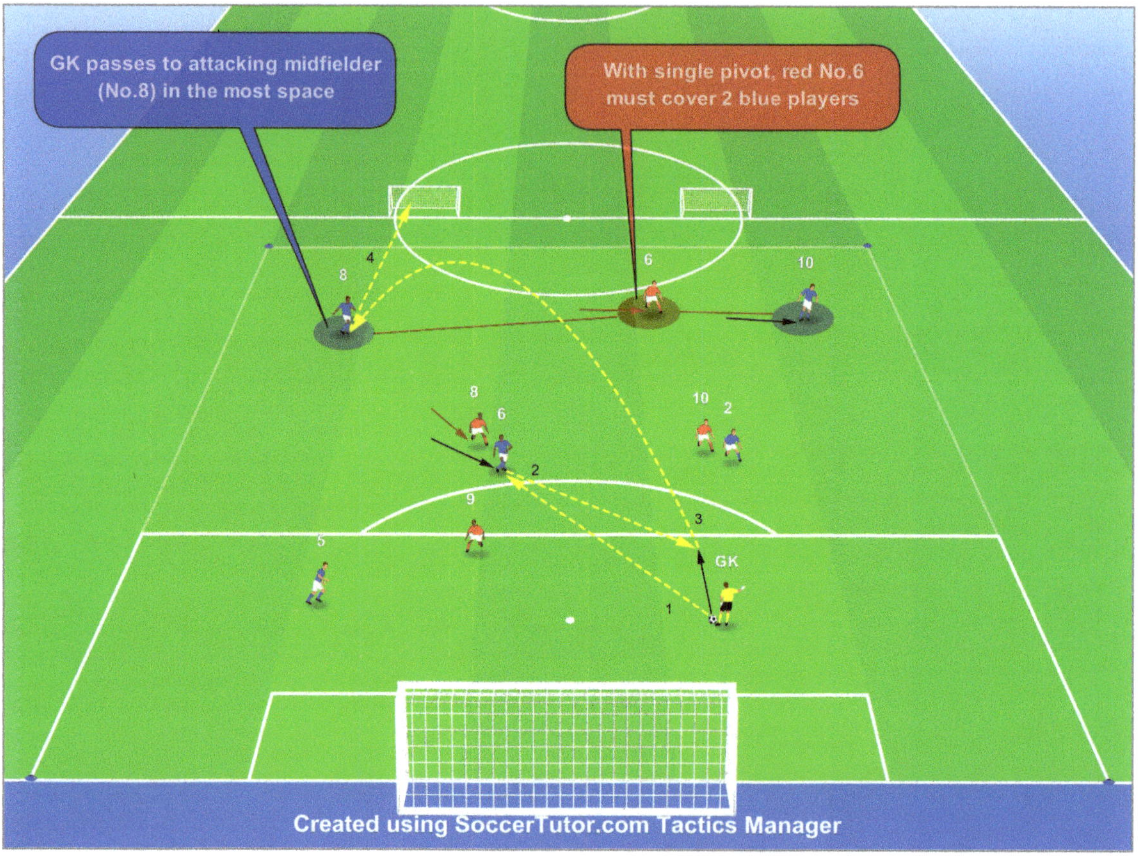

GK passes to attacking midfielder (No.8) in the most space

With single pivot, red No.6 must cover 2 blue players

Practice Description

- This is a variation of the previous practice. Now the blues build up in a 2-at-the-back box midfield shape, while the reds press high with man marking.
- The **single red pivot** (**N°6**) **must cover both blue attacking midfielders** (**N°8 and N°10**), so they shift wider to increase their distance and stretch the press.
- The **blue defensive midfielders** (**N°6 and N°2**) **drop back** centrally to create more space for the attacking midfielders.

- **Blue Objective:** Find the **free attacking midfielder** (**N°8**) and progress to score.
- **Red Objective:** Press to win the ball and counter to score within 8–12 seconds.
- **Coaching Points:** Movement and timing create passing lanes. Success depends on reading the press, quick decisions, and accurate line breaking passes.
- **Variation:** Adapt by alternating between a single or double pivot red midfield.

©SOCCERTUTOR.COM

BEAT THE PRESS WITH A BOX MIDFIELD

Box Midfield Session 5: Against High Press with Zonal Defending and Man Marking

PROGRESSION

5. Find the Free Midfielder Against a High Press with Zonal Defending and Man Marking Conditioned Game

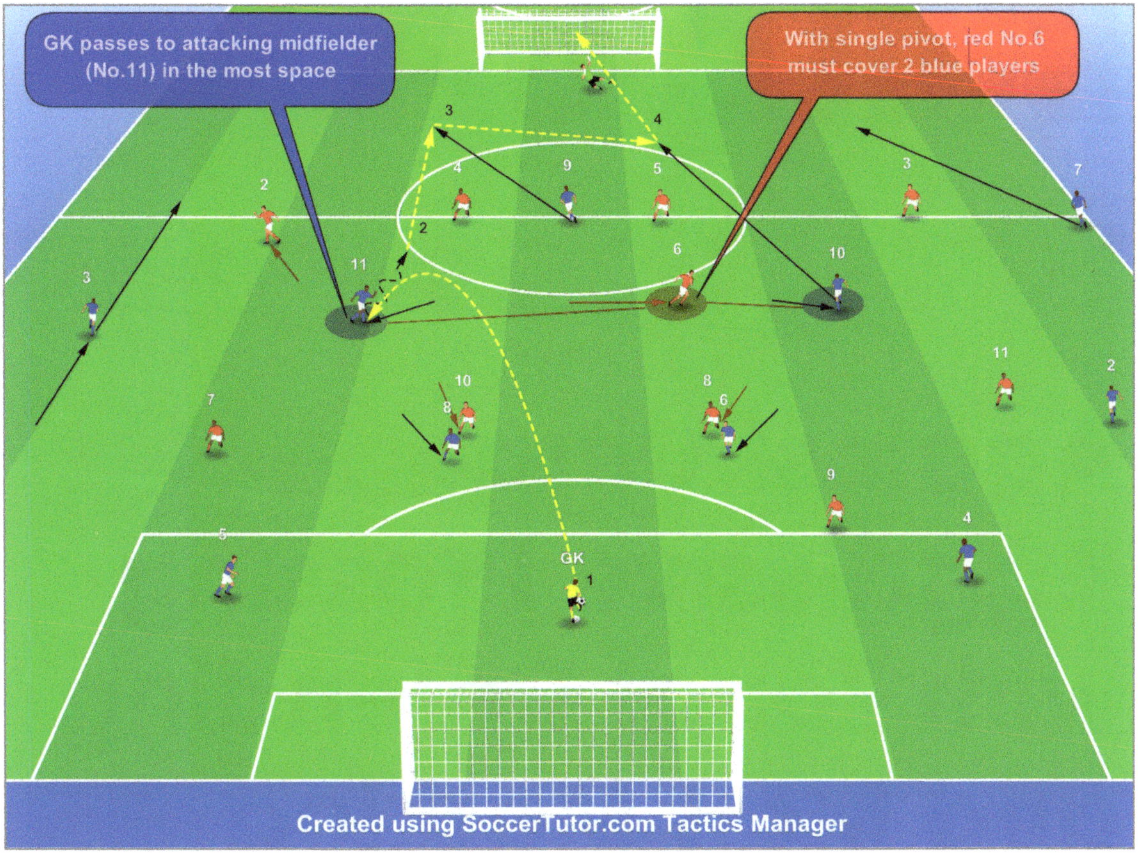

GK passes to attacking midfielder (No.11) in the most space

With single pivot, red No.6 must cover 2 blue players

Practice Description

- This final practice is an 11v11 game. The attacking team either build up play using a 2-at-the-back box midfield or 3-at-the-back (diagram example). This setup allows the players to **apply the principles outlined earlier in the session** into a realistic match-like situation.
- The red defending team press high after the first pass, using man marking in midfield.
- In this example, the **reds defend with a single pivot, leading the goalkeeper (GK)** to play aerial passes to the attacking midfielders (**Nº10 and Nº11**), who increase their distance from the red Nº6 who is trying to cover both of them.
- **Coaching Points:** Create distance from the opposing midfielder marking 2 players, using coordinated movements to open passing lanes and create space. Recognise pressing triggers early and make quick, effective decisions.
- **Variation:** Adapt by alternating between a single or double pivot red midfield.

BOX MIDFIELD BUILD UP

Tactical Analysis

Against Ultra-Aggressive Pressing with Zonal Defending and Man Marking

Build up play patterns from Guardiola, Alonso, and Arteta's teams

Build Up Against Ultra-Aggressive Pressing with Zonal Defending and Man Marking

We have already mentioned that when a high press is applied, there is a 7 (+GK) v 6 situation in favour of the possession team. When pressing is applied up to the goalkeeper (ultra-aggressive pressing), the defending team has to deal with an extra player.

The **possession team again has a +2 numerical advantage** (**8 +GK v7**) when building up play from the goalkeeper.

When the objective of the defending team is to apply ultra-aggressive pressing, some principles have to be applied.

1. **First Principle:** When pressing is applied to the goalkeeper, it is to **block the passing lane towards one of the centre backs**, who stays free. This eliminates the first numerical advantage problem.

   If the first principle is not applied properly, a pass to the centre back would at least neutralise the player who presses the goalkeeper.

2. **Second Principle:** Set up to **control all the receivers of a potential short pass** from the goalkeeper.

   If the second principle is not applied properly, an easy short pass can be played to a free player. This pass will again at least neutralise the player who presses the goalkeeper, and potentially more players.

To achieve the second principle, the defending team must apply close marking to all opponents near the ball. One way to carry this out is by using a **hybrid of zonal defending and man marking in midfield**, which we will fully analyse in this section.

This means that the **midfielders should mark the opponents within their zone of responsibility** and especially the defensive midfielders, who are potential receivers of a short first pass. If they do receive, the aim is to use close marking to prevent them from turning.

Note: Although we set out the opposition's pressing structure and aims, the **focus of this section is on how to build up play with a box midfield against this type of defending/pressing**, with tactical solutions provided.

Build Up Against Ultra-Aggressive Pressing with Zonal Defending and Man Marking (3 at Back)

1. Opposition Positioning Adjustments (4-2-3-1 to 3-2-3-2) to Apply Marking Against a Box Midfield

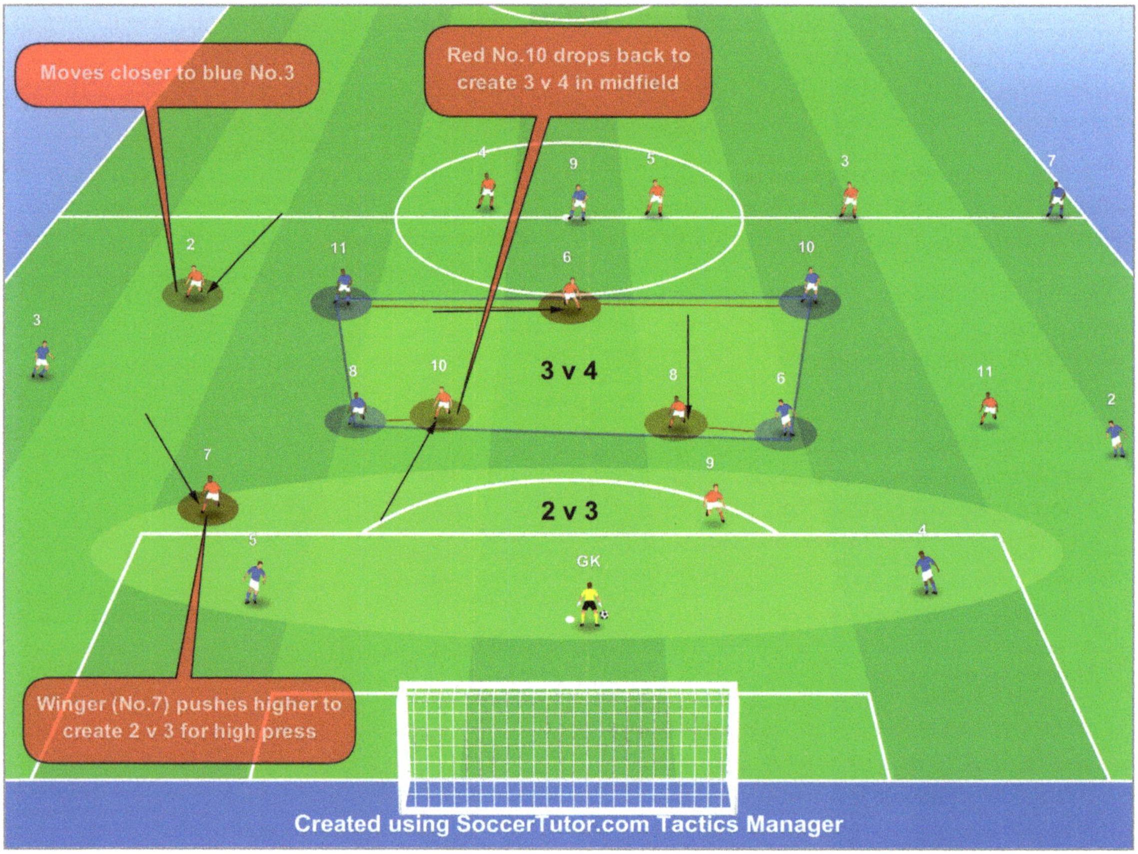

When using a 3-at-the-back box midfield (goalkeeper and 2 centre backs), the defending team must adjust accordingly.

A **red forward (N°10) drops back into midfield**, creating a 3v4 situation in the centre, which is easier to manage than a 2v4 disadvantage. This movement triggers the **winger on that side (N°7) to push higher and create a 2v3 press in the forward line**.

The **red full back on that side (N°2) steps forward** closer to the blue left back (N°3), **preventing an easy outlet pass**.

The midfielders adjust their positioning with **N°6** moving between blue N°11 and N°10, and **N°8** advancing to mark blue N°6.

Note: All potential short passing options are marked, limiting the blue team's ability to play through the press.

Box Midfield: Against Ultra-Aggressive Pressing with Zonal Defending and Man Marking

2. Opposition Press the Goalkeeper and Ensure All Nearby Passing Options are Marked

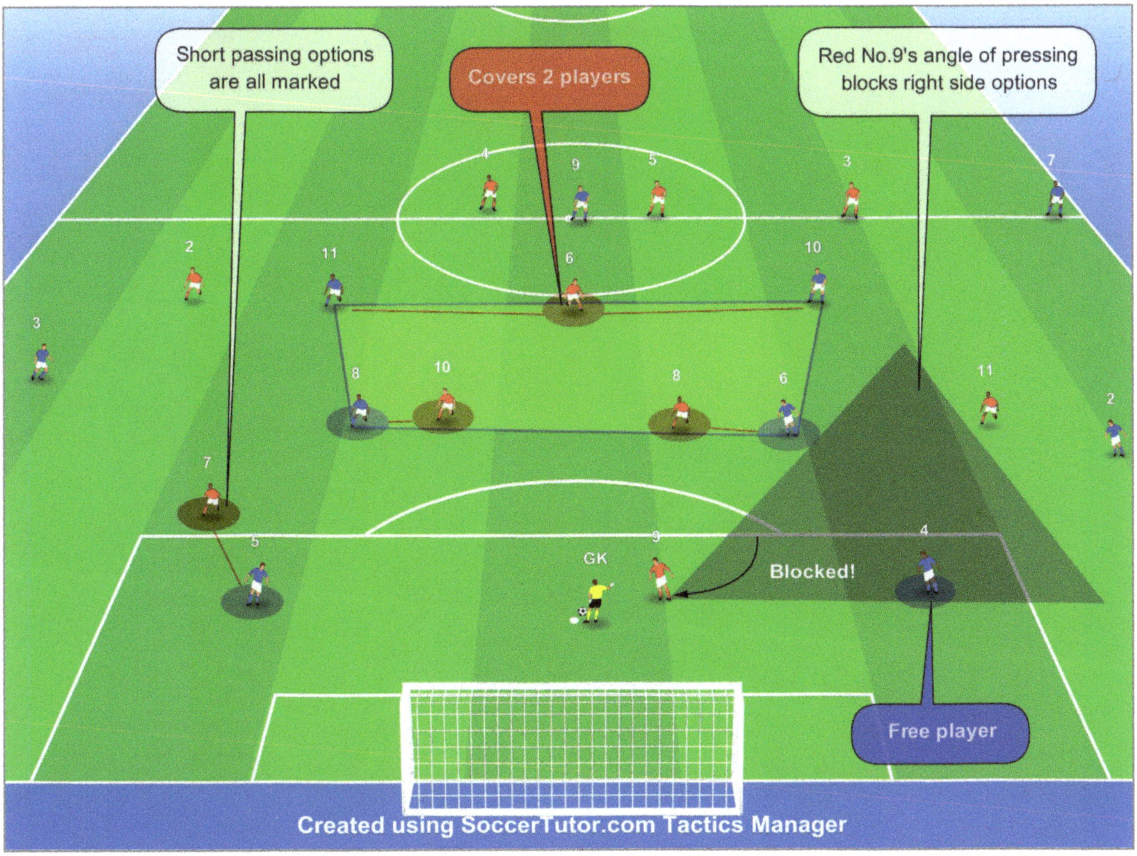

When the red forward (N°9) presses the **goalkeeper (GK)**, the passing lane towards the **right centre back (N°4)** is blocked, although he remains unmarked.

Meanwhile, all the **other nearby players are tightly marked to limit the GK's short passing options** and restrict safe outlets under pressure.

However, the **red defensive midfielder (N°6) positions himself between the 2 blue attacking midfielders (N°11 and N°10)**, rather than committing to one, which **allows both blue players to find space**. This makes it easier for the blues to bypass the press and progress the ball forward.

Note: If red N°6 decides to close down blue **N°11**, who is more likely to receive based on the angle of the press, then **N°10** becomes free.

BEAT THE PRESS WITH A BOX MIDFIELD

Box Midfield: Against Ultra-Aggressive Pressing with Zonal Defending and Man Marking

3. Potential Link Player Positioning and Scanning to Support the Free Defender Before Pressure is Applied

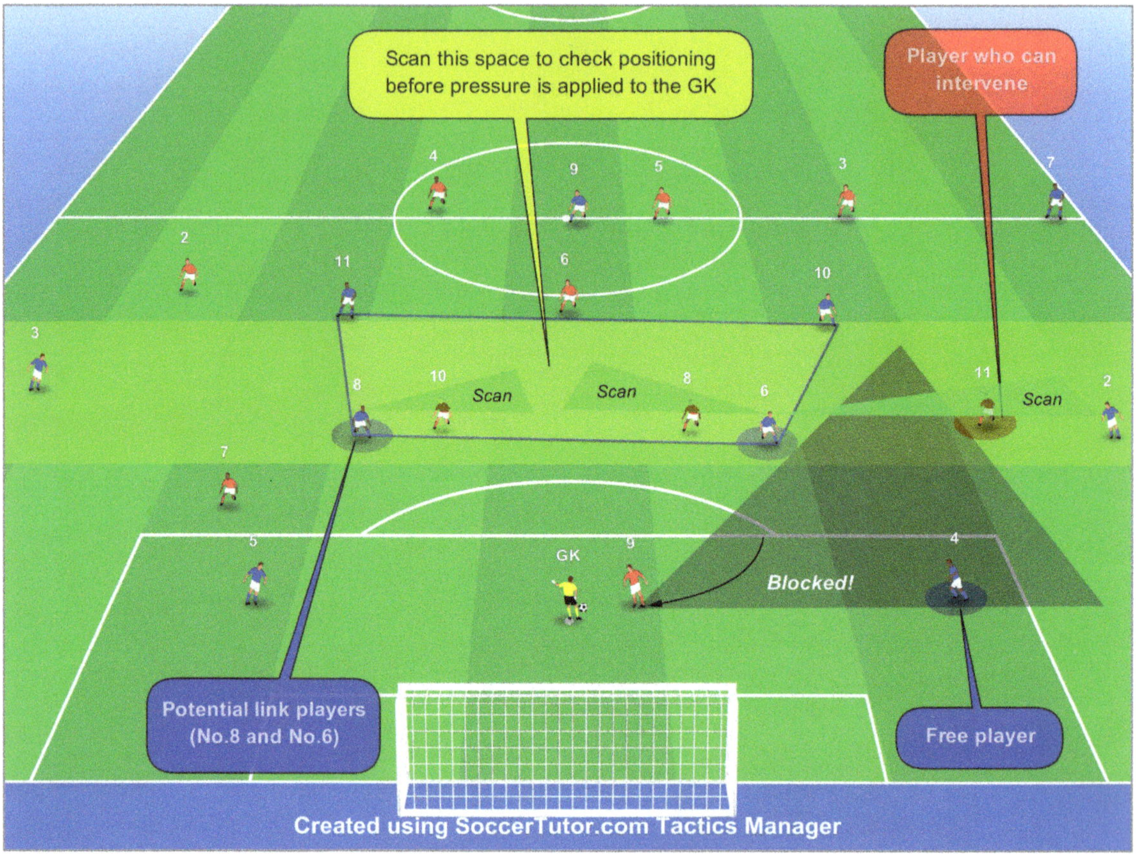

Principles to Attack Effectively Against this Type of Defending:

1. Use the link players near the ball carrier to move the ball to the free defender.
2. Move the ball to the free midfielder (directly or indirectly via a link player).

The blues should either use a nearby link player to move the ball to the free defender or play directly to an unmarked midfielder. **With a box midfield, 2 link players (Nº8 and Nº6 in diagram) are often available to support** and break the press effectively.

Key Principles Link Players Follow to be Effective:

1. Stay high enough to form an effective passing angle.
2. Constantly scan for teammates and opposing players' positions, especially in the area likely to be used after the goalkeeper (GK) is pressed.

The highlighted yellow zone is where the potential blue link players must focus before pressing is applied.

Once the red forward (Nº9) presses GK, the right centre back (Nº4) becomes the free defender. At that point, the **blue defensive midfielder (Nº6) should scan again to track the red winger (Nº11)**, who poses the greatest interception risk.

Box Midfield: Against Ultra-Aggressive Pressing with Zonal Defending and Man Marking

4a. Timing of Link Player's Movement Creates a Narrow Passing Angle to Prevent Interceptions

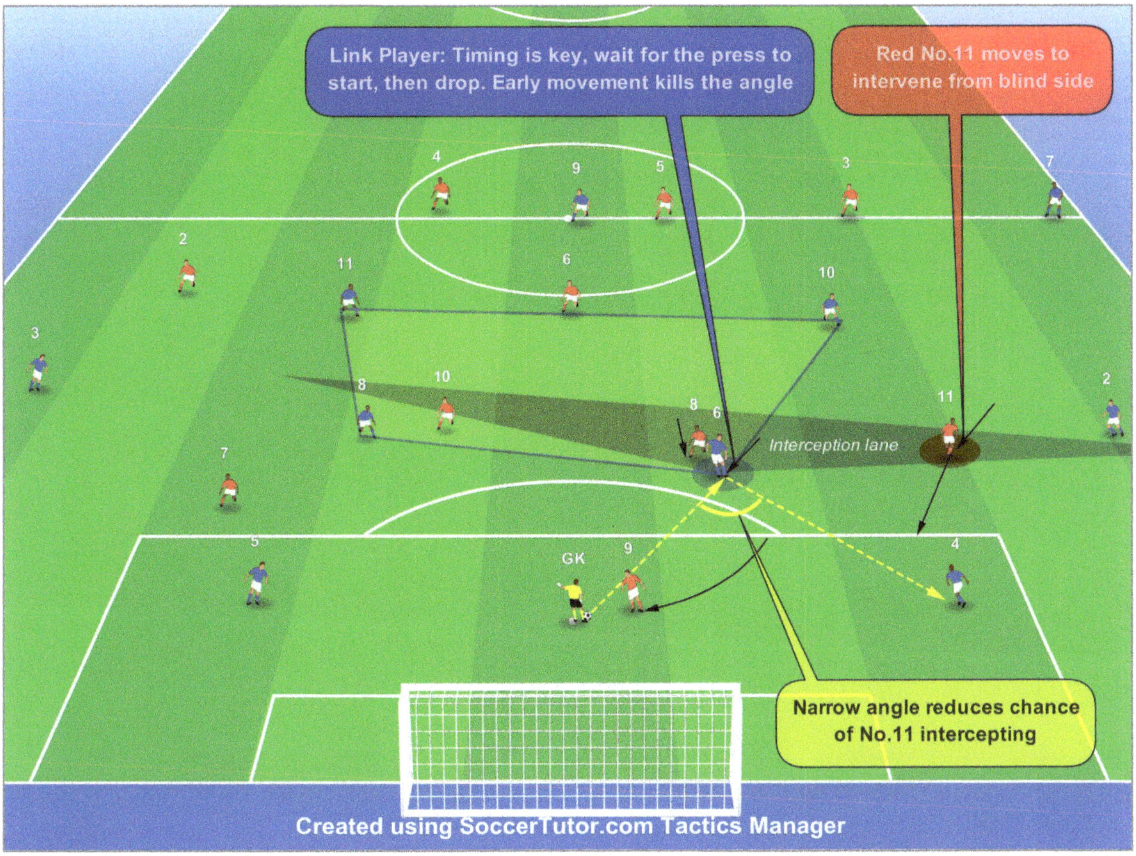

Another key principle for the link player is timing. **Support must be offered only after the press starts (not before).** Otherwise, the passing angle becomes ineffective and easily predictable. Movement must be carefully synchronised with the press.

Starting high, the **link player drops only when the opponent commits to press the goalkeeper (GK).** This timed movement allows them to stay high but still receive freely.

As shown in the diagram example with the **defensive midfielder (N°6)**, this creates a narrow passing angle to the free **right centre back (N°4)**.

The **narrow passing angle helps limit the influence of the red winger (N°11)**, who approaches from the blind side.

Note: Although the link player may have seen him earlier during scanning, red N°11 may be outside his field of view during the pass. Proper timing keeps him far enough away from the line of the pass to successfully intercept.

BEAT THE PRESS WITH A BOX MIDFIELD

Box Midfield: Against Ultra-Aggressive Pressing with Zonal Defending and Man Marking

4b. Variation: Early or Deep Movement by the Link Player Creates a Wide Passing Angle that Increases Risk

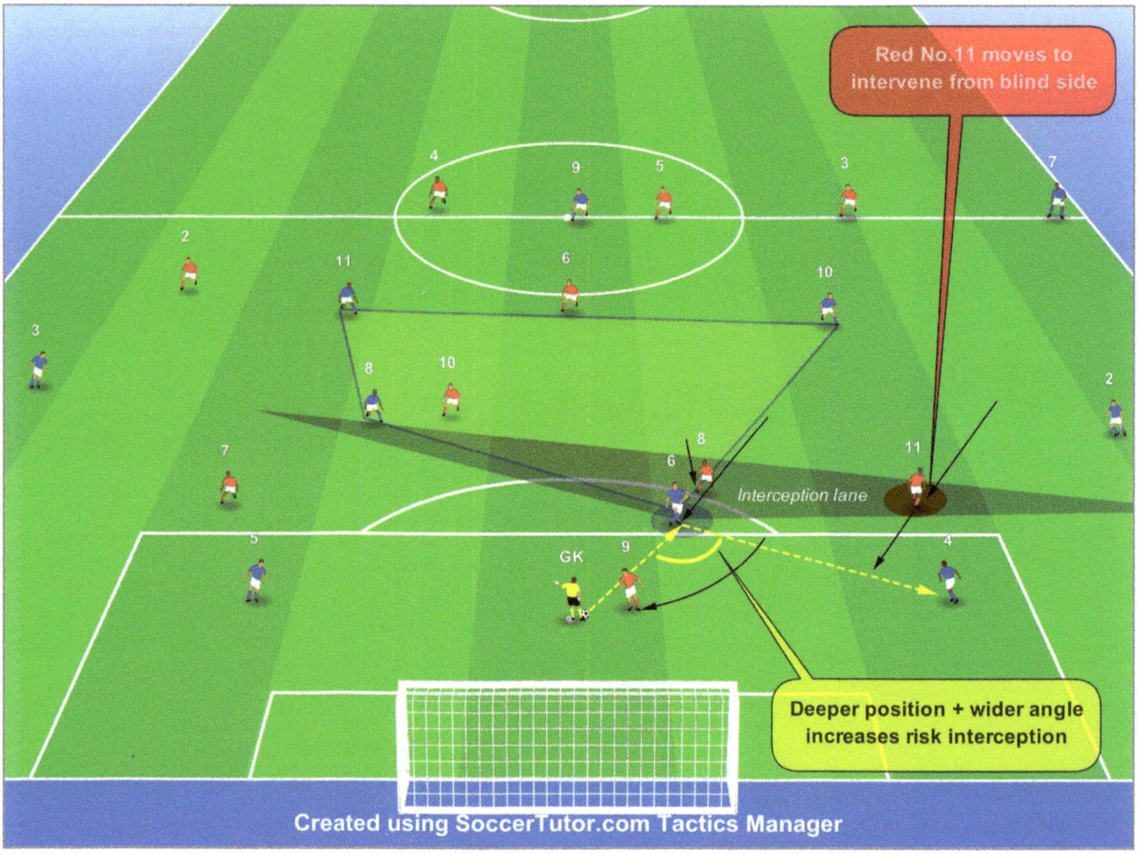

If the link player starts too deep or drops too early, he receives the pass from the goalkeeper (GK) in a deep position, which flattens the angle of the pass and makes it easier to predict and intercept. A deep starting position leads to a more horizontal or wide passing line.

In this situation, the **blue centre back (N°4)** is still the target player, but the red winger (N°11), coming from the blind side, is much closer to the path of the ball and more likely to intercept. **Early or deep movement disrupts the purpose of link players, allowing opponents to recover and block forward ball progression**.

Note: To create a sharper, more effective passing angle, the **link player must start higher and move at the correct time**.

BEAT THE PRESS WITH A BOX MIDFIELD

Box Midfield: Against Ultra-Aggressive Pressing with Zonal Defending and Man Marking

5. Free Defender Must Act Quickly to Exploit Available Space or 2v1 Situation Near the Ball

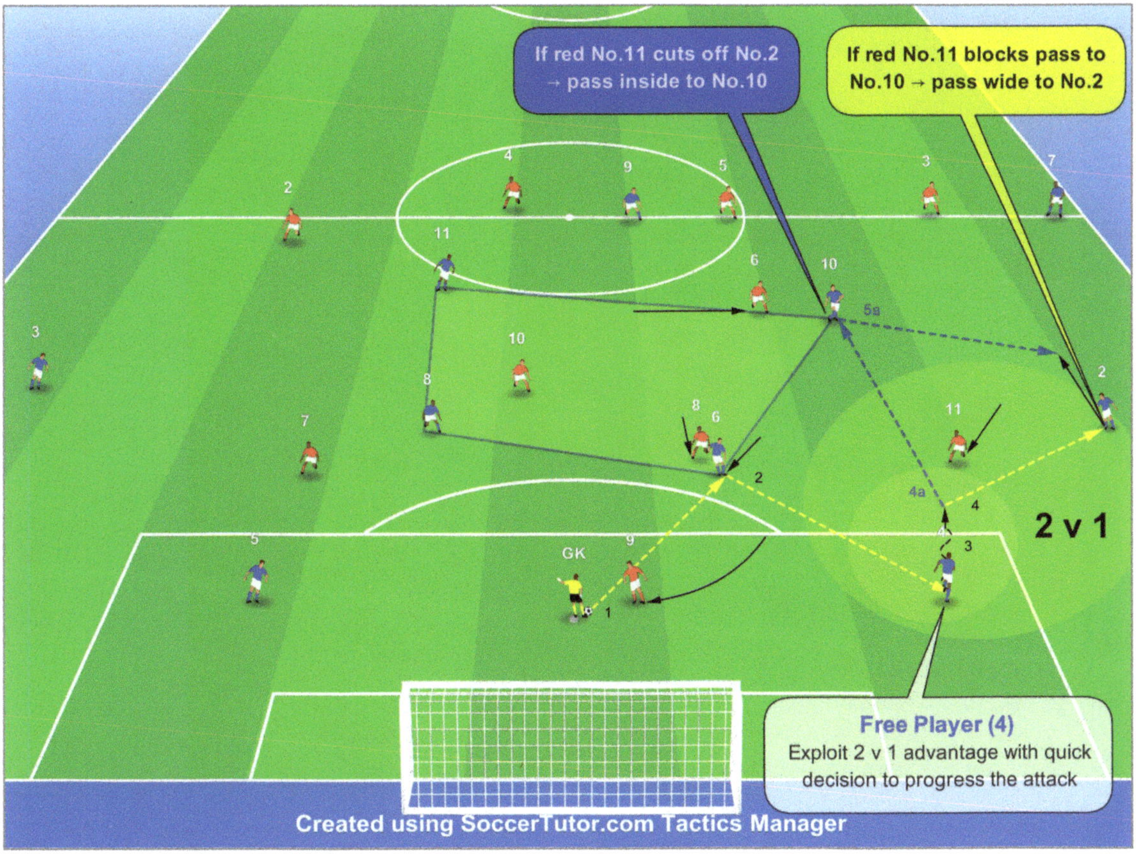

Once the ball is moved to the free defender (**N°4**) through the link player (**N°6**), the receiver must react quickly.

N°4 can either drive forward with the ball into the available space or exploit the 2v1 numerical advantage (**highlighted**) to progress the attack.

If the red winger (N°11) presses **N°4** and blocks the passing lane towards the **attacking midfielder (N°10)**, **N°4** passes to the **right back** (**N°2** - yellow arrow).

If red N°11 blocks the pass to **N°2** instead, **N°10** becomes the link player to move the ball to **N°2** (blue arrows).

If red N°11 drops back (retreats), **N°4** has space to dribble the ball forward.

Note: Quick decision making is crucial. If **N°4** hesitates, the red central midfielder (**N°8**) may recover and block the passing lane towards **N°10**. If red N°11 focuses fully on tracking **N°2**, effectively exploiting the situation depends on a fast execution.

Box Midfield: Against Ultra-Aggressive Pressing with Zonal Defending and Man Marking

6. Potential Options to Move the Ball to the Free Defender or Attacking Midfielder when the Goalkeeper is Pressed

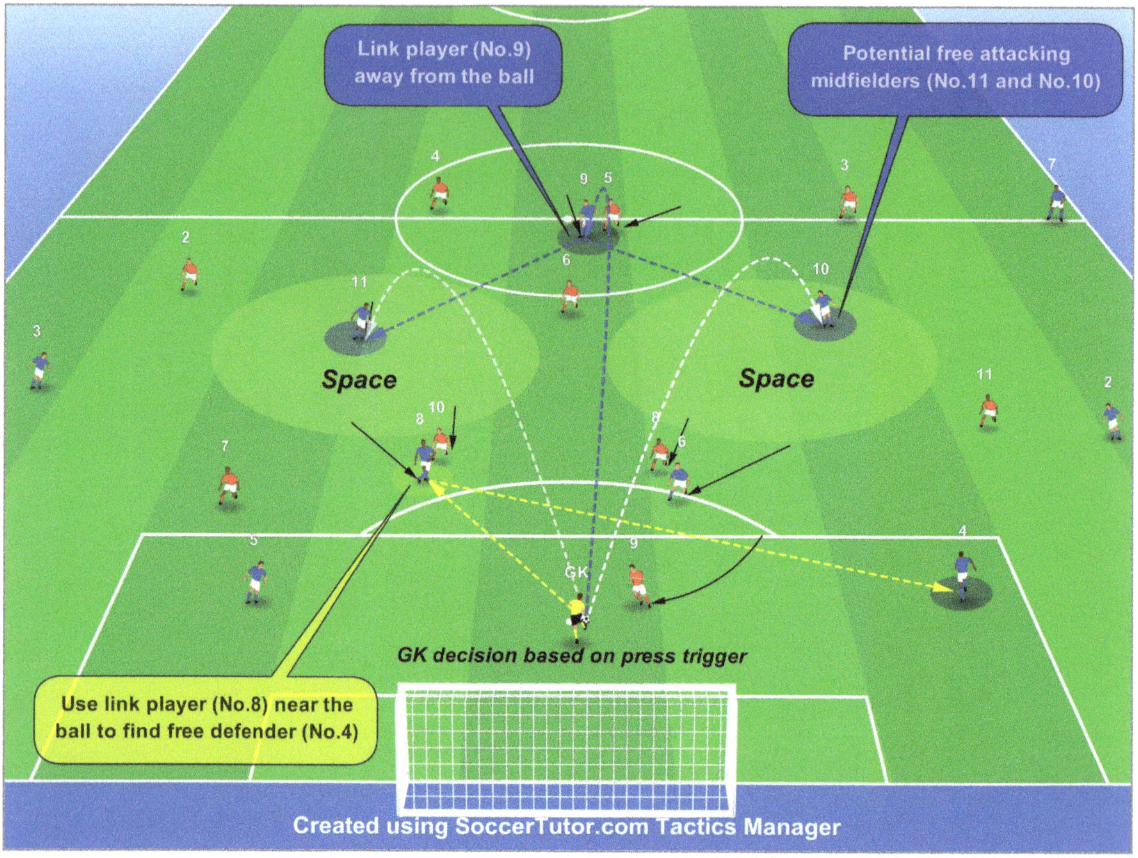

This diagram shows the goalkeeper's (**GK**) passing options against ultra-aggressive pressing with zonal defending and man marking with a 3-at-the-back box midfield.

As soon as the red Nº9 presses **GK**, Nº10 and Nº8 move to mark the **blue defensive midfielders (Nº6 and Nº8)** closely, as they can act as link players to move the ball to the **free centre back (Nº4** - yellow arrows).

Red Nº10 and Nº8's movement creates more space for the **attacking midfielders (Nº11** and **Nº10)**. If the red defensive midfielder (Nº6) stays between them, they **both have available space to receive free of marking either directly** (white arrows)

or indirectly via the **forward (Nº9** - blue arrows). **GK decides which option is best** depending on the available time to make the decision.

If red Nº6 decides to move closer to either **Nº11** or **Nº10**, then the other one will be completely free of marking and becomes the clear target player.

Note: Both link players (Nº8 and Nº6) can be effective in moving the ball to Nº4. However, Nº6's pass to Nº4 is shorter and safer as it gives less chance for red Nº11 to move forward from the blind side and intercept.

BEAT THE PRESS WITH A BOX MIDFIELD

Box Midfield: Against Ultra-Aggressive Pressing with Zonal Defending and Man Marking

Build Up Against Ultra-Aggressive Pressing with Zonal Defending and Man Marking (2 at Back)

1. Opposition Positioning Adjustments (4-4-2 to 4-1-4-1) to Apply Marking Against a Box Midfield

Against a 2-at-the-back box midfield (goalkeeper and centre back), the red defending team must adjust to apply man marking in midfield. A 2v4 disadvantage makes standard man marking ineffective, requiring an additional player to drop back. The **best solution is for the red N°10 to drop into midfield, while N°9 stays forward to mark the blue centre back (N°5)**. This reinforces defensive coverage while maintaining a 1v2 press in the front line.

Red N°10 marking blue N°2 triggers position shifts in midfield. Red N°6 moves centrally to cover both blue N°8 and N°10, while red N°8 pushes forward to mark blue N°6, ensuring defensive compactness and control in key areas.

There is no need for additional forward movement, as the **reds focus on keeping their defensive shape balanced while limiting the blue team's build up options**.

Box Midfield: Against Ultra-Aggressive Pressing with Zonal Defending and Man Marking

2. Goalkeeper's Potential Options for Playing to the Free Defender or Midfielder

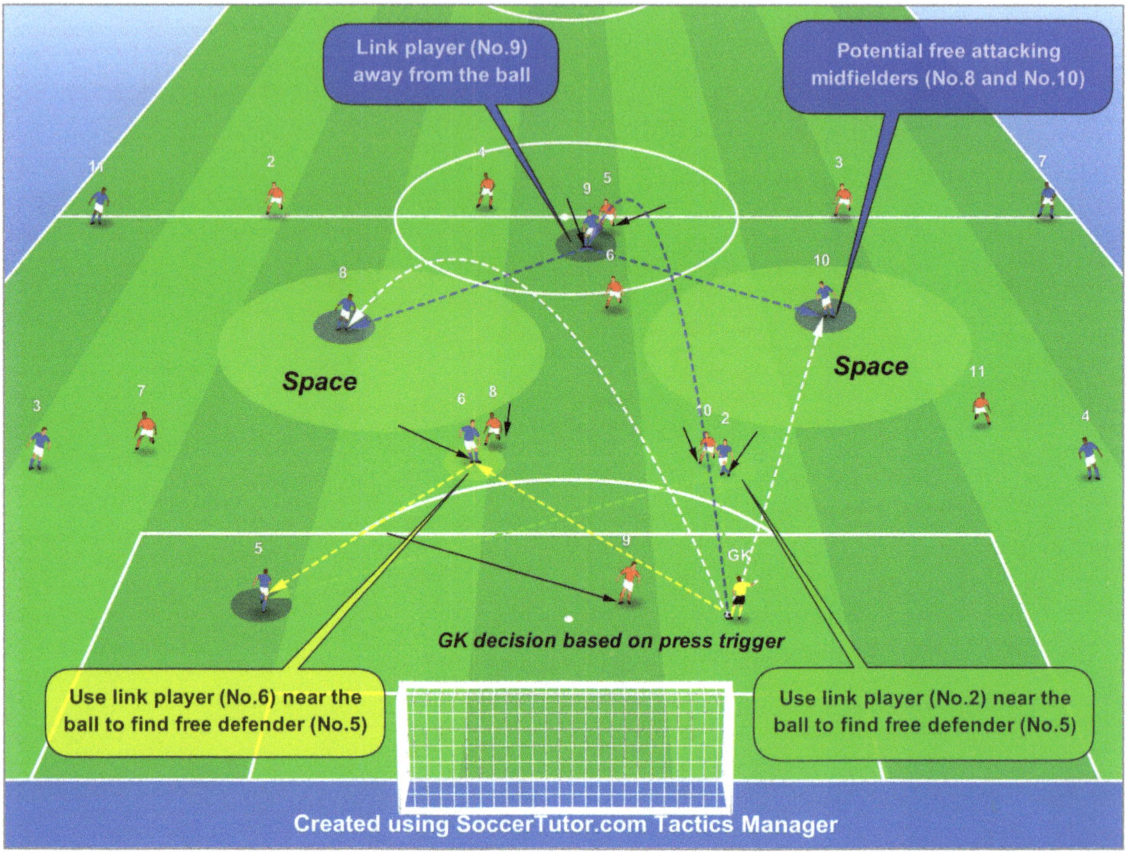

This diagram shows the potential options to build up play against ultra-aggressive pressing with zonal defending and man marking with a 2-at-the-back box midfield.

As the red forward Nº9 presses **GK**, the **defensive midfielders (Nº2 and Nº6) are 2 potential link players near the ball to move the ball to the free blue centre back (Nº5 - green and yellow arrows)**.

Nº2 and Nº6 draw the press of red Nº8 and Nº10, so space is created for the blue attacking midfielders (Nº8 and Nº10). They can receive from **GK** directly (white arrows) or indirectly via the **forward (Nº9)**, who acts as a link player (blue arrows).

Note 1: If red Nº6 decides to move closer to one of the blue attacking midfielders, the other one will be completely free of marking and become the clear target player.

Note 2: The goalkeeper's decision making is crucial to the effectiveness of the build up play and largely depends on the time available with the ball.

Note 3: The link players have to apply the link player principles *(see page 134)*.

BOX MIDFIELD SESSION

Training Session 6 (6 Practices)

Against Ultra-Aggressive Pressing with Zonal Defending and Man Marking

Based on Guardiola, Alonso, and Arteta build up patterns

Box Midfield Session 6: Against Ultra-Aggressive Pressing

TRAINING SESSION (6 PRACTICES)
1. Passing Combinations to Move the Ball to the Free Player via a Link Player

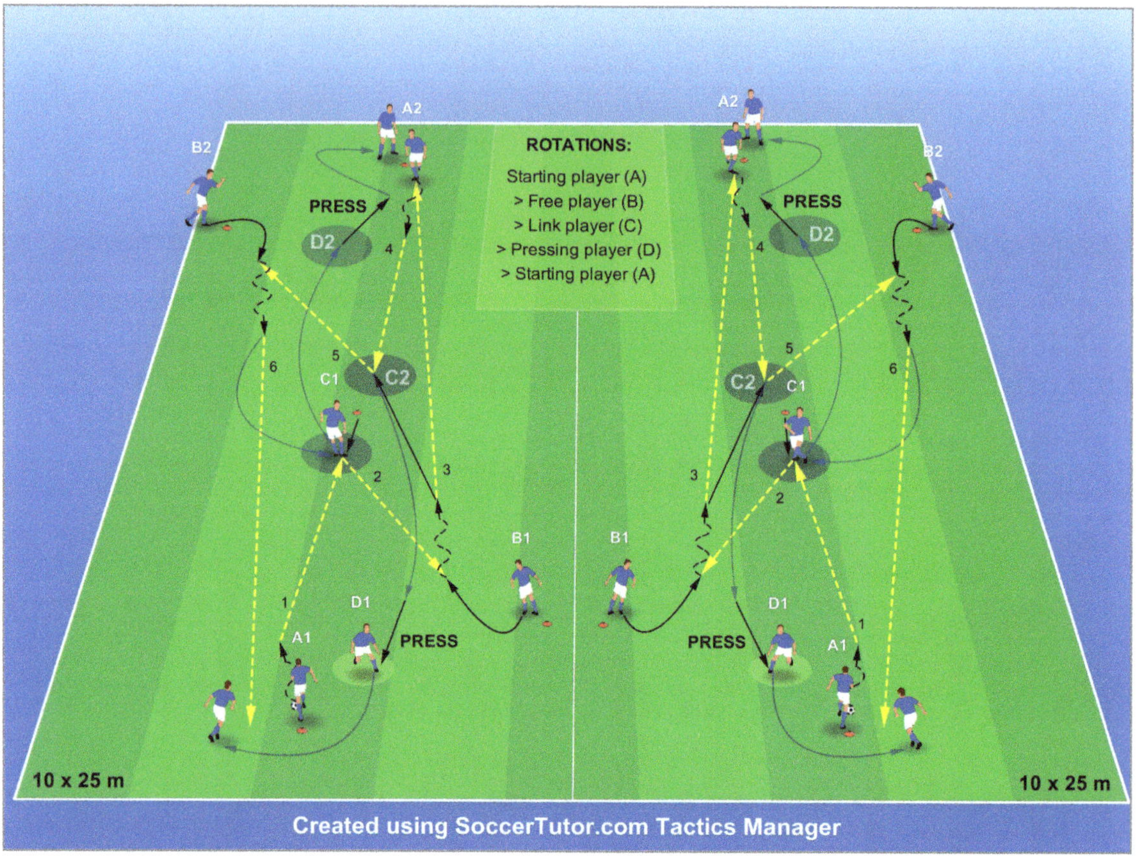

ROTATIONS:
- Starting player (A)
- > Free player (B)
- > Link player (C)
- > Pressing player (D)
- > Starting player (A)

10 x 25 m

Created using SoccerTutor.com Tactics Manager

Practice Description

1-2. **A1** dribbles forward and **D1** presses, blocking the passing lane to **B1**. **A1** passes to **C1** (**link player**), who drops back. **C1** passes to **B1** (**free player**).

3. **B1** dribbles forward and passes to **A2**, while **C1** moves towards the opposite end (to Position D2).

4. **A2** dribbles forward → **C1** (Position D2) is triggered to **press**, blocking the passing lane to **B2**. **A2** then passes to **B1**, who is now the **link player** in Position C2.

5. **B1** passes to **B2** (**free player**).

6. **B2** dribbles forward and passes to the next player waiting at Position A1 (**start**).

→ **B1** moves to become the **pressing player** at Position D1.

→ **B2** moves to become the **link player** at Position C2 and play to **A1**, who has become the **free player** at Position B1.

Player Rotations:

- From bottom: **A1** → **B1** → **C2** → **D1** → **A1**.
- From top: **A2** → **B2** → **C1** → **D2** → **A2**.

BEAT THE PRESS WITH A BOX MIDFIELD

Box Midfield Session 6: Against Ultra-Aggressive Pressing

PROGRESSION

2. Using the Link Player to Move the Ball to the Free Player Continuous 3v2 Wave Game

1/2: Creating and Exploiting a 3v2 Situation

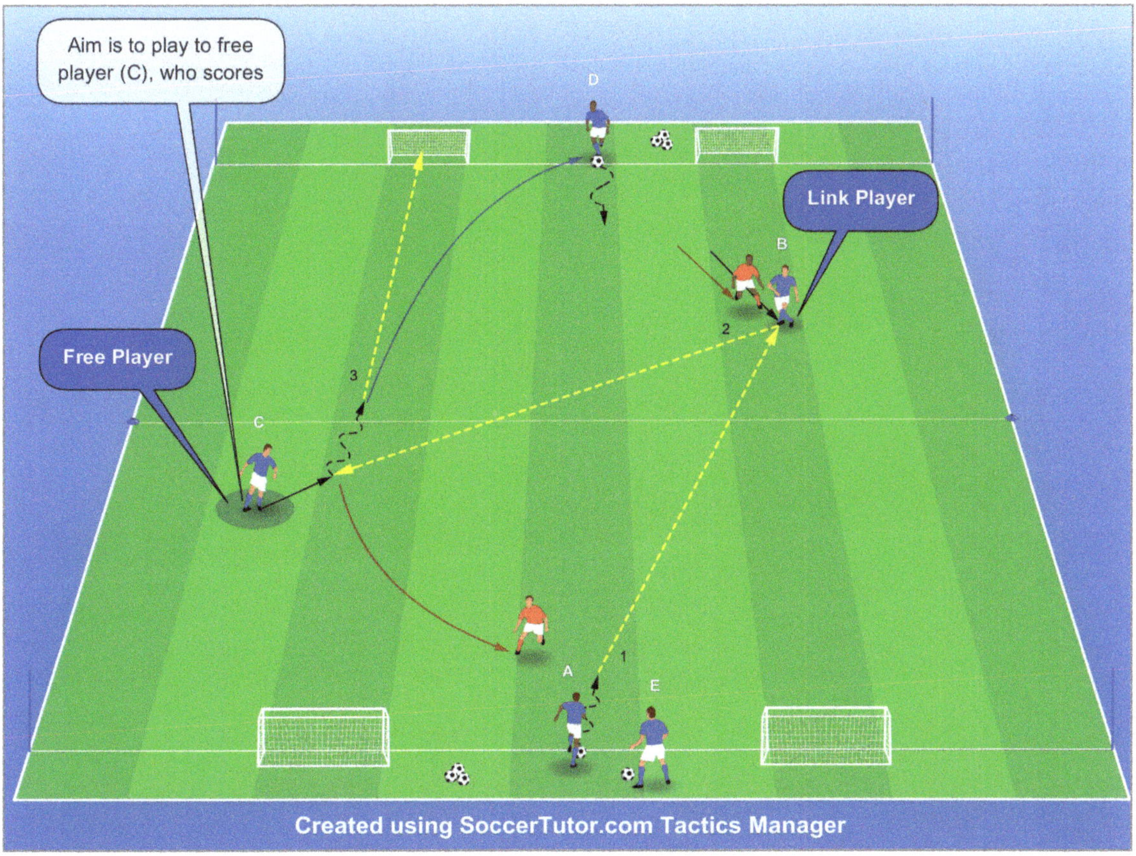

Diagram labels: Aim is to play to free player (C), who scores · Link Player · Free Player

Practice Description (1/2)

- Inside the 10 x 20m area, there is a 2v2 situation, with 3 additional blue players positioned outside. The area is divided into 2 halves (1v1 in both).
- The game starts with **A** dribbling into the area and creating a 3v2 numerical advantage. The nearest red defender steps forward to press **A**, so **C is left unmarked and becomes the free target player**.

- The ball can be played to **C** either directly or through **B**, who acts as the link player to find the free player.
- **C** receives and passes into either small goal before exiting the area and moving outside to Position D.
- **D** dribbles into the area, initiating a new 3v2 situation in the opposite direction *(see phase 2/2 on the next page).*

BEAT THE PRESS WITH A BOX MIDFIELD

Box Midfield Session 6: Against Ultra-Aggressive Pressing

2/2: Continuous Waves (End to End)

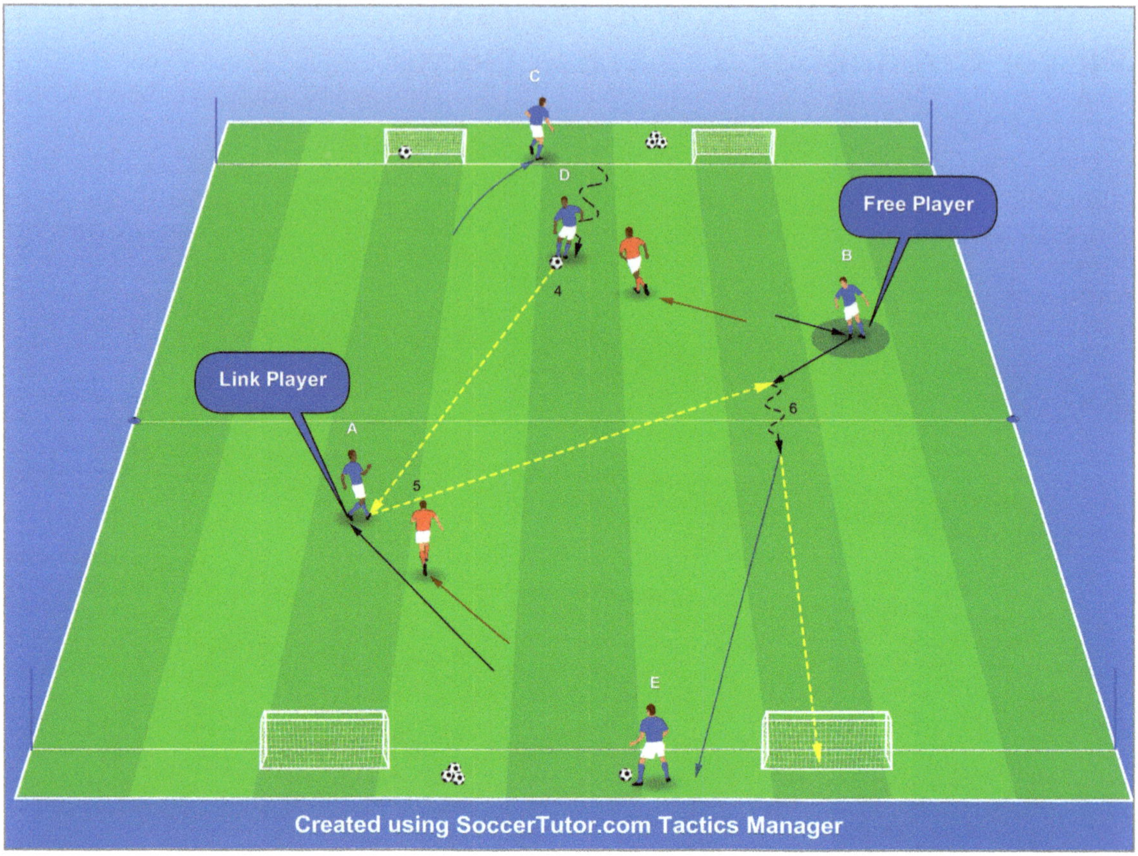

Practice Description (2/2)

- **D** dribbles in to create a new 3v2 and the nearest red player moves to press.
- The aim is to move the ball to the new free player (**B**), either directly or via the new link player (**A**).
- **B** receives and passes into either small goal before exiting the area and moving outside to Position E.
- The blues **circulate possession, identify free players**, and make **quick decisions** to sustain numerical superiority.
- **Red Objective:** Press to win the ball and counter to score within 10-12 seconds.
- The red defenders rotate out (rest) after a set number of repetitions to maintain intensity and vary the player roles.

Coaching Points

1. **Effective use of the link player** to help with ball movement.
2. **Synchronisation in movements** to maintain structure and passing options.
3. **Quick and accurate passing**.
4. **Decision making** based on defensive movements and the pressing applied.
5. **High tempo execution** to make it challenging and match realistic.

BEAT THE PRESS WITH A BOX MIDFIELD

Box Midfield Session 6: Against Ultra-Aggressive Pressing

PROGRESSION
3. Moving the Ball to the Free Player Directly or via Link Player and Finish 3v2 (+GK) Game

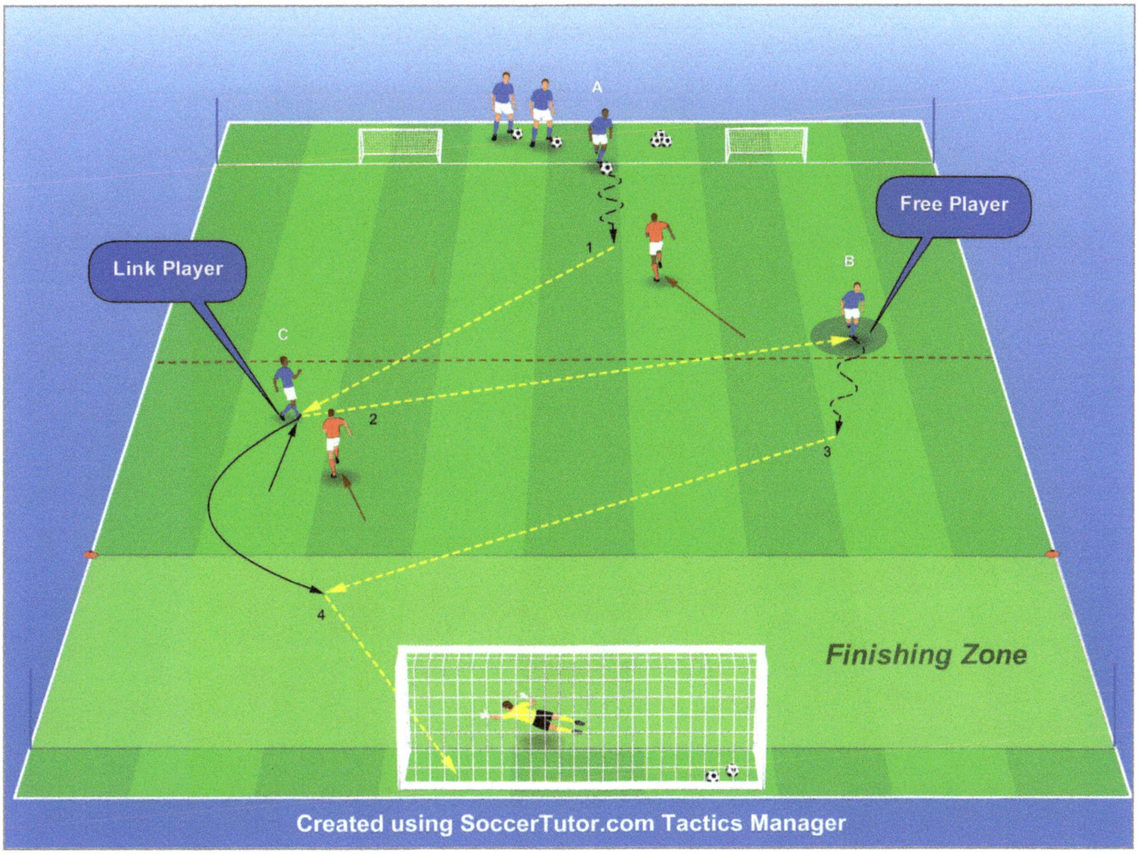

Practice Description

- Inside a 10 x 20m area, there is a 2v2 situation (1v1 in each half of largest zone) +3 additional blue players positioned outside. Inside the finishing zone (5m), there is a large goal and goalkeeper.
- The game starts with **A** dribbling into the area and creating a 3v2 numerical advantage.
- The nearest red player moves forward to press **A**. The **blues must identify the free player** (**B in diagram**) and play to them directly or via the link player (**C**).

- **Blue Objective: Receive inside the finishing zone or dribble into it and score.** The player who shoots moves to the start and a new blue player dribbles into the area for the next repetition.
- **Red Objective:** Win the ball and counter to score in the 2 small goals.
- The red defenders rotate out (rest) after a set number of repetitions.
- **Rules:** Red players cannot enter the finishing zone. You can increase the amount of extra outside players.

BEAT THE PRESS WITH A BOX MIDFIELD

Box Midfield Session 6: Against Ultra-Aggressive Pressing

PROGRESSION

4. Finding Free Player Against Ultra-Aggressive Pressing 8+1 (+GK) v 7 Game (3-at-the-Back Box Midfield)

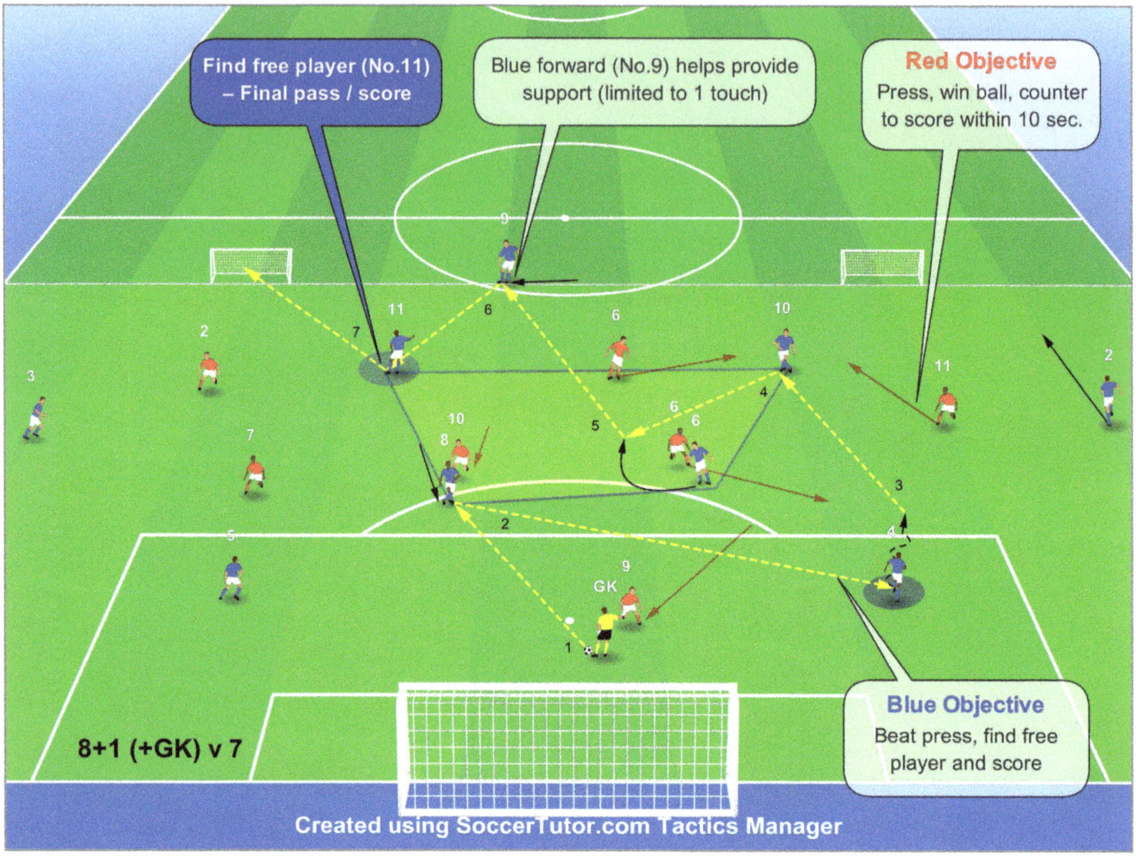

Find free player (No.11) – Final pass / score

Blue forward (No.9) helps provide support (limited to 1 touch)

Red Objective
Press, win ball, counter to score within 10 sec.

Blue Objective
Beat press, find free player and score

8+1 (+GK) v 7

Created using SoccerTutor.com Tactics Manager

Practice Description

- The blues have a **numerical advantage of 10 v 7 including the goalkeeper (GK) and outside forward (N°9)**.
- **Blue Objective:** Progress the ball from the **GK** and score. **See previous practices + analysis pages for different solutions**. The diagram shows an example.
- **Red Objective:** Apply full pitch man marking and force the blues to find the free player with a direct pass or via a link player. Win the ball and counter to score within 8-10 seconds.

- **Note:** This game reinforces quick decision making, ball circulation, and positioning to break the press under realistic match conditions.

Restrictions

1. A red player must press the goalkeeper immediately.
2. The blue **forward (N°9)** can help provide support but is limited to only playing one touch passes back into the area.
3. If the ball goes out of play, the coach restarts with a pass to the red team.

BEAT THE PRESS WITH A BOX MIDFIELD

Box Midfield Session 6: Against Ultra-Aggressive Pressing

VARIATION

5. Finding Free Player Against Ultra-Aggressive Pressing 7+1 (+GK) v 6 Game (2-at-the-Back Box Midfield)

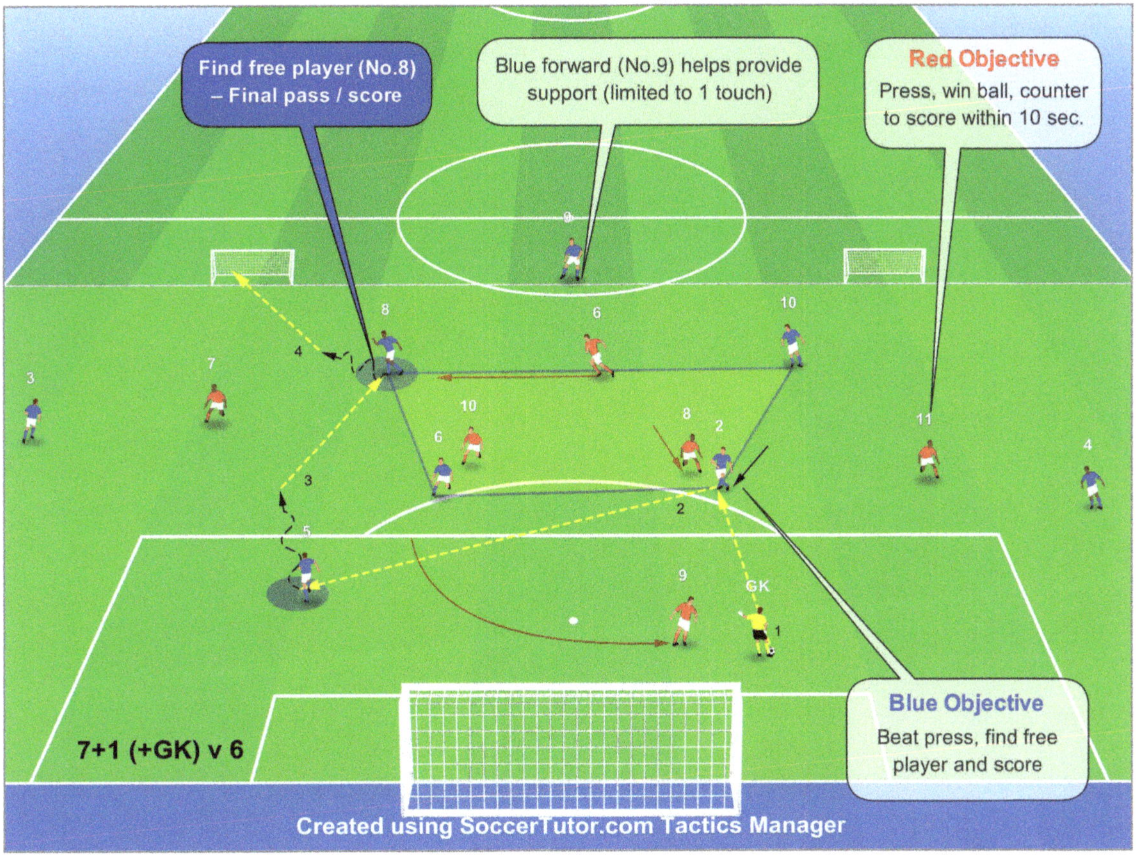

Diagram annotations:
- Find free player (No.8) – Final pass / score
- Blue forward (No.9) helps provide support (limited to 1 touch)
- **Red Objective:** Press, win ball, counter to score within 10 sec.
- **Blue Objective:** Beat press, find free player and score
- 7+1 (+GK) v 6

Practice Description

- In this variation of the previous practice, the blues now build up play with 2 players at the back (goalkeeper + centre back Nº5).

- The blues have a **numerical advantage of 9 v 6 including the goalkeeper (GK) and outside forward (Nº9)**.

- While the numerical setup differs, the core objective remains the same, which is to **identify the free player and move the ball to them** against ultra-aggressive high pressing (up to goalkeeper).

- The **blue attacking team must use the link player effectively (Nº2 in diagram)** to progress play and bypass defensive pressure.

- The same rules and restrictions apply, ensuring tactical continuity while allowing the players to experience a key variation to the box midfield build up structure.

- **Note:** The link players have to apply the appropriate link player principles to avoid mistakes *(see page 134)*.

BEAT THE PRESS WITH A BOX MIDFIELD

Box Midfield Session 6: Against Ultra-Aggressive Pressing

PROGRESSION

6. Finding the Free Player Against Ultra-Aggressive Pressing 11 v 11 Game (3-at-the-Back Box Midfield)

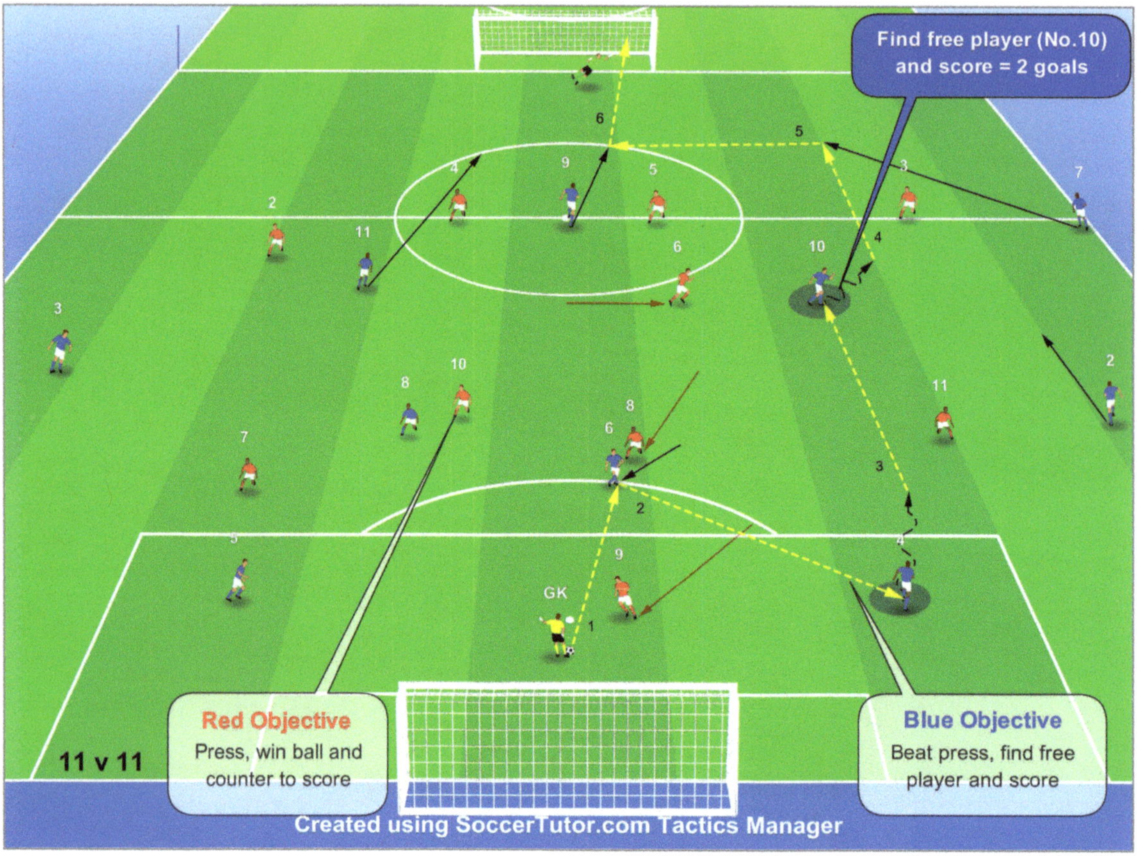

Find free player (No.10) and score = 2 goals

Red Objective
Press, win ball and counter to score

11 v 11

Blue Objective
Beat press, find free player and score

Practice Description

- We play an 11v11 game with the reds applying ultra-aggressive high pressing (up to goalkeeper) with man marking.

- **Note:** See previous practices (+ analysis pages) for build up solutions/principles.

- **Blue Objective:** Build up play and score (1 goal). If they successfully find the free player with a direct pass or via a link player before scoring = 2 goals.

- **Red Objective:** Press to win the ball and counter to try and score.

- Play always restarts with the blue **GK**. Team roles are reversed after a set time.

Coaching Points

1. **Synchronised off-the-ball movements** to maintain structure and passing options.

2. **Quick and accurate passing** to exploit gaps in the press.

3. **Decision making under pressure** - when to use link player or direct option.

4. **The link player principles should be applied** (see page 134).

©SOCCERTUTOR.COM

BEAT THE PRESS WITH A BOX MIDFIELD

BOX MIDFIELD BUILD UP

Tactical Analysis

Against Full Pitch Man Marking

Build up play patterns from Guardiola, Alonso, and Arteta's teams

BEAT THE PRESS WITH A BOX MIDFIELD

Box Midfield Build Up: Against Full Pitch Man Marking

Box Midfield Build Up Solutions Against Full Pitch Man Marking (2 at Back)

1. Opposition's Man Marking Across the Pitch Against a Box Midfield with 2-at-the-Back

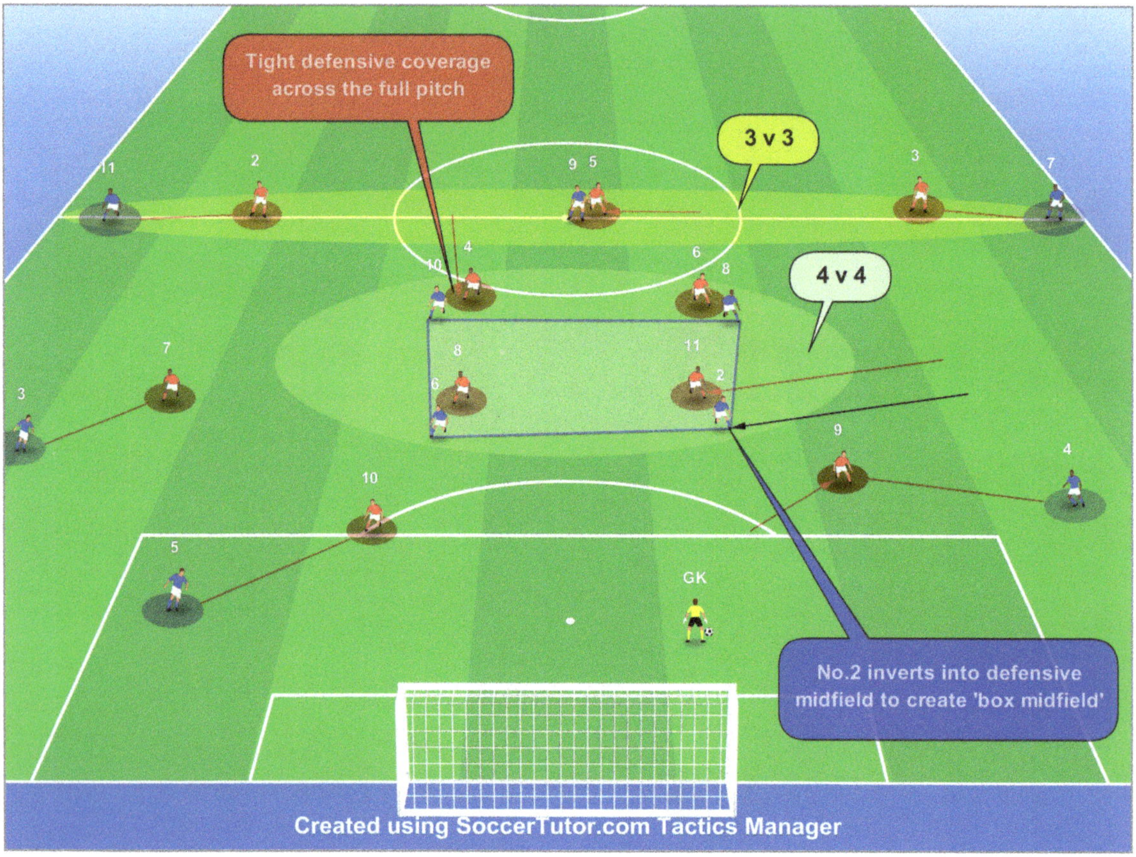

When using a 2-at-the-back box midfield, the defending team must adjust their structure to apply full pitch man marking.

As it is most often the **full back (blue Nº2) inverting into central midfield to create the box midfield**, the opposing wide player (red Nº11) is responsible for them. Additionally, to maintain tight marking, a **red centre back (Nº4 in diagram) must step forward to mark the free attacking midfielder (blue Nº10)**.

These adjustments create tight defensive coverage across the pitch, limiting the blue team's passing options and their ability to progress the ball through central areas.

©SOCCERTUTOR.COM   BEAT THE PRESS WITH A BOX MIDFIELD

Box Midfield Build Up: Against Full Pitch Man Marking

2. Utilising a Target Player with Goalkeeper's Long Pass and Support Play Movements

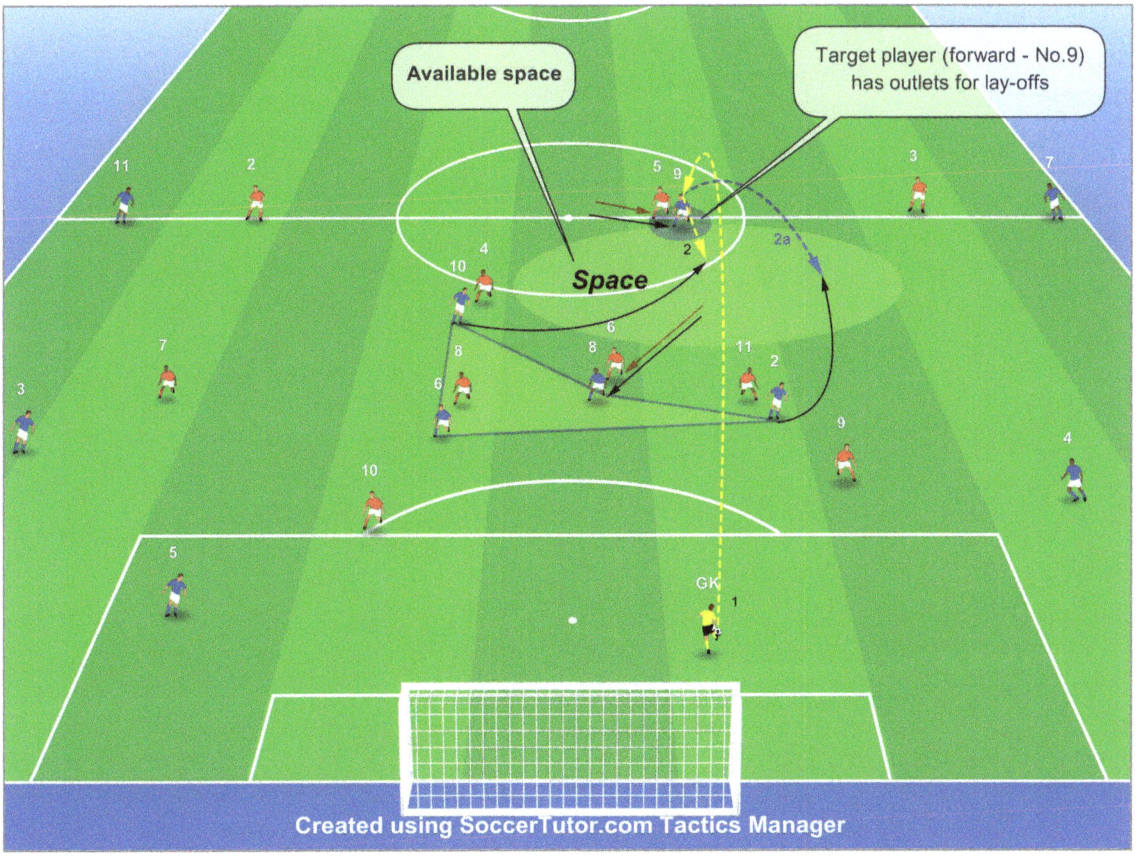

To maximise the effectiveness of a target player forward (Nº9), one of the attacking midfielders must drop back to create space for them to operate.

In the diagram, **blue Nº8 drops back** and red Nº6 is forced to track him. This **movement pulls a key defensive midfielder out of position**, opening up valuable space for **Nº9** to receive.

With this space created, **Nº9 can receive without being double marked**, increasing the chances of holding up play effectively. The role is not just to receive but also to link up with supporting teammates to progress the attack.

Blue Nº10 and Nº2 make support runs to provide passing options and ensure Nº9 has outlets for quick lay-offs or combinations. If **Nº9** can release the ball at the right moment, the **blues can neutralise 6 or 7 red opponents immediately**.

The **receiver will be running forward into available space, facing the opponent's goal**.

This sequence creates attacking momentum while maintaining positional superiority. **Nº9's** ability to hold up play with well-timed support runs provides a **direct route to goal scoring opportunities while preventing the opposition from regaining defensive compactness**.

Box Midfield Build Up: Against Full Pitch Man Marking

3. Using Link Players to Find the Free Player Near the Ball with the Goalkeeper in Possession Against Ultra-Aggressive High Pressing

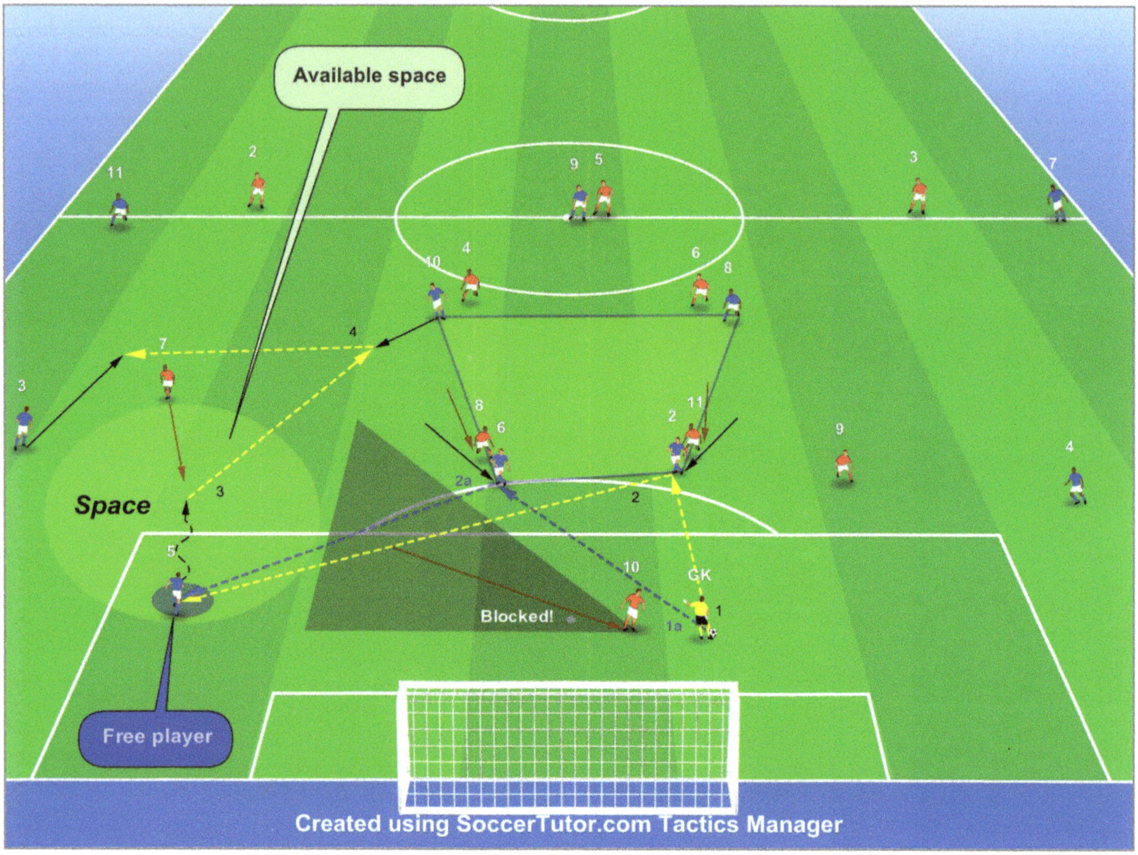

When ultra-aggressive high pressing is applied, the option on the previous page is still viable but there is less time for the **goalkeeper** (**GK**) and the players to synchronise their movements in order to apply it. The **attacking team have to use the link players to find the free man**. Here we show the best option. The blue team must **quickly identify the free player**, react quickly, and ensure **precise execution to break through the press using one of 2 link players**.

If the red N°10 presses the GK, the centre back (N°5) is left unmarked, creating an opportunity to receive a pass from either **defensive midfielder** (**N°6** or **N°2**).

After receiving, **N°5** will be able to exploit the available space ahead and if pressure is applied, another player will be free of marking e.g. the **left back N°3** in the diagram example.

The ball can be directed to **N°3** directly or through a link player (**N°10**). This situation can be repeated multiple times against a man marking pressing team.

Note: Remain aware of shifting defensive movements and adjust positioning to ensure fluid ball progression. Applying the **principles outlined on page 134** are vital to avoid mistakes. **Focus: Use the link players to find the free player.**

Box Midfield Build Up: Against Full Pitch Man Marking

Box Midfield Build Up Solutions Against Full Pitch Man Marking (3 at Back)

1. Opposition's Man Marking Across the Pitch Against a Box Midfield with 3-at-the-Back

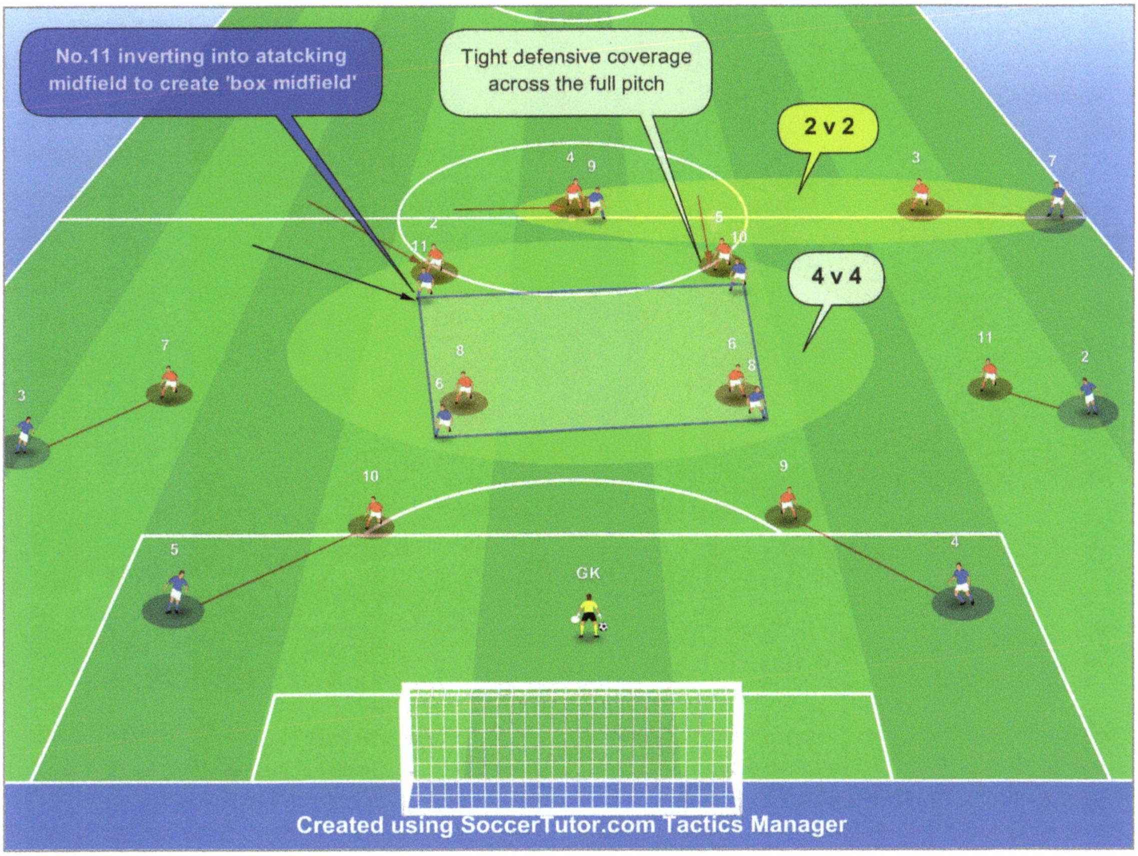

When using a 3-at-the-back box midfield (goalkeeper and 2 centre backs), the defending team must adjust their structure to apply full pitch man marking.

As it is most often the **winger (blue Nº11 in diagram) inverting into an attacking midfielder role to create the box midfield, the opposing full back (red Nº2) is the one primarily responsible for tracking/marking them**.

Additionally, to maintain tight marking, a **red centre back (Nº5 in diagram) must step forward to mark the free attacking midfielder (blue Nº10)**. This ensures there is defensive coverage in central areas.

The result is a **2 v 2 situation in defence and 4 v 4 in midfield**, requiring the red team to remain disciplined and compact to limit the blue team's attacking progression.

BEAT THE PRESS WITH A BOX MIDFIELD

Box Midfield Build Up: Against Full Pitch Man Marking

2. Exploiting a Target Player with Goalkeeper's Long Pass and Support Play Movements

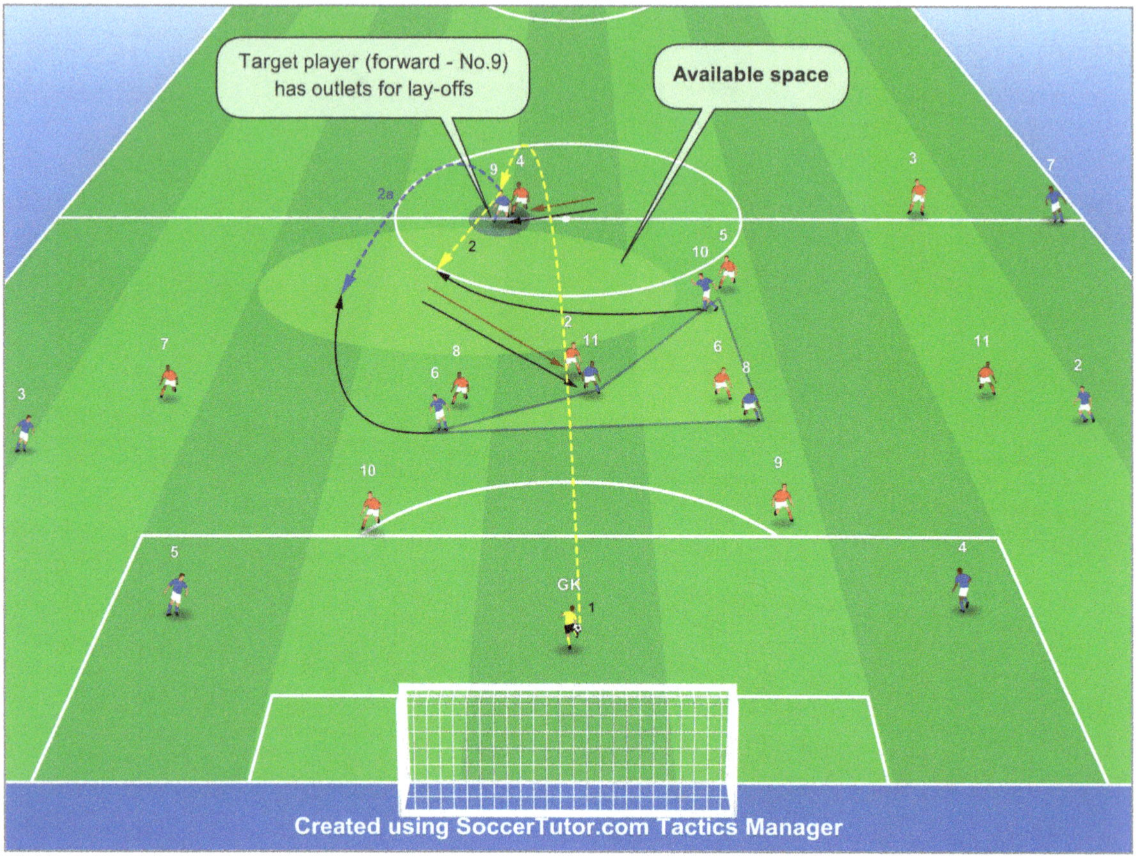

To maximise the effectiveness of a target man forward (**N°9**), one of the players in the attacking midfield positions must drop back to create space for them to operate.

In the diagram, **blue N°11 drops back** and forces red N°2 to track him. This **movement pulls a key defensive midfielder out of position**, opening up valuable space for **N°9** to receive.

N°9 can receive without being double marked, increasing his chances of holding up play effectively. **Blue N°10 and N°6 make quick forward runs** and position themselves to receive a potential lay-off pass from **N°9**.

If executed correctly, this **tactic can neutralise at least 7 red opponents**, which beats the press and significantly increases the blue team's chances of launching an effective attack.

As explained earlier, it provides a **direct route to goal scoring opportunities while preventing the opposition from regaining defensive compactness**.

Box Midfield Build Up: Against Full Pitch Man Marking

3. Exploiting a Forward's Speed with the Goalkeeper's Long Pass into Available Space in Behind

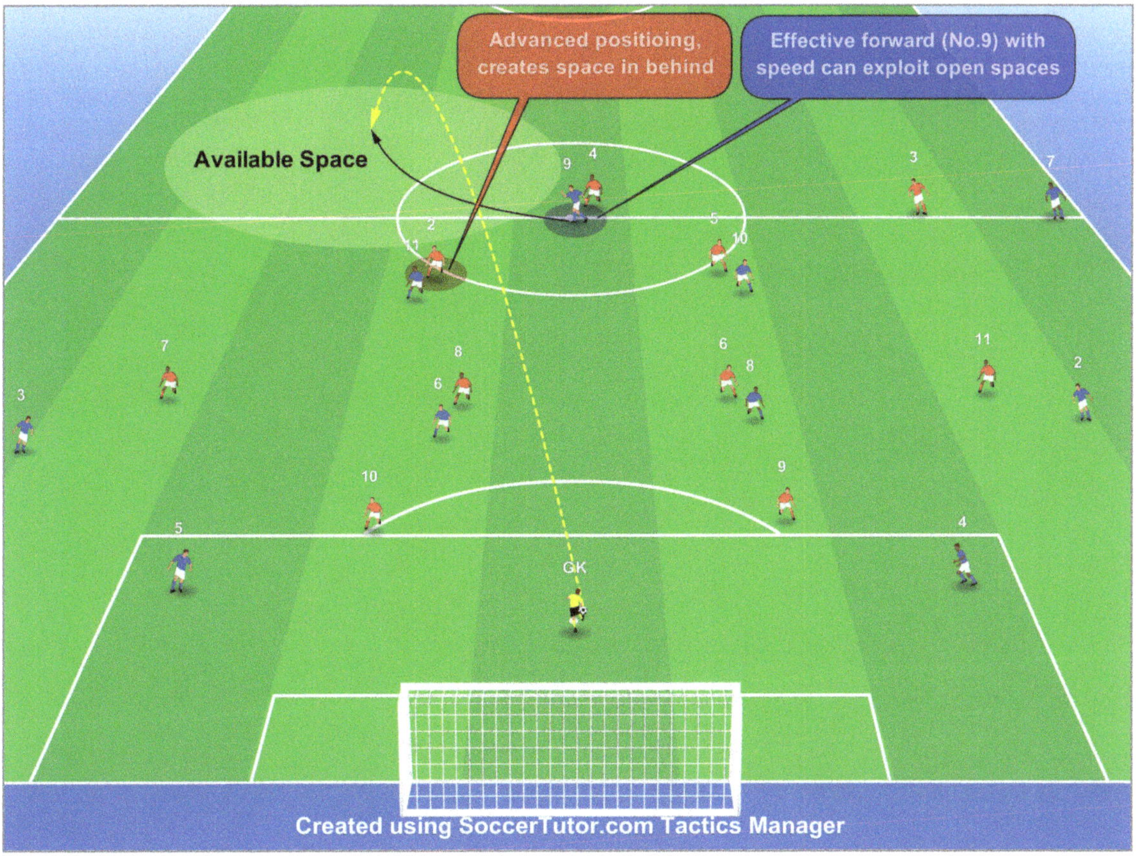

The opposition's defensive setup in this situation provides an opportunity to utilise a pacey forward who thrives in open spaces. The **advanced positioning of the red full back (N°2), which is explained on page 153, leaves space high on the left flank, allowing the blues to exploit this defensive imbalance**.

An accurate pass from the **goalkeeper (GK)** enables the **forward (N°9)** to run into space and engage in a 1v1 against the red centre back (N°4). With momentum and space to attack, **N°9 can drive towards goal or shift the ball into a more dangerous area before engaging the defender**.

Note 1: Additional support from attacking midfielders or overlapping wingers further increases the threat to the opposition's defensive structure.

Note 2: This approach capitalises on a defensive gap, allowing the blue team to **bypass the press and create a direct goal scoring opportunity**.

BEAT THE PRESS WITH A BOX MIDFIELD

Box Midfield Build Up: Against Full Pitch Man Marking

4. Advanced Full Back's Run for Goalkeeper's Long Pass into Available Space Out Wide

A **full back with strong attacking qualities is crucial in a 3-at-the-back box midfield** as they are responsible for covering the entire flank on their own.

If this player is capable of exploiting open space, they can **take advantage of gaps left by the opposition's shifting defence.**

As the opposing wide player (red N°7) is positioned towards the inside, space is available behind him.

A **precise long ball from the goalkeeper (GK) can release blue N°3**, who must have the speed and technical ability to drive forward effectively after receiving.

Note 1: If executed correctly, at least 6 red opponents can be neutralised, which creates a dangerous attacking opportunity.

Note 2: By using an attacking full back, the team can stretch the opposition, break lines, and progress into advanced areas while maintaining defensive balance.

BEAT THE PRESS WITH A BOX MIDFIELD

BOX MIDFIELD SESSION

Training Session 7 (5 Practices)

Against Full Pitch Man Marking

Based on Guardiola, Alonso, and Arteta build up patterns

BEAT THE PRESS WITH A BOX MIDFIELD

Box Midfield Session 7: Against Full Pitch Man Marking

TRAINING SESSION (5 PRACTICES)
1. Beating a Full Pitch Man Marking Press by Finding the Free Player Support Play Zones

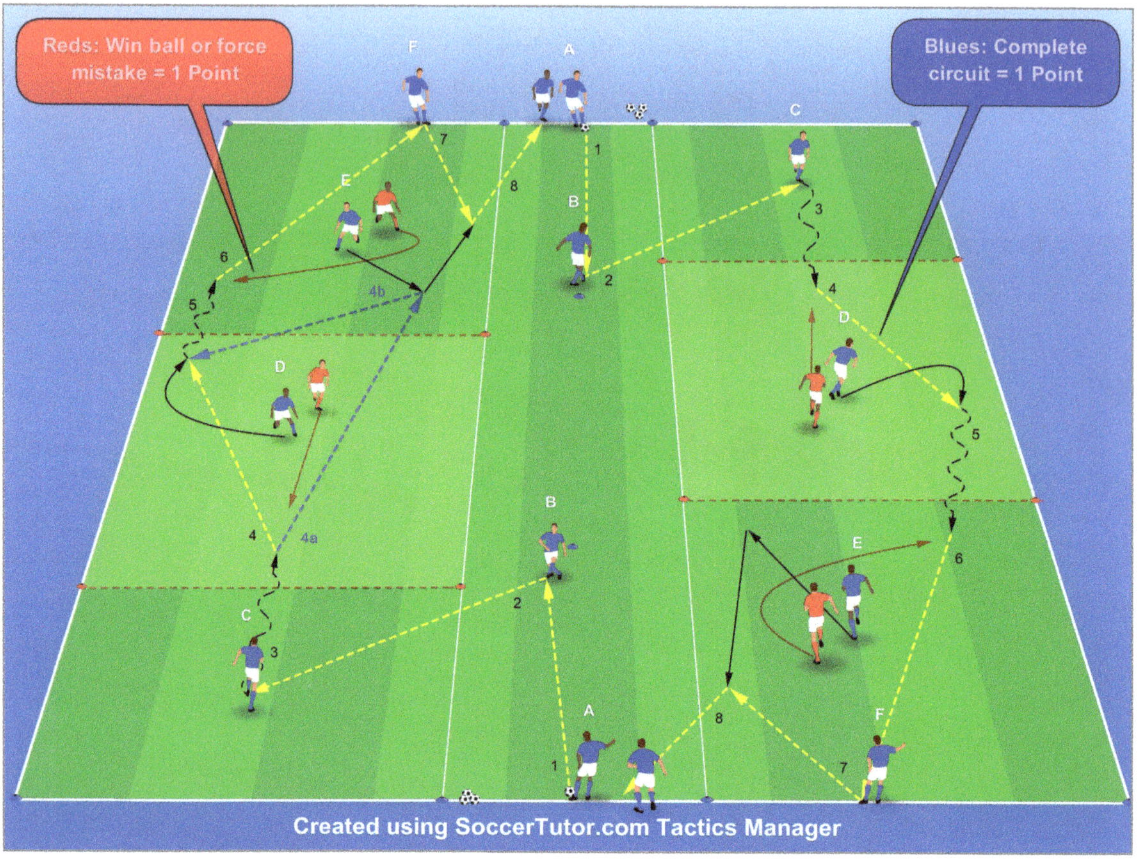

Practice Description

- This practice is played simultaneously on both sides. There is 1 low zone (8x5m) and 2 larger zones (8x8m).

- The sequence starts with **A** passing to **B**, who plays it diagonally back to **C**.

- **C** dribbles from **Zone 1** into **Zone 2**, triggering the red player to press.

- **D** moves into a passing lane to become the free player, with **E** mirroring this movement on the opposite side to provide **C** with 2 passing options.

- **C** can pass directly to **D** (yellow arrow) or play to **E**, who acts as a link player to move the ball to **D** (blue arrows).

- Once **D** receives, they dribble into **Zone 3**. **E** moves to offer a passing option. As the red player presses the ball, the pass is directed to **E** (free player) either directly or via **F** (as shown). **E** passes to the start (1 point for complete circuit). All blue players rotate to the next position and the sequence repeats.

- **Defending Objective:** Score 1 point for winning the ball or forcing a mistake.

Box Midfield Session 7: Against Full Pitch Man Marking

PROGRESSION
2. Beating a Full Pitch Man Marking Press with a Long Pass and Support Runs Functional Combinations

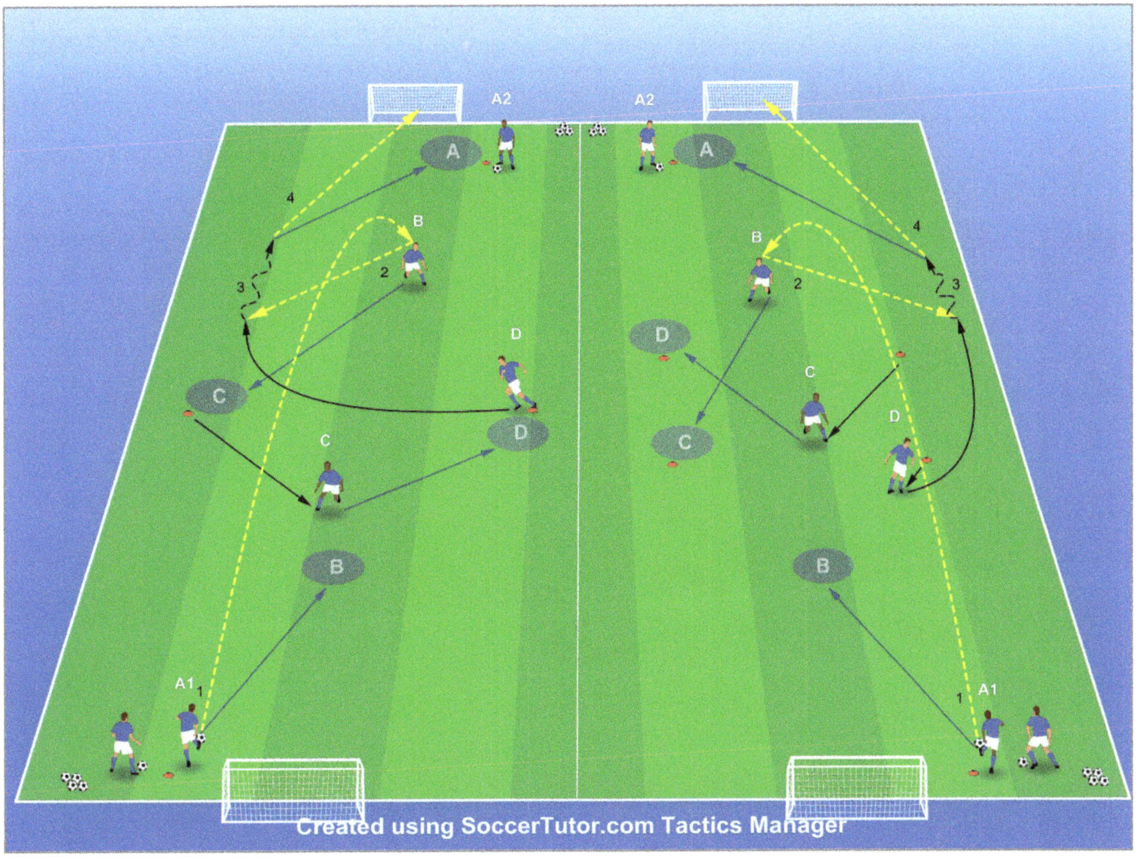

Practice Description

- This practice is played simultaneously on both sides and each player has a defined role. **A1** = Long passer. **B** = Receiver. **C** = Create space. **D** = Exploit space.

- **On the left**, **C** drops back as if to draw an opponent out of position, while **D** makes a run into the vacated space.

- **A1** plays a long pass to **B**, who directs the ball into **D's** path. **D** finishes the sequence by dribbling forward, passing into the small goal, and moving to **A2**.

- **On the right**, **C** drops back while **D** makes an overlapping run into the vacated space. **D** receives, passes into the small goal, and moves to **A2**.

- **Player Rotations:** A1 → B → C → D → A2.

→ Repeats sequence in opposite direction.

Coaching Points

1. **Intelligent well-timed movement** to disrupt man marking.

3. **Accurate passing** with the correct weight (short and long).

BEAT THE PRESS WITH A BOX MIDFIELD

Box Midfield Session 7: Against Full Pitch Man Marking

PROGRESSION

3. Beat Ultra-Aggressive Man Marking Press with a Box Midfield and Link Players in a Half Pitch Game

Variation 1: Box Midfield with 2-at-the-Back (7 +GK vs 7)

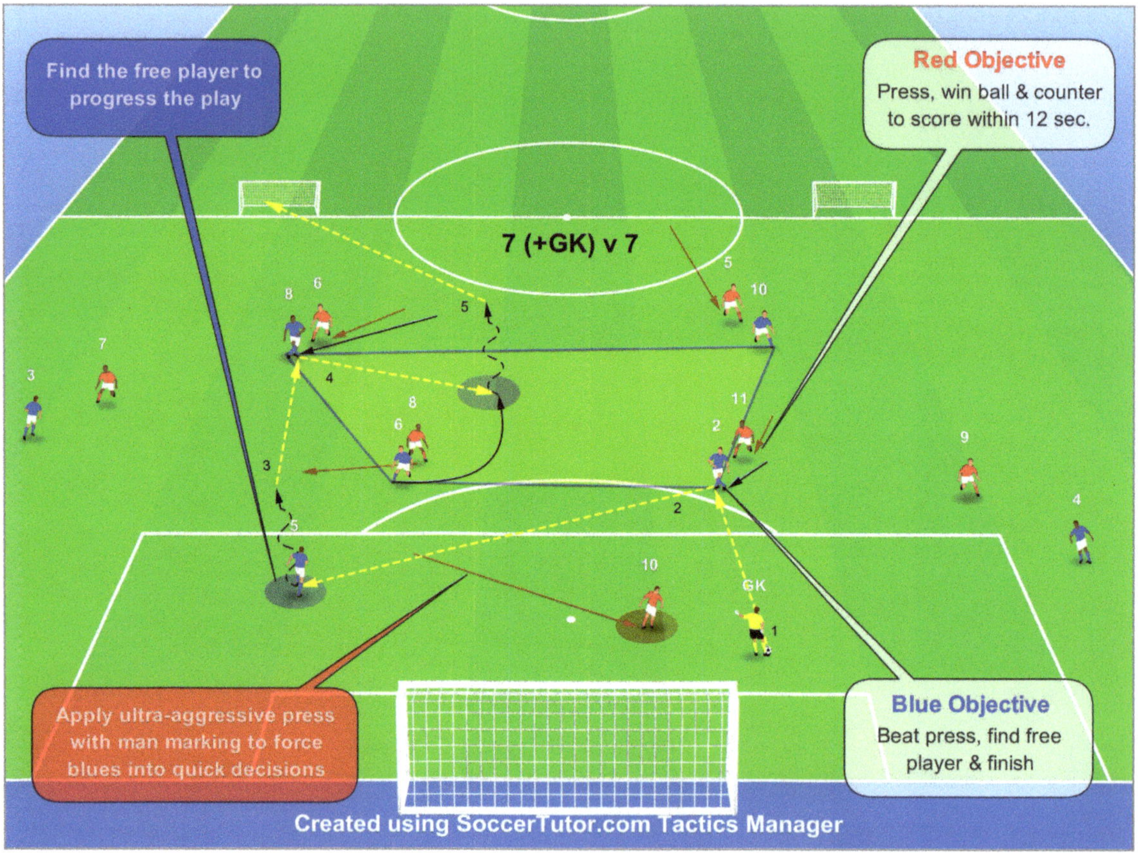

Practice Description (Variation 1)

- This 7v7 (+GK) game is played in the low half of the pitch. The blues use a box midfield with 2-at-the-back. The 2 wingers and forward are not involved.

- **Blue Team Objective:** Find the free player to **progress play against ultra-aggressive pressing up to the goalkeeper (GK)** and use any numerical advantages to break forward and score in either of the 2 small goals.

- **Red Team Objective:** Apply a full pitch man marking press to force the blues into quick decisions. Win the ball and counter to score within 10-12 seconds.

- **Note:** This practice sharpens quick decision making, movement, passing to break through ultra-aggressive pressing, and exploiting numerical advantages in match-like conditions.

©SOCCERTUTOR.COM

BEAT THE PRESS WITH A BOX MIDFIELD

Box Midfield Session 7: Against Full Pitch Man Marking

Variation 2: Box Midfield with 3-at-the-Back (8 +GK vs 8)

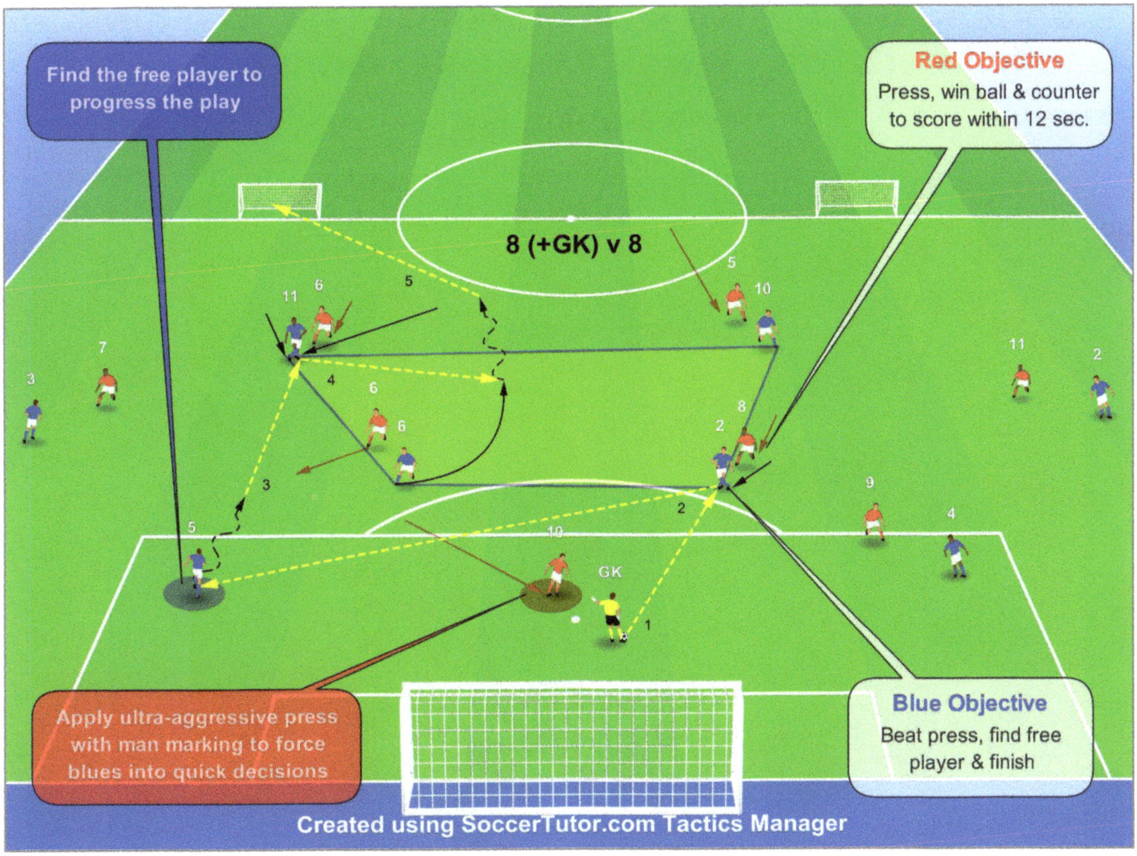

Practice Description (Variation 2)

- The structure remains the same, but the blue team now uses a 3-at-the-back box midfield. The game changes from 7v7 (+GK) to an 8v8 (+GK) game.
- All players are again tightly man marked by the red team.
- **Blue Team Objective:** Find the free player, use link players, break pressing lines and create/exploit available spaces to progress the ball forward and score in the small goals.
- **Red Team Objective:** Press to win the ball and counter to score within 10–12 seconds, just like in Variation 1.

Coaching Points

1. **Intelligent off-ball movements** to lose markers.
2. **Timing and synchronisation** of supporting runs.
3. **Accuracy in passing** to ensure effective ball circulation (well-weighted under pressure).
4. **Reading the pressing cues** to identify the free player.
5. **Using the link player principles (see page 134) effectively** to connect lines and beat the press.

BEAT THE PRESS WITH A BOX MIDFIELD

Box Midfield Session 7: Against Full Pitch Man Marking

PROGRESSION

4. Beating a Full Pitch Man Marking Press with the Goalkeeper's Long Pass 7v7 (+GKs) Game

Variation 1: Box Midfield with 3-at-the-Back

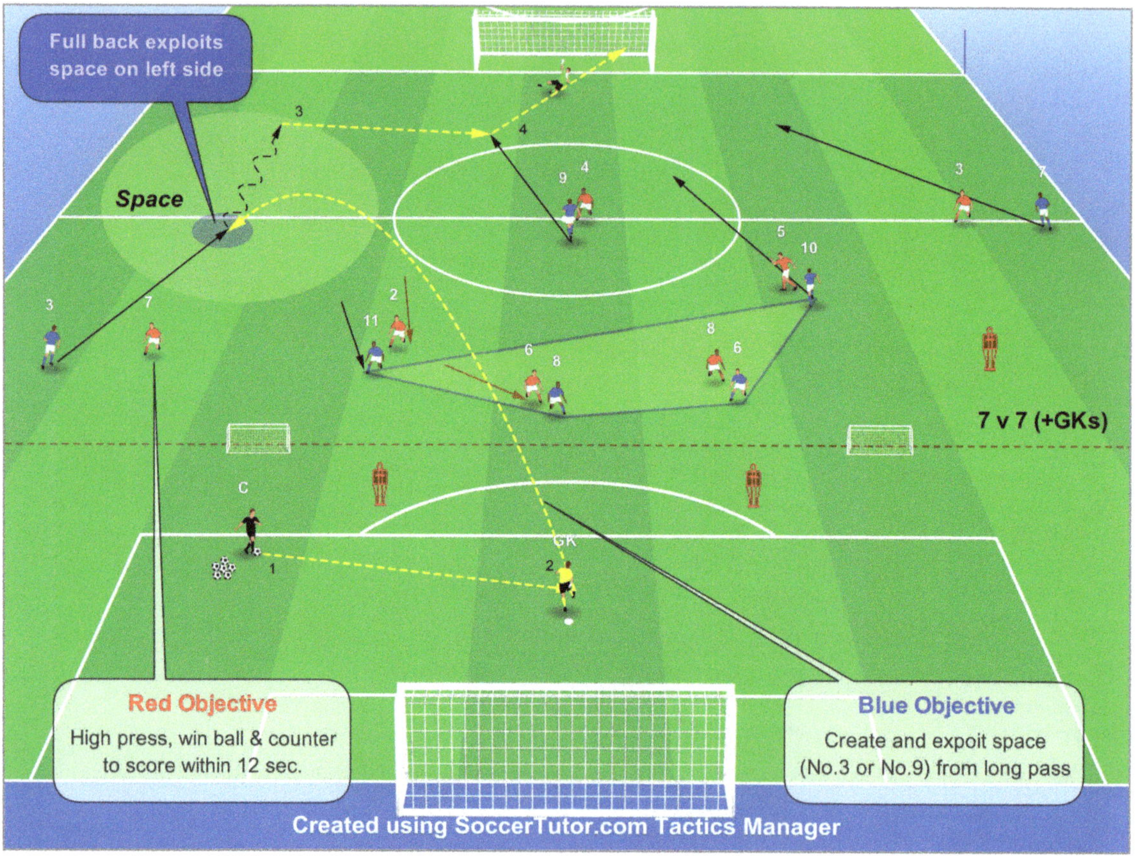

Red Objective
High press, win ball & counter to score within 12 sec.

Blue Objective
Create and expoit space (No.3 or No.9) from long pass

Practice Description (Variation 1)

- This practice simulates **build up play against full pitch man marking**, focusing on **creating and exploiting space using the goalkeeper's (GK) long pass**.
- In this 7v7 (+GKs) game, the blues set up with a **box midfield, left back (Nº3), right winger (Nº7)**, and **forward (Nº9)**.
- We start with the coach's pass to the blue **GK**. The centre backs and right back are not involved.

- **Blue Team Objective:** Create space through off-ball movement, **play a long pass from the GK to the forward (Nº9) or the left back (Nº3), and score**.
- *See analysis pages 153-156 for the full explanation of the tactics in this situation.*
- **Red Team Objective:** Apply high press man marking across the whole area. Win the ball and counter to score in the small goals within 10-12 seconds.

BEAT THE PRESS WITH A BOX MIDFIELD

Box Midfield Session 7: Against Full Pitch Man Marking

Variation 2: Box Midfield with 2-at-the-Back

(Diagram: 7 v 7 (+GKs) practice setup with Target player annotation, Red Objective: High press, win ball & counter to score 2 small goals within 12 sec. Blue Objective: Create and exploit space (No.9) from long pass)

Practice Description (Variation 2)

- In this variation, the same game structure and objectives apply, but the build up is practiced using a 2-at-the-back box midfield. The **left back (N°3) is removed and a left winger (N°11) is introduced** to change the shape and attacking dynamics.

- **Blue Team Objective:** Create space through movement and **use the goalkeeper's (GK) long pass to find the forward (N°9), provide support, and score**.

- **See analysis pages 150-151 for the full explanation of the tactics in this situation**.

- **Red Team Objective:** Apply high press man marking. Win the ball and counter attack to score in either of the 2 small goals within 10-12 seconds.

- **Restriction:** The goalkeeper must play within 4–5 seconds of receiving to maintain game intensity and decision making under pressure.

Box Midfield Session 7: Against Full Pitch Man Marking

PROGRESSION

5. Reading Tactical Triggers to Beat the Press Against Full Pitch Man Marking Game

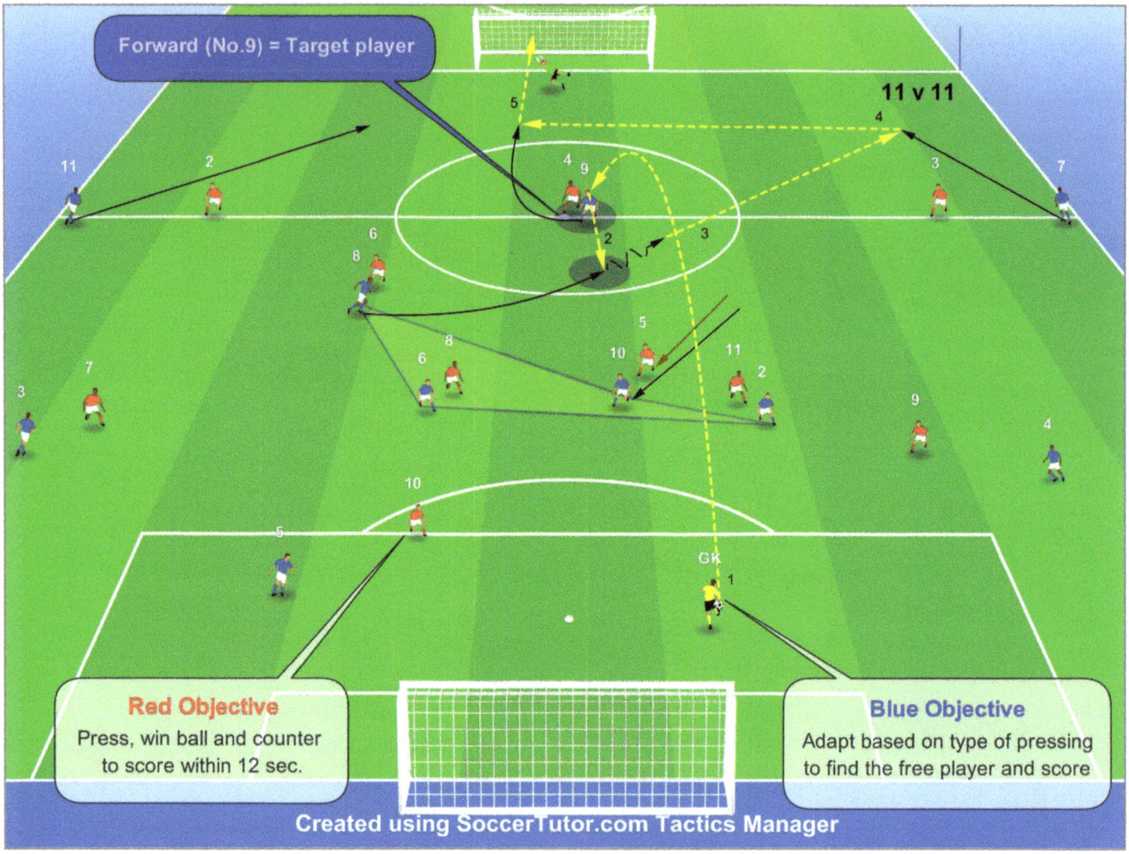

Red Objective
Press, win ball and counter to score within 12 sec.

Blue Objective
Adapt based on type of pressing to find the free player and score

Practice Description

- **Tactical Objective:** Finding the free player against ultra-aggressive pressing (up to goalkeeper) or creating and exploiting space against high pressing (on first receiver).

- In 3/4 of a full pitch, we play an 11v11 game.

- The red team apply full pitch man marking using ultra-aggressive pressing or high pressing (*see previous practices + all analysis pages*) to disrupt the blue team's build up play.

- **Blue Team Objective:** Adapt based on the type of pressing applied and progress the ball forward to score.

- **Against ultra-aggressive pressing (up to goalkeeper)**, the blues must find and use the free player to beat the press.

- **Against high pressing (on first receiver)**, they must coordinate synchronised movements to create and exploit space.

- **Red Team Objective:** Win the ball and counter to score within 10-12 seconds.

BEAT THE PRESS WITH A BOX MIDFIELD

FINAL MESSAGE FOR COACHES

Athanasios Terzis
- Football Tactics Expert
- Award Winning Author
- PAOK U23 Assistant Coach
- UEFA 'A' Coaching Licence
- Greek Football Federation Instructor

- Building up from the back **must be developed step by step** for success.

- The **risk factor is high** since the build up play happens near your team's goal.

- Losing possession in this area **can lead to dangerous situations**, including goal scoring opportunities for the opposition.

- Players need to **gradually gain confidence** in the process to become more effective.

- Coaches must **introduce build up play progressively** to ensure players are comfortable and limit costly mistakes.

Free Trial

Football Coaching Specialists Since 2001

Tactics Manager
Create your own Practices, Tactics & Plan Sessions!

Tactics Manager App

SoccerTutor.com

Football Coaching Specialists Since 2001

Coaching Books Available in Full Colour Print and eBook
PC | Mac | iPhone | iPad | Android Phone / Tablet | Chromebook

 **FREE** Coach Viewer **APP**

SoccerTutor.com

Football Coaching Specialists Since 2001

Xabi Alonso

82 Passing, Positional Possession, Games, Patterns and Attacking Practices Direct from Bayer Leverkusen Training Sessions

+ Tactical Analysis

SoccerTutor.com - Football Coaching Specialists Since 2001

Coaching Books Available in Full Colour Print and eBook
PC | Mac | iPhone | iPad | Android Phone / Tablet | Chromebook

 **FREE** Coach Viewer **APP**

SoccerTutor.com

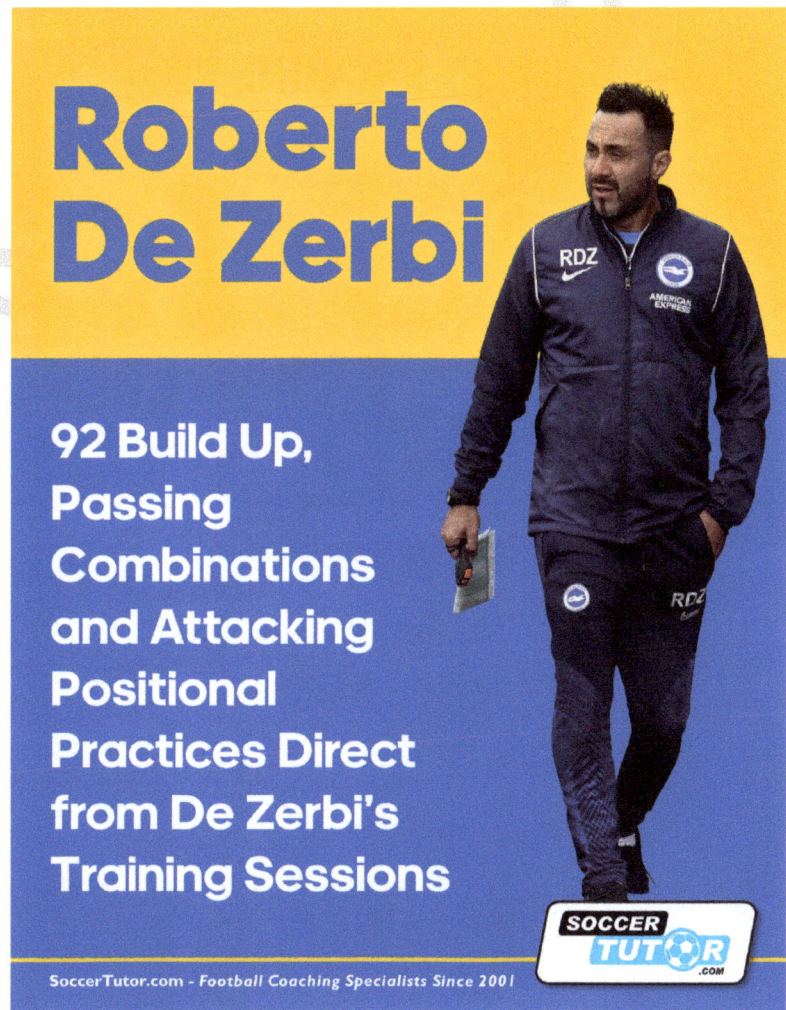

Football Coaching Specialists Since 2001

More Coaching Books Available from Athanasios Terzis
PC | Mac | iPhone | iPad | Android Phone / Tablet | Chromebook

FREE Coach Viewer **APP**

SoccerTutor.com

Football Coaching Specialists Since 2001

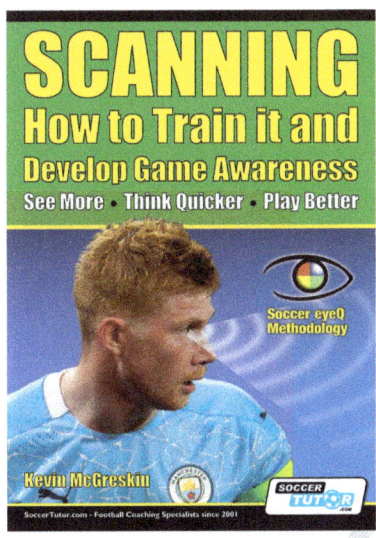

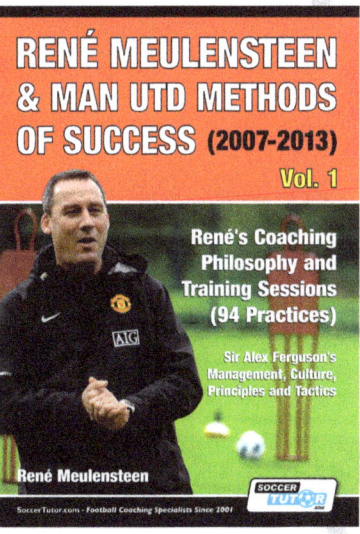

More Coaching Books Available in Full Colour Print and eBook
PC | Mac | iPhone | iPad | Android Phone / Tablet | Chromebook

 **FREE** Coach Viewer **APP**

SoccerTutor.com

www.ingramcontent.com/pod-product-compliance
Lightning Source LLC
Chambersburg PA
CBHW040932240426
43673CB00051B/1958